TRADIVOX
VOLUME VI

TRADIVOX

CATHOLIC CATECHISM INDEX

VOLUME VI

Thomas Aquinas
John Pecham
William of Pagula

Edited by
Aaron Seng

SOPHIA INSTITUTE PRESS
MANCHESTER, NEW HAMPSHIRE

© 2021 by Tradivox, Inc.
South Bend, Indiana
www.Tradivox.com

This book is an original derivative work comprised of newly typeset and
reformatted editions of the following Catholic catechisms, once issued with ecclesiastical
approval and now found in the public domain:

Translation of the Athanasian Creed, *Quicumque Vult*, is by John Marquess of Bute, cited in:
Herbermann, Charles G., Edward A. Pace, Conde B. Pallen, Thomas J. Shahan, and John J.
Wynne, eds. *The Catholic Encyclopedia*. Vol. 2. New York: Robert Appleton Company, 1907.
Inset image provided courtesy of The Morgan Library, New York.

Translation of the "Opuscula" is by Fr. Joseph Collins, from:
Aquinas, Thomas. *The Catechetical Instructions*. New York: Joseph F. Wagner, Inc., 1939.
Inset image provided courtesy of Corpus Christi College, Cambridge.

Translations of the "Medieval Manuals of Instruction" are by Drs. Shinners and Dohar, from:
Shinners, John, and William J. Dohar, eds. *Pastors and the Care of Souls in Medieval England*.
Notre Dame: University of Notre Dame Press, 1998. Used with permission.
Inset images provided courtesy of the Bodleian Library, Oxford.

Scripture references follow the Douay-Rheims Bible,
per the imprint of John Murphy Company (Baltimore, 1899).

Printed in the United States of America. All rights reserved.

Cover and interior design by Perceptions Design Studio.
Unless otherwise noted, all illustrations are in the public domain.

Sophia Institute Press
Box 5284, Manchester, NH 03108
1-800-888-9344

www.SophiaInstitute.com

Sophia Institute Press® is a registered trademark of Sophia Institute.

ISBN 978-1-64413-360-6
LCCN 2021947917

The Manner of Execution at Tyburn.

Dedicated with love and deepest respect
to all the English Martyrs and Confessors.
Orate pro nobis.

CONTENTS

ACKNOWLEDGMENTS

THE publication of this series is due primarily to the generosity of countless volunteers and donors from several countries. Special thanks are owed to Mr. and Mrs. Phil Seng, Mr. and Mrs. Michael Over, Mr. and Mrs. Jim McElwee, Mr. and Mrs. John Brouillette, Mr. and Mrs. Thomas Scheibelhut, as well the visionary priests and faithful of St. Stanislaus Bishop and Martyr parish in South Bend, Indiana, and St. Patrick's Oratory in Green Bay, Wisconsin. May God richly reward their commitment to handing on the Catholic faith.

FOREWORD

The Catholic faith remains always the same throughout the centuries and millennia until the coming of our Lord at the end of the time, likewise "Jesus Christ is the same yesterday, today and forever" (Heb 13:8). The Catholic faith is "the faith, which was once delivered unto the saints" (Jude 1:3). The Magisterium of the Church teaches us solemnly the same truth in the following words of the First Vatican Council: "The doctrine of the faith which God has revealed, is put forward not as some philosophical discovery capable of being perfected by human intelligence, but as a divine deposit committed to the spouse of Christ to be faithfully protected and infallibly promulgated. Hence, too, that meaning of the sacred dogmas is ever to be maintained, which has once been declared by holy mother Church, and there must never be any abandonment of this sense under the pretext or in the name of a more profound understanding. May understanding, knowledge and wisdom increase as ages and centuries roll along, and greatly and vigorously flourish, in each and all, in the individual and the whole Church: but this only in its own proper kind, that is to say, in the same doctrine, the same sense, and the same understanding (cf. Vincentius Lerinensis, *Commonitorium*, 28)."[1]

An authentically Catholic catechism has the function of learning and teaching the unchanging Catholic faith throughout all generations. The Roman Pontiffs indeed, taught: "There is nothing more effective than catechetical instruction to spread the glory of God and to secure the salvation of souls."[2] Saint Pius X said, that "the great loss of souls is due to ignorance

---

[1] Vatican I, Dogmatic Constitution *Dei Filius de fide catholica*, Ch. 4
[2] Pope Benedict XIV, Apostolic Constitution *Etsi minime*, n. 13

of divine things."[3] Therefore, the traditional catechisms have enduring value in our own day and age, which is marked by an enormous doctrinal confusion, which reigns in the life of the Church in the past six decades, and which reaches its peak in our days.

I welcome and bless the great project of the "Tradivox" in cataloguing and preserving the hundreds of long-lost Catholic catechisms issued with episcopal approval over the last millennium. This project will convincingly show the essentially unchanging nature of the apostolic doctrine across time and space, and so I invite the faithful of the entire world to support this historic effort, as we seek to restore the perennial catechism of the Church. The project of a catechism restoration on behalf of "Tradivox" will surely be of great benefit not only to many confused and disoriented Catholic faithful, but also to all people who are sincerely seeking the ultimate and authentic truth about God and man, which one can find only in the Catholic and apostolic faith, and which is the only religion and faith willed by God and to which God calls all men.

+Athanasius Schneider, O.R.C.,
Titular Bishop of Celerina
Auxiliary Bishop of the Archdiocese of Saint Mary in Astana

---

[3] Cf. Pope St. Pius X, Encyclical *Acerbo nimis*, n. 27

SERIES EDITOR'S
PREFACE

S OME are surprised to find that when a given Catholic is asked to "look something up in the catechism," he may well respond: "Which one?" The history of the Catholic Church across the last millennium is in fact filled with the publication of numerous catechisms, issued in every major language on earth; and for centuries, these concise "guidebooks" to Catholic doctrine have served countless men and women seeking a clear and concise presentation of that faith forever entrusted by Jesus Christ to his one, holy, Catholic, and apostolic Church.

Taken together, the many catechisms issued with episcopal approval can offer a kind of "window" on to the universal ordinary magisterium—a glimpse of those truths which have been held and taught in the Church *everywhere, always, and by all*. For, as St. Paul reminds us, the tenets of this Faith do not change from age to age: "Jesus Christ yesterday and today and the same for ever. Be not led away with various and strange doctrines" (Heb 13:8-9).

The catechisms included in our *Tradivox Catholic Catechism Index* are selected for their orthodoxy and historical significance, in the interest of demonstrating to contemporary readers the remarkable continuity of Catholic doctrine across time and space. Long regarded as reliable summaries of Church teaching on matters of faith and morals, we are proud to reproduce these works of centuries past, composed and endorsed by countless priests, bishops, and popes devoted to "giving voice to tradition."

IN THIS VOLUME

It is sometimes claimed that catechisms were first conceived of in the six-teenth century, whether due to more efficient printing, higher literacy rates, the appearance of protestantism with its emphasis on didactic instruction, or a combination of all these factors. Some have even credited Martin Luther, in his catechisms of 1529, with the invention of the entire genre. However, although the prevalence of catechisms certainly grew exponentially in the mid-1500s, the origins of this textual form must be sought much earlier.

Leaving aside the theological treatises and mystagogical sermon-cycles of many early fathers and doctors of the Church, there are concise works of systematic religious instruction that come down to us from even the ninth century, many having been written for a lay audience in Latin as well as translated into other spoken languages of the time. There are works in Old German such as the Weissenburg Catechism (ca. 800), the Frankish *Liber Manualis* of Dhuoda (ca. 842), the *Elucidarium* of Honorius (ca. 1096), and numerous works throughout the medieval period that served as catechisms "for simple folk"[1] — all appearing well before Luther was born. Indeed, by the time the monumental *Roman Catechism*[2] appeared in 1566, published as the first universal catechism for priests by order of the Council of Trent, the genre of Catholic catechisms was already long established, and populated by texts in every major language.

Prior to the late Middle Ages, most Catholic catechisms were included within larger, sometimes multi-volume works of *pastoralia*: books intended for clergy to use in their work of shepherding souls. These texts often included directions for the assigning of suitable penances, admonitions for spiritual directees, relevant portions of canon law and liturgical rubrics, and other content helpful to parish priests in their daily tasks. In the thirteenth century, demand for concise manuals of instruction in doctrine, morals, and prayer grew significantly, especially in the wake of the

---

[1] As one such text was entitled, namely Jean Gerson's *ABC for Simple Folk*, ca. 1401-2.

[2] Included in Volume VII of this series.

epochal Fourth Lateran Council (1215), which issued universal decrees regarding religious instruction for the faithful. Although the majority of publications in this period were authored for Catholic clerics, the laity also invested in copies for private study and home-based instruction, often posting portions of such works in public places for others to read. Given the typical brevity of medieval catechetical texts, this volume recovers four such works, alongside one of the major credal statements that was in frequent use at the time, each with a corresponding original manuscript image. The texts themselves are rendered here in English to show the continuity of Catholic doctrine as taught in those centuries, as well as to give an intriguing insight into the work of medieval parish priests, exhorted to "edify everyone with their knowledge both about the faith and about good behavior; and…[to] mold their subjects with the food of God's word according to how he inspires them, lest they are deservedly blamed because of their idleness."[3]

FIRST IN THIS VOLUME is one of the principal symbols, or creeds: the *Quicumque Vult*, titled after its initial words and often referred to as the Athanasian Creed. Long believed to be the work of the great saint and doctor of the Church for whom it is named, its authorship is yet a matter of some uncertainty, given its uncharacteristic Western structure and phrasing, as well as the lack of clear contemporary witness to its composition. While some portions of this creed do appear in the writings of St. Vincent of Lerins around the year 440, the earliest known manuscript copy is from a homily collection by Caesarius of Arles (d. 542). Internal evidence confirms the antiquity and unmistakable influence of St. Athanasius in any case, and given the frequency of local synods in that period—one of which convened in Alexandria under his presidency—many scholars are content to date *Quicumque Vult* to around the end of Athanasius' life (296-373), if not to his direct authorship.

Regardless of its precise historical origin, by the time of the early Middle Ages this creed was held as so significant for the Catholic profession of

---

[3] See p. 209–210, below.

faith that it had been drawn into the regular liturgical life of the Church, perhaps warranting its consideration as a kind of "dogmatic hymn" of the fathers. Manuscripts from the ninth century attest to its mandatory recitation in the divine office, with the Sarum Breviary prescribing it for daily recitation at the hour of prime. By the 1500s, the Athanasian Creed was spoken or chanted nearly every Sunday in the Roman Breviary, and remained so until the sweeping liturgical changes of the mid-twentieth century reduced its appearance to once per year, at prime on Trinity Sunday.

The Athanasian Creed was also a common feature in medieval catechesis, being variously reprinted in catechetical texts and devotional manuals up until the Council of Trent; after which, the *Professio Fidei Tridentina*[4] tended to feature more often. Even so, *Quicumque Vult* was still employed as a pedagogical tool in the centuries following Trent, often for instruction on the dogmas of the Trinity and the Incarnation, or to inculcate the need for right faith as a prerequisite for salvation. "Whosoever will be saved," thunders the Athanasian Creed, "before all things it is necessary that he hold the Catholic faith. Which faith, except everyone do keep whole and undefiled, without doubt he shall perish everlastingly." Amid the errors of religious pluralism that were beginning to emerge in the nineteenth century, it is worth quoting one of the more prominent exponents of *Quicumque Vult* from that time: John Henry Cardinal Newman. In his *Essay in Aid of a Grammar of Assent*, Newman highlights both the didactic and latreutic character of this ancient profession of faith, against the credal dangers of his day:

> It must be recollected especially that the Athanasian Creed has sometimes been called the "*Psalmus Quicunque.*" It is not a mere collection of notions, however momentous. It is a psalm or hymn of praise, of confession, and of profound, self-prostrating homage, parallel to the canticles of the elect in the Apocalypse. It appeals to the imagination quite as much as to the intellect. It is the war-song of faith, with which we warn, first ourselves, then each other, and then all those who are within its hearing, and the hearing of the truth, who our God is, and

---

[4] Included in Volume III of this series.

how we must worship him, and how vast our responsibility will be, if we know what to believe, and yet believe not. For myself, I have ever felt it as the most simple and sublime, the most devotional formulary to which Christianity has given birth, more so even than the *Veni Creator* and the *Te Deum*.[5]

Given such a commendation from so outstanding a catechist, surely Catholics of our own time do well to revisit this venerable creed, making it their own psalm and confession in a world now immersed in religious pluralism and dogmatic errors particularly regarding the Holy Trinity and Incarnation.

THE SECOND TEXT included in this volume is *The Catechetical Instructions of St. Thomas Aquinas* (ca. 1260), consisting of five of Aquinas' *Opuscula* or "Little Treatises." These were a series of doctrinal talks composed by the brilliant saint and doctor of the Church for the benefit of his students and the lay faithful of Naples. Inasmuch as Aquinas bears the accolade of Universal Doctor and is regarded as the most eminent Catholic theologian of the past eight centuries, no introduction to the significance of his little catechism may be required. However, in this English translation, provided from the erudite Sulpician Fr. Joseph Collins, we have retained the translator's introduction to the person and writings of St. Thomas for greater insight, along with his more germane annotations and original textual divisions.

THE OTHER THREE TEXTS in this volume are included under their proper Latin titles, derived from the initial words of the documents themselves. Each is a brief medieval manual of catechetical instruction in its own right; in them, the concerns of the English Middle Ages may be clearly felt, and the attention of priests is repeatedly directed to the moral perfection of his parishioners as well as their instruction in right doctrine. While we have

---

[5] John Henry Newman, *Essay in Aid of a Grammar of Assent* (Burns, Oates, & Co., London: 1870), 128-129.

introduced some section divisions to these texts for further clarity, we have retained the original English translations of Drs. Shinners and Dohar.[6]

The first of these medieval manuals is the *Ignorantia Sacerdotum* or "Ignorance of Priests," which comprises the text of the ninth canon of the Provincial Council of Lambeth (1281), convoked by the renowned Archbishop of Canterbury, John Pecham. A Franciscan friar consecrated and installed by Pope Nicholas III, Pecham showed the reforming zeal and pastoral focus of a true shepherd of souls over more than a decade in the see of Canterbury. Among his many efforts at correcting abuses and raising moral and educational standards, he enacted a visitation of the entire province that went so far as to compel the submission of the royal chapels which claimed exemption—a courageous act at the time. Pecham's efforts to instruct, govern, and sanctify his flock found their peak at the Council of Lambeth, wherein he required all priests to offer quarterly a vernacular exposition of the articles of faith, which he then proceeded to outline in the tract-sized catechism included here. This little text was reprinted as a standalone work in both Latin and English for the next two hundred fifty years, inspiring a significant number of similar works along the way.

The next of these little manuals is *Quinque Verba*, or "Five Words"—an anonymous work likely from the early 1300s, designed to be highly informative and inexpensively replicable in order to "remedy the ignorance of simple priests...lest anyone try to excuse himself from knowing this material."[7] Like innumerable later catechisms, it endeavors to use content divisions for rapid indexing; in this case, a five-fold explication of "things which must be believed...loved...done...avoided...[and] things that priests should do."[8] While certainly a case-study in balanced pastoral wisdom and moral guidance, it is most instructive to find that *Quinque Verba* begins with the assertion that "since faith is the foundation of every spiritual good, the first thing that should be known are matters of faith."[9] In a

---

[6] John Shinners and William J. Dohar, eds., *Pastors and the Care of Souls in Medieval England* (Notre Dame: University of Notre Dame Press, 1998).

[7] See p. 199, below.

[8] See ibid.

[9] See ibid.

kingdom that had been predominantly and enduringly Catholic since the sixth century—Our Lady's Dowry, as England was so long known—it is remarkable to find such insistence on right faith among English Catholics of the fourteenth century.

The last of the three shorter texts in this volume is a single chapter from William of Pagula's sizeable *Oculus Sacerdotis* or "Priest's Eye," composed circa 1320 as a meticulously detailed guide for priestly ministry. A studied theologian and canonist with extensive pastoral experience, William of Pagula (d. 1332) was well-equipped to compose this work, viewed as one of tremendous utility at the time and for which he is most remembered. Employing the medieval motif of the eye containing and representing different things to the soul, William warns that the priest's eye especially must be entirely sound: "lest, out of ignorance, the blind take it upon themselves to lead others and they both fall into the pit."[10] The chapter included in this volume is from *Liber Secunda* (*Dextera pars oculi*), a portion that was frequently excerpted and circulated as a standalone text for religious instruction, particularly on matters of sacramental and moral theology, with which it is chiefly concerned.

In the four unique catechisms contained in this volume, drawn from a Europe now some eight centuries past, one may certainly find elements of limited relevance to our own historical context, such as the admissibility of "scot-ales" or the proper collection of "garb tithes." However, an attentive reading of the articles of faith and principles of moral action presented here have much to reveal to our own age of enlightened self-aggrandizement. In ways often as surprising as they are resonant, one may find that the times and concerns of Catholics in the Middle Ages were not so very different from ours today; and their religion, *Deo gratias*, was no different at all.

[10] See p. 213, below.

EDITORIAL NOTE

Our *Catholic Catechism Index* series generally retains only the doctrinal content of those catechisms it seeks to reproduce, as well as that front matter most essential to establishing the credibility of each work as an authentic expression of the Church's common doctrine, e.g., any episcopal endorsement, *nihil obstat*, or *imprimatur*. However, it should be noted that especially prior to the eighteenth century, a number of catechisms were so immediately and universally received as reliably orthodox texts (often simply by the reputation of the author or publisher), that they received no such "official" approval; or if they did, it was often years later and in subsequent editions. We therefore include both the original printing date in our Table of Contents, and further edition information in the Preface above.

Our primary goal has been to bring these historical texts back into publication in readable English copy. Due to the wide range of time periods, cultures, and unique author styles represented in this series, we have made a number of editorial adjustments to allow for a less fatiguing read, more rapid cross-reference throughout the series, and greater research potential for the future. While not affecting the original content, these adjustments have included adopting a cleaner typesetting and simpler standard for capitalization and annotation, as well as remedying certain anachronisms in spelling or grammar.

Woodcut depicting an early method used in the production of Catholic catechisms, circa 1568.

At the same time, in deepest respect for the venerable age and subject matter of these works, we have been at pains to adhere as closely as possible to the original text: retaining archaisms such as "doth" and "hallowed," and avoiding any alterations that might affect the doctrinal content or authorial voice. We have painstakingly restored original artwork wherever possible, and where the rare explanatory note has been deemed necessary, it is not made in the text itself, but only in a marginal note. In some cases, our editorial refusal to "modernize" the content of these classical works may require a higher degree of attention from today's reader, who we trust will be richly rewarded by the effort.

We pray that our work continues to yield highly readable, faithful reproductions of these time-honored monuments to Catholic religious instruction: catechisms once penned, promulgated, and praised by bishops across the globe. May these texts that once served to guide and shape the faith and lives of millions now do so again; and may the scholars and saints once involved in their first publication now intercede for all who take them up anew. *Tolle lege!*

Sincerely in Christ,
Aaron Seng

TRADIVOX
VOLUME VI

ducas in temptationem. Sed libera
nos a malo amen. Symbolum apłorum.

Petr.
CREDO in deum patrem omnipo
tentem. creatorem celi & terre.
Andreas
& in ihm xpm filium eſ unicū
Iacob:
dūm nrm. qui conceptus est de spū
Mach̄s. *Ioħs.*
sco. natus ex maria uirgine. passus
Thomas
sub pontio pilato. crucifixus. mortuus.
Iacob: *Philipp.*
& sepultus. descendit ad inferna. ter
Bartholom̄s.
cia die resurrexit a mortuis. Ascendit
ad celos. sedet ad dexteram dei patris
Simō.
omnipotentis. inde uenturus iudicare
Taddeus.
uiuos & mortuos. Credo in spm scm. scam
ecclam catholicam. scōr communionē.
Machias.
remissionem peccōr. carnis resurrecti
onem. & uitam etnam amen.

QVICUMQVE fides athanasie.
uult saluus esse. ante omnia
opus est ut teneat catholicā fidē.
Quam nisi quisq; integram inuiolatāq;
seruauerit. absq; dubio meternū pibit.
Fides autē catholica hec ē. ut unum dm

Page from a Psalter, including the beginning of the Athanasian Creed with a portrait of the Saint; MS G.43 from The Morgan Library, New York. Scribe unknown, England ca. 1180.

Quicumque Vult

Quicumque Vult

Whosoever will be saved, before all things it is necessary that he hold the Catholic faith. Which faith except everyone do keep whole and undefiled, without doubt he shall perish everlastingly. And the Catholic faith is this, that we worship one God in Trinity and Trinity in Unity. Neither confounding the Persons, nor dividing the substance. For there is one Person of the Father, another of the Son, and another of the Holy Ghost. But the Godhead of the Father, of the Son and of the Holy Ghost is all one, the glory equal, the majesty co-eternal. Such as the Father is, such is the Son, and such is the Holy Ghost. The Father uncreate, the Son uncreate, and the Holy Ghost uncreate. The Father incomprehensible, the Son incomprehensible, and the Holy Ghost incomprehensible. The Father eternal, the Son eternal, and the Holy Ghost eternal and yet they are not three eternals but one eternal. As also there are not three uncreated, nor three incomprehensibles, but one uncreated, and one incomprehensible. So likewise the Father is Almighty, the Son Almighty, and the Holy Ghost Almighty. And yet they are not three almighties but one Almighty.

So the Father is God, the Son is God, and the Holy Ghost is God. And yet they are not three gods, but one God. So likewise the Father is Lord, the Son Lord, and the Holy Ghost Lord. And yet not three lords but one Lord. For, like as we are compelled by the Christian verity to acknowledge every Person by himself to be God and Lord, so are we forbidden by the Catholic religion to say, there be three gods or three lords. The Father is made of none: neither created, nor begotten. The Son is of the Father alone: not made, nor created, but begotten. The Holy Ghost is of the Father, and of the Son: neither made, nor created, nor begotten, but proceeding.

So there is one Father, not three fathers; one Son, not three sons; one Holy Ghost, not three holy ghosts. And in this Trinity none is afore or after other, none is greater or less than another, but the whole three Persons are co-eternal together, and co-equal. So that in all things, as is aforesaid, the Unity in Trinity, and the Trinity in Unity is to be worshipped. He therefore that will be saved, must thus think of the Trinity.

Furthermore, it is necessary to everlasting salvation, that he also believe rightly the incarnation of our Lord Jesus Christ. For the right faith is, that we believe and confess, that our Lord Jesus Christ, the Son of God, is God and man.

God, of the substance of the Father, begotten before the worlds; and man, of the substance of his Mother, born into the world. Perfect God and perfect man, of a reasonable soul and human flesh subsisting. Equal to the Father as touching his Godhead, and inferior to the Father as touching his manhood. Who, although he be God and man, yet he is not two, but one Christ. One, not by conversion of the Godhead into flesh, but by taking of the manhood into God. One altogether, not by confusion of substance, but by unity of Person. For as the reasonable soul and flesh is one man, so God and man is one Christ. Who suffered for our salvation, descended into hell, rose again the third day from the dead. He ascended into heaven, he sitteth on the right hand of the Father, God Almighty, from whence he shall come to judge the quick and the dead. At whose coming all men shall rise again with their bodies, and shall give account for their own works. And they that have done good shall go into life everlasting, and they that have done evil into everlasting fire. This is the Catholic faith, which except a man believe faithfully and firmly, he cannot be saved.

AMEN

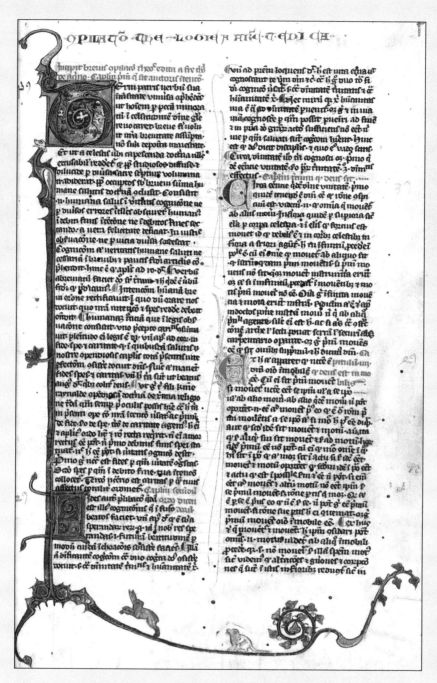

Initial page of one of the earliest compilations of St. Thomas Aquinas'
Opuscula; MS 035 from Corpus Christi College, Cambridge. Scribe and
location unknown, dated from the late 1200s to early 1300s.

The

Catechetical Instructions

of

St. Thomas Aquinas

Translated with a Commentary by
Rev. Joseph B. Collins, S.S., D.D., Ph.D.

Introduction by
Rev. Rudolph G. Bandas, Ph.D., S.T.D. et M.

New York City

JOSEPH F. WAGNER, INC.
LONDON: B. HERDER

Nihil Obstat:
E. A. Connolly, S.S., J.C.D.
Censor Deputatus

Imprimatur:
+Most Reverend Michael J. Curley, D. D.
Archbishop of Baltimore

Baltimore, February 9, 1939

Translator's Preface

St. Thomas Aquinas

St. Thomas Aquinas was born about the year 1225.[1] The name Aquinas derived from the territory of his father, Count Landulf of Aquina, in the vicinity of Naples. The mother of Thomas was Theodora, countess of Teano, and his family was related to the emperors Henry VI and Frederick II, and to the kings of France, Aragon, and Castile. "He could have quartered half the kingdoms of Europe in his shield," wrote Chesterton, "if he had not thrown away the shield. He was Italian and French and German and in every way European."[2] At the early age of five, Thomas was sent to school at the Benedictine Monastery of Monte Cassino. He showed at once the great gifts of intellect with which he had been endowed. His biographers attest to the piety and inquiring nature of this young pupil, who would surprise his master with the oft-repeated question: "What is God?" The early Benedictine training left Thomas with a lifelong devotion to the liturgy, and prepared him for further studies at the famed University of Naples where he was enrolled in or about the year 1239. While at Naples, Thomas met with the members of the Order of St. Dominic, which had been founded some twenty years earlier. He made known his desire to be a Dominican about 1240, and instantly met with strong opposition from his family, but especially from his mother. At length he received the Dominican habit in April, 1244, and was chosen to continue his studies at the Dominican school of studies at the University of Paris.

Countess Theodora completely disapproved of this journey, and sent two of her sons and a detachment of soldiers to intercept Friar Thomas on his way to Paris. In this she was successful, and for nearly two years he was held a virtual prisoner in the family castle. This period was well spent by

---

[1] P. Mandonnet, "Date de la naissance de S. Thomas d'Aquin," *Revue Thomiste* (1914), 652-662.

[2] G. K. Chesterton, *St. Thomas Aquinas* (New York: Sheed & Ward, 1933), 43.

Thomas in study and meditation. Here he was constantly urged to forsake his vocation, and on one occasion he was tempted by a woman who had been thrust into his chamber by his own brothers. Thomas arose and, grasping a burning brand from the fire, forced the temptress from his room. Then with characteristic vigor, he burned deep in the door the potent sign of the cross. In later years he confided to his secretary and companion, Reginald of Piperno, that immediately after this event he was granted his urgent prayer for the gift of perpetual chastity, and thereafter had complete freedom from the motions of concupiscence. It seems probable that this gave first basis for his title of Angelic Doctor.

In 1245, St. Thomas began to attend the lectures in theology of St. Albert the Great at the University of Paris. He made extraordinary progress in his studies, and three years later he accompanied St. Albert to Cologne there to continue his study. He was engaged in teaching in 1250. This same year marks his ordination to the priesthood. Thomas accompanied his teacher, Albert the Great, back to Paris in 1252, where he continued his lecturing and at the same time prepared for the examinations for the degree of Master in Theology. He was awarded the degree in 1257 from the University of Paris. He continued to lecture at this world-famous institution during these early years in his career, which was marked by developing intellectual power and originality and growing familiarity with the vast field of theological and philosophical learning.

St. Thomas was called to Rome in 1259, and for nine busy years was teaching, lecturing, and writing as the theologian of the Papal Court. He continued his study of Aristotle, and was deeply engrossed in the literature of the fathers of the Church. "He worked with the spirit of a missionary," says Maritain, "in the cause of truth against error."[3] His chief writings of this period were a number of philosophical works, commentaries on various books of the old and new testaments, theological disputations; above all, in 1267 or 1268 he completed the First Part of his masterpiece, the *Summa Theologica*.

---

[3] J. Maritain, *The Angelic Doctor* (New York: Dial Press, 1931), 35.

St. Thomas was already widely known as a great theologian and scholar in this century which abounded in great theologians and scholars. Recalled to Paris to replace a stricken master of theology at the university, he began the last period of his life. He was to live less than six more years. They were crowded years of writing, teaching, and preaching. His sermons, which fill a good-sized volume, were begun in the early years of his priestly life, and he continued to preach until his death. He was an authority on the spiritual life, and personally experienced the trials and consolations of the trained ascetic and the true contemplative. His writings on ascetic and mystical theology are original and permanent contributions to the science of the saints. It is related of him that, after having written the sublime treatise on the Holy Eucharist, he was seen to fall into an ecstasy, and a voice from the crucifix above the altar was heard to say: "Thou hast written well of me, Thomas. What reward wilt thou have?" To this the saint replied: "None, Lord, other than thyself."

Thomas remained in Paris for three years, from 1269 to 1272,[4] in the full maturity of his powers and the manifold outpourings of his genius. All of the Second Part of the *Summa Theologica* was written at this time, and the Third Part was begun. In 1272, he was recalled to Naples by order of the king to teach at the University of Naples which he had attended as a boy. He put the finishing touches on his numerous projects, completed the Third Part of the *Summa* up to Question 90, and then laid down his pen already worn out at the early age of 48. "I can do no more," he said on the morning of December 6, 1273. He had experienced an ecstasy during Mass and said to Reginald, his secretary: "Such secrets have been revealed to me that all I have written now appears of little value." During the following Lenten season, Thomas gave to the students and townsfolk of Naples the series of catechetical instructions on the Creed, commandments, and prayer which make up part of this volume. They are his last words. He died on March 7, 1274, at Fossanuova in Northern Italy while on his way to

---

[4] For the vexed question of exact dates in the life of St. Thomas, I have relied chiefly on Cayre, *Precis de Patrologie* (Paris, 1930), II, 526-536, who in turn is largely indebted to the researches of Mandonnet.

attend the Council of Lyons. St. Thomas Aquinas lived in an age of great scholars and great saints. He is the "prince and master of all."[5]

St. Thomas was canonized in 1323. St. Pius proclaimed him a Doctor of the Universal Church in 1567. When Pope Leo XIII wrote his famous encyclical, *Aeterni Patris*, on the restoration of Christian philosophy, he urged his readers with all the force of his apostolic office "to restore the golden wisdom of St. Thomas and to spread it far and wide for the defense and beauty of the Catholic faith, for the good of society, and for the advantage of all sciences." The same pontiff, in a brief dated August 4, 1880, designated St. Thomas patron of all Catholic universities, and his successors, including Pope Pius XI, have ordered Catholic teachers to make the explanations of Christian doctrine by St. Thomas the basis for all their teaching.

Chief Works of St. Thomas

More than sixty separate works, some of great length and some brief, came from the fertile mind of the Angelic Doctor.[6] Most important and, one would wish, most familiar of all his writings is the *Summa Theologica*. This is a complete scientific exposition of theology and at the same time a summary of Christian philosophy. St. Thomas considered this work simply as a manual of Christian doctrine for the use of students. He thus announced its division: "Since the chief aim of this sacred science is to give a knowledge of God, not only as he is in himself, but also as he is the beginning of all things and the end of all, especially of all rational creatures — we shall treat first of God; secondly, of rational creatures' advance towards God; thirdly, of Christ who as man is the way by which we tend to God." These are the leading ideas of his *Summa*, and upon them he based the three Parts of this great work.

The *Summa contra Gentiles*, whose full title is *Treatise on the Truth of the Catholic Faith against Unbelievers* (1258-1261), is the most profound

[5] Leo XIII, *Aeterni Patris*, n. 17

[6] For a complete list of St. Thomas' writings: Cayre, *Precis*, II, 526-536; Maritain, *Angelic Doctor*, 179-183; *Catholic Encyclopedia*, XIV, 666ff.

and doubtless the most powerful apologetical work ever written. It is St. Thomas' "*Summa philosophica*," taking philosophy in the modern sense. The long list of commentaries on the sacred scriptures are exhaustive, of great depth, and of permanent value. The *Perfection of the Spiritual Life* is one of the classics in the field of ascetical and mystical theology, and together with pertinent parts of the *Summa* forms a complete explanation of the Christian higher life.[7] St. Thomas also wrote the admirable *Office for the Feast of Corpus Christi* with its familiar prayers and hymns.[8]

The Opuscula

The *Opuscula* or *Little Treatises* are very numerous. In the course of time, works were listed among the *Opuscula* which were not written by St. Thomas. In the "official" catalogue of Reginald of Piperno, the *Opuscula* number seventy. They may be roughly classified as philosophical and theological, on moral and canonical questions, on liturgy and the religious life, and catechetical instructions. There are some *Opuscula* not listed in the "official" catalogue which are now considered authentic. The five *Opuscula* which are translated in the present volume are undoubtedly authentic.[9] The "Explanations" of the "Creed," the "Our Father," and the "Ten Commandments" are numbers 66, 65, 68 respectively in the catalogue which was prepared for the process of canonization of St. Thomas. The "Explanation of the Hail Mary" is listed in the catalogue of Bernard Guidonis and in later lists. This is noteworthy, since Bernard had before

---

[7] Cf. Hugh Pope, O. P., *On Prayer and the Contemplative Life by St Thomas* (Benziger Bros., 1914).

[8] It contains the *Pange lingua* with "*Tantum ergo*" among its verses, *Sacris Solemnis* with the lines of "*Panis angelicus,*" *Verbum supernum* with its concluding verse, "*O salutaris hostia.*" The antiphon of the office is the beautiful "*O Sacrum Convivium.*" The prayer said by the celebrant at benediction of the Blessed Sacrament, "*Deus qui nobis sub Sacramento mirabili,*" etc., is also a part of this office. The Eucharistic poem, *Adoro te devote*, is also probably by St. Thomas, who is rightly called the Doctor of the Eucharist.

[9] The authoritative studies on the authenticity of the *Opuscula* are: M. Mandonnet, O. P., *Des Ecrits Authentiques de S. Thomas d'Aquin* (Fribourg, 1910), and "Les Opuscules de S. Thomas d'Aquin," in *Revue Thomiste* (1927), 121-157; M. Grabmann, *Die echten Schriften des hl. Thomas v. Aquin* (Munster, 1920).

him the official list. Both Mandonnet and Grabmann consider the work authentic.[10] St. Thomas gave these "Explanations" to the students and people of Naples during his last Lenten season on earth. The talks on the ten commandments were written down by Peter d' Andrea, and the explanation of the other prayers were faithfully reported by his secretary and companion, Reginald of Piperno.

The "Explanation of the Seven Sacraments" is the second part of the treatise, *De Fidei Articulis et Septem Sacramentis*, which St. Thomas wrote at the request of the Archbishop of Palermo in 1261-1262. It is noteworthy that the famed *Decretum pro Armenis* ("Instruction for the Armenians"), issued by the authority of the Council of Florence, is taken almost verbatim from the second part of this *opusculum* (i.e., the "Explanation of the Seven Sacraments"). It is not a definition of the Council, but a practical instruction, as Denzinger points out.[11]

The latest editions of the *Opuscula* are the Vives edition (Paris) of 1871-80 and the Parma edition of 1852-73. This latter edition is reedited by Mandonnet with a new order and an introduction (Lethielleux, Paris, 1927). The "catechetical" *Opuscula* are here given in one volume in English for the first time. An English translation of two of these under the title, "On the Commandments" and "On the Lord's Prayer," was made by the Reverend H. A. Rawes in England in 1891. It is now out of print and practically inaccessible. Recently an English translation was made by Rev. Lawrence Shapcote, O. P., in two small volumes with the titles, "The Three Greatest Prayers" and "The Commandments of God" (Burns and Oates, 1937). The "Explanation of the Seven Sacraments," however, is here given for the first time in English.

St. Thomas in the History of Catechetics

The original and traditional meaning of *catechesis* (from the Greek: "teaching by word of mouth") was oral teaching or instruction by word. It is used in this sense in the new testament (e.g., in Luke 1:4; Acts 18:25).

---

[10] Mandonnet, *Des Ecrits*, 66; Grabmann, *Die echten Schriften*, 232-337.
[11] Denzinger, *Enchiridion Symbolorum*, n. 695.

Catechetical referred solely to this form of oral explanation of Christian doctrine. This is the meaning that *catechetical instruction* had in the time of St. Thomas and throughout the Middle Ages.[12] "In this connection," says one authority, "it must be remembered that the term *catechetical* was very often applied to sermons and instructions for grown people, not for children."[13] The conception of "catechetical" and "catechism" as referring to the question-and-answer method of teaching became general only during the Counter-Reformation. Thus, St. Augustine's classic work on teaching religion, *De Rudibus Catechizandis* (*On Instructing the Ignorant*), is straight exposition without question and answers. The famed *Roman Catechism* (*Catechism of the Council of Trent*)[14] is not in question-and-answer form. Hence, the catechetical instructions of St. Thomas, which are oral explanations of Christian doctrine, entitle him to a place in the history of catechetics with St. Augustine, Gerson, St. Charles Borromeo, St. Peter Canisius and others.[15]

The method of explaining Christian doctrine by giving detailed attention to the Creed, the commandments, the Our Father and Hail Mary, goes back to the early centuries of the Church. One of the first great works which embody this fourfold division is the *Catechetical Instructions* of St. Cyril of Jerusalem (d. 386). This division became general throughout the medieval period, and the "Creed, code, sacraments, and prayer" came to be a formula of the faith. Numerous synods and councils of the Church at this time decreed that sermons and instructions must be given the faithful

---

[12] "By the catechism of St. Thomas is generally understood his explanation of the Apostles' Creed, the Lord's Prayer, the Hail Mary, and the decalogue" [Gatterer-Kruz, *The Theory and Practice of the Catechism* (1914), 47].

[13] Spirago-Messmer, *Spirago's Method of Christian Doctrine* (1901), 508.

[14] Editor's note: Included in Volume VII of this series.

[15] John Gerson, the saintly chancellor of the University of Paris, wrote *On Leading the Little Ones to Christ* in the early fifteenth century. St. Charles Borromeo, Archbishop of Milan, was one of the founders of the Confraternity of Christian Doctrine and one of the authors of the *Roman Catechism*. St. Peter Canisius, the great Jesuit teacher of religion in the Counter-Reformation, wrote the well-known Canisian catechisms. Editor's note: St. Peter Canisius in fact composed three catechisms, two of which are included in Volume IX of this series.

according to this fourfold division.[16] The *Roman Catechism* follows this arrangement, as do most of the catechisms of modern times.

The Catechetical Instructions of St. Thomas were used generally throughout the thirteenth and fourteenth centuries as manuals and textbooks for priests and teachers of religion.[17] "The 'Explanations' of St. Thomas," wrote Spirago, "are remarkable for their conciseness and their simplicity of language; they are especially noteworthy because the main parts of the catechetical course of instruction are brought into connection with one another so that they appear as one harmonious whole."[18] The influence of these works is especially prominent in the *Roman Catechism* which the Council of Trent ordered written for parish priests and for all teachers of religion. Many of the explanatory passages in both works are almost identical.

Translator's Note

The edition used in this translation is the Parma, edited by P. Mandonnet, O. P., *Opuscula Omnia* (Lethielleux, Paris, 1927). Where the Vives edition is used, the change is noted in the footnotes. The edition of the *Roman Catechism* (*Catechism of the Council of Trent*) used in the commentary is *Catechismus Concilii Tridentini ad Parochos*, Romae, Ex Typog. Polyglotta, S. Cong, de Prop. Fide, 1891. To Reverend E. A. Connolly, S. S., for reading the manuscript and for many helpful suggestions the translator is very grateful.

Joseph B. Collins, S.S., D.D., Ph.D.

---

[16] Cf. Callan-McHugh, *Catechism of the Council of Trent*, Introduction, xiv and xvi. See also Spirago Messmer, *Christian Doctrine*, 507.

[17] Spirago-Messmer, *Christian Doctrine*, 513-514.

[18] Ibid.

The Apostles' Creed

WHAT IS FAITH?

The Nature and Effects of Faith. — The first thing that is necessary for every Christian is faith, without which no one is truly called a faithful Christian. Faith brings about four good effects. The first is that through faith the soul is united to God, and by it there is between the soul and God a union akin to marriage: "I will espouse thee in faith."[19] When a man is baptized, the first question that is asked him is: "Do you believe in God?"[20] This is because baptism is the first sacrament of faith. Hence, the Lord said: "He that believeth and is baptized shall be saved."[21] Baptism without faith is of no value. Indeed, it must be known that no one is acceptable before God unless he have faith. "Without faith it is impossible to please God."[22] St. Augustine explains these words of St. Paul, "All that is not of faith is sin,"[23] in this way: "Where there is no knowledge of the eternal and unchanging truth, virtue even in the midst of the best moral life is false."

The second effect of faith is that eternal life is already begun in us; for eternal life is nothing else than knowing God. This the Lord announced when he said: "This is eternal life, that they may know thee, the only true God, and Jesus Christ whom thou hast sent."[24] This knowledge of God begins here through faith, but it is perfected in the future life when we shall know God as he is. Therefore, St. Paul says: "Faith is the substance of things to be hoped for."[25] No one then can arrive at perfect happiness

---

[19] Os 2:20

[20] Translator's note: In the ceremony of administering the sacrament of baptism, the priest asks the sponsor: "N., do you believe in God the Father Almighty, Creator of heaven and earth?"

[21] Mk 16:16

[22] Heb 11:6

[23] Rom 14:23

[24] Jn 17:3

[25] Heb 11:1

of heaven, which is the true knowledge of God, unless first he knows God through faith. "Blessed are they that have not seen and have believed."[26]

The third good that comes from faith is that right direction which it gives to our present life. Now, in order that one live a good life, it is necessary that he know what is necessary to live rightly; and if he depends for all this required knowledge on his own efforts alone, either he will never attain such knowledge, or if so, only after a long time. But faith teaches us all that is necessary to live a good life. It teaches us that there is one God who is the rewarder of good and the punisher of evil; that there is a life other than this one, and other like truths whereby we are attracted to live rightly and to avoid what is evil. "The just man liveth by faith."[27] This is evident in that no one of the philosophers before the coming of Christ could, through his own powers, know God and the means necessary for salvation as well as any old woman since Christ's coming knows him through faith. And, therefore, it is said in Isaias that "the earth is filled with the knowledge of the Lord."[28]

The fourth effect of faith is that by it we overcome temptations: "The holy ones by faith conquered kingdoms."[29] We know that every temptation is either from the world or the flesh or the devil. The devil would have us disobey God and not be subject to him. This is removed by faith, since through it we know that he is the Lord of all things and must therefore be obeyed. "Your adversary the devil, as a roaring lion, goeth about seeking whom he may devour. Whom resist ye, strong in faith."[30] The world tempts us either by attaching us to it in prosperity, or by filling us with fear of adversity. But faith overcomes this in that we believe in a life to come better than this one, and hence we despise the riches of this world and we are not terrified in the face of adversity. "This is the victory which overcometh the world: our faith."[31] The flesh, however, tempts us by attracting us to the

---

[26] Jn 20:29
[27] Hb 2:4
[28] Is 11:9
[29] Heb 11:33
[30] 1 Pt 5:8
[31] 1 Jn 5:4

swiftly passing pleasures of this present life. But faith shows us that, if we cling to these things inordinately, we shall lose eternal joys. "In all things taking the shield of faith."[32] We see from this that it is very necessary to have faith.

"The Evidence of Things That Appear Not."—But someone will say that it is foolish to believe what is not seen, and that one should not believe in things that he cannot see. I answer by saying that the imperfect nature of our intellect takes away the basis of this difficulty. For if man of himself could in a perfect manner know all things visible and invisible, it would indeed be foolish to believe what he does not see. But our manner of knowing is so weak that no philosopher could perfectly investigate the nature of even one little fly. We even read that a certain philosopher spent thirty years in solitude in order to know the nature of the bee. If, therefore, our intellect is so weak, it is foolish to be willing to believe concerning God only that which man can know by himself alone. And against this is the word of Job: "Behold, God is great, exceeding our knowledge."[33] One can also answer this question by supposing that a certain master had said something concerning his own special branch of knowledge, and some uneducated person would contradict him for no other reason than that he could not understand what the master said! Such a person would be considered very foolish. So, the intellect of the angels as greatly exceeds the intellect of the greatest philosopher as much as that of the greatest philosopher exceeds the intellect of the uneducated man. Therefore, the philosopher is foolish if he refuses to believe what an angel says, and a far greater fool to refuse to believe what God says. Against such are these words: "For many things are shown to thee above the understanding of men."[34]

Then, again, if one were willing to believe only those things which one knows with certitude, one could not live in this world. How could one live unless one believed others? How could one know that this man is one's own father? Therefore, it is necessary that one believe others in matters which one cannot know perfectly for oneself. But no one is so worthy of

[32] Eph 6:16
[33] Jb 36:26
[34] Ecclus 3:25

belief as is God, and hence they who do not believe the words of faith are not wise, but foolish and proud. As the apostle says: "He is proud, knowing nothing."[35] And also: "I know whom I have believed; and I am certain."[36] And it is written: "Ye who fear the Lord, believe him and your reward shall not be made void."[37] Finally, one can say also that God proves the truth of the things which faith teaches. Thus, if a king sends letters signed with his seal, no one would dare to say that those letters did not represent the will of the king. In like manner, everything that the saints believed and handed down to us concerning the faith of Christ is signed with the seal of God. This seal consists of those works which no mere creature could accomplish; they are the miracles by which Christ confirmed the sayings of the apostles and of the saints.

If, however, you would say that no one has witnessed these miracles, I would reply in this manner. It is a fact that the entire world worshipped idols and that the faith of Christ was persecuted, as the histories of the pagans also testify. But now all are turned to Christ—wise men and noble and rich—converted by the words of the poor and simple preachers of Christ. Now, this fact was either miracle or it was not. If it is miraculous, you have what you asked for, a visible fact; if it is not, then there could not be a greater miracle than that the whole world should have been converted without miracles. And we need go no further. We are more certain, therefore, in believing the things of faith than those things which can be seen, because God's knowledge never deceives us, but the visible sense of man is often in error.[38]

---

[35] 1 Tm 6:4

[36] 2 Tm 1:12

[37] Ecclus 2:8

[38] Translator's note: For the meaning of the word *faith* see the *Catholic Encyclopedia*, vol. V. The necessity of faith is explained in St. Thomas, *Summa Theologiae*, II-II, q. 2, a. 3, 4.

THE FIRST ARTICLE

"I believe in one God."

Among all the truths which the faithful must believe, this is the first—that there is one God. We must see that God means the ruler and provider of all things. He, therefore, believes in God who believes that everything in this world is governed and provided for by him. He who would believe that all things come into being by chance does not believe that there is a God. No one is so foolish as to deny that all nature, which operates with a certain definite time and order, is subject to the rule and foresight and an orderly arrangement of someone. We see how the sun, the moon, and the stars, and all natural things follow a determined course, which would be impossible if they were merely products of chance. Hence, as is spoken of in the psalm, he is indeed foolish who does not believe in God: "The fool hath said in his heart: There is no God."[39]

There are those, however, who believe that God rules and sustains all things of nature, and nevertheless do not believe God is the overseer of the acts of man; hence they believe that human acts do not come under God's providence. They reason thus because they see in this world how the good are afflicted and how the evil enjoy good things, so that divine providence seems to disregard human affairs. Hence the words of Job are offered to apply to this view: "He doth not consider our things; and he walketh about the poles of heaven."[40] But this is indeed absurd. It is just as though a person who is ignorant of medicine should see a doctor give water to one patient and wine to another. He would believe that this is mere chance, since he does not understand the science of medicine which for good reasons prescribes for one wine and for another water. So is it with God. For God in his just and wise providence knows what is good and necessary for men; and hence he afflicts some who are good and allows certain wicked men to prosper. But he is foolish indeed who believes this is due to chance, because he does not know the causes and method of God's

[39] Ps 13:1
[40] Jb 22:14

dealing with men. "I wish that God might speak with thee, and would open his lips to thee, that he might show thee the secrets of wisdom, and that his law is manifold: and thou mightest understand that he exacteth much less of thee than thy iniquity deserveth."[41]

We must, therefore, firmly believe that God governs and regulates not only all nature, but also the actions of men. "And they said: The Lord shall not see; neither shall the God of Jacob understand. Understand, ye senseless among the people, and, you fools, be wise at last. He that planted the ear, shall he not hear? He that formed the eye, doth he not consider?... The Lord knoweth the thoughts of men."[42] God sees all things, both our thoughts and the hidden desires of our will. Thus, the necessity of doing good is especially imposed on man since all his thoughts, words and actions are known in the sight of God: "All things are naked and open to his eyes."[43]

We believe that God who rules and regulates all things is but one God. This is seen in that wherever the regulation of human affairs is well arranged, there the group is found to be ruled and provided for by one, not many. For a number of heads often brings dissension in their subjects. But since divine government exceeds in every way that which is merely human, it is evident that the government of the world is not by many gods, but by one only.

Some Motives for Belief in Many Gods

There are four motives which have led men to believe in a number of gods.

1. The dullness of the human intellect. Dull men, not capable of going beyond sensible things, did not believe anything existed except physical bodies. Hence, they held that the world is disposed and ruled by those bodies which to them seemed most beautiful and most valuable in this world. And, accordingly, to things such as the sun, the moon and the stars, they attributed and gave a divine worship. Such men are like to one who,

[41] Jb 11:5-6
[42] Ps 93:7-11
[43] Heb 4:13

going to a royal court to see the king, believes that whoever is sumptuously dressed or of official position is the king! "They have imagined either the sun and moon or the circle of the stars…to be the gods that rule the world. With whose beauty, if they being delighted, took them to be gods."[44]

2. The second motive was human adulation. Some men, wishing to fawn upon kings and rulers, obey and subject themselves to them and show them honor which is due to God alone. After the death of these rulers, sometimes men make them gods, and sometimes this is done even whilst they are living. "That every nation may know that Nabuchodonosor is god of the earth, and besides him there is no other."[45]

3. The human affection for sons and relatives was a third motive. Some, because of the excessive love which they had for their family, caused statues of them to be erected after their death, and gradually a divine honor was attached to these statues.[46] "For men serving either their affections or their kings, gave the incommunicable name to stones and wood."[47]

4. The last motive is the malice of the devil. The devil wished from the beginning to be equal to God, and thus he said: "I will ascend above the height of the clouds. I will be like the Most High."[48] The devil still entertains this desire. His entire purpose is to bring about that man adore him and offer sacrifices to him; not that he takes delight in a dog or cat that is offered to him, he does relish the fact that thereby irreverence is shown to God. Thus, he spoke to Christ: "All these will I give thee, if falling down thou wilt adore me."[49] For this reason those demons who entered into idols said that they would be venerated as gods. "All the gods of the Gentiles are demons."[50] "The things which the heathens sacrifice, they sacrifice to devils, and not to God."[51]

---

[44] Ws 13:2-3
[45] Jdt 5:29
[46] Cf. Ws 14:15-21
[47] Ws 14:21
[48] Is 14:14
[49] Mt 4:9
[50] Ps 95:5
[51] 1 Cor 10:20

Although all this is terrible to contemplate, yet at times there are many who fall into these above-mentioned four causes. Not by their words and hearts, but by their actions, they show that they believe in many gods. Thus, those who believe that the celestial bodies influence the will of man and regulate their affairs by astrology, really make the heavenly bodies gods, and subject themselves to them. "Be not afraid of the signs of heaven which the heathens fear. For the laws of the people are vain."[52] In the same category are all those who obey temporal rulers more than God, in that which they ought not; such actually set these up as gods. "We ought to obey God rather than men."[53] So also those who love their sons and kinsfolk more than God show by their actions that they believe in many gods; as likewise do those who love food more than God: "Whose god is their belly."[54] Moreover, all who take part in magic or in incantations believe that the demons are gods, because they seek from the devil that which God alone can give, such as revealing the future or discovering hidden things. We must, therefore, believe that there is but one God.

THE FIRST ARTICLE (CONTINUED)

"The Father Almighty, Creator of heaven and earth."

It has been shown that we must first of all believe there is but one God. Now, the second is that this God is the Creator and Maker of heaven and earth, of all things visible and invisible. Let us leave more subtle reasons for the present and show by a simple example that all things are created and made by God. If a person, upon entering a certain house, should feel a warmth at the door of the house, and going within should feel a greater warmth, and so on, the more he went into its interior, he would believe that somewhere within was a fire, even if he did not see the fire itself which caused this heat which he felt. So also is it when we consider the things of this world. For one finds all things arranged in different degrees of beauty

[52] Jer 10:2-3
[53] Acts 5:29
[54] Phil 3:19

and worth, and the closer things approach to God, the more beautiful and better they are found to be. Thus, the heavenly bodies are more beautiful and nobler than those which are below them; and, likewise, the invisible things in relation to the visible. Therefore, it must be seen that all these things proceed from one God who gives his being and beauty to each and everything. "All men are vain, in whom there is not the knowledge of God: and who by these good things that are seen could not understand him that is. Neither by attending to the works have acknowledged who was the workman…For by the greatness of the beauty, and of the creature, the creator of them may be seen, so as to be known thereby."[55] Thus, therefore, it is certain for us that all things in the world are from God.

Errors Relating to the First Article

There are three errors concerning this truth which we must avoid.

First, the error of the Manicheans, who say that all visible created things are from the devil, and only the invisible creation is to be attributed to God. The cause of this error is that they hold that God is the highest good, which is true; but they also assert that whatsoever comes from good is itself good. Thus, not distinguishing what is evil and what is good, they believed that whatever is partly evil is essentially evil—as, for instance, fire because it burns is essentially evil, and so is water because it causes suffocation, and so with other things. Because no sensible thing is essentially good, but mixed with evil and defective, they believed that all visible things are not made by God who is good, but by the evil one. Against them St. Augustine gives this illustration. A certain man entered the shop of a carpenter and found tools which, if he should fall against them, would seriously wound him. Now, if he would consider the carpenter a bad workman because he made and used such tools, it would be stupid of him indeed. In the same way it is absurd to say that created things are evil because they may be harmful; for what is harmful to one may be useful to another. This error is contrary to the faith of the Church, and against it we say: "Of all

---

[55] Ws 13:1, 5

things visible and invisible."[56] "In the beginning God created heaven and earth."[57] "All things were made by him."[58]

The second error is of those who hold the world has existed from eternity: "Since the time that the fathers slept, all things continue as they were from the beginning of the creation."[59] They are led to this view because they do not know how to imagine the beginning of the world. They are, says Rabbi Moses, in like case to a boy who immediately upon his birth was placed upon an island, and remained ignorant of the manner of child-bearing and of infants' birth, thus, when he grew up, if one should explain all these things to him, he would not believe how a man could once have been in his mother's womb. So also those who consider the world as it is now, do not believe that it had a beginning. This is also contrary to the faith of the Church, and hence we say: "the Maker of heaven and earth."[60] For if they were made, they did not exist forever. "He spoke and they were made."[61]

The third is the error which holds that God made the world from prejacent matter (*ex praejacenti materia*). They are led to this view because they wish to measure divine power according to human power; and since man cannot make anything except from material which already lies at hand, so also it must be with God. But this is false. Man needs matter to make anything, because he is a builder of particular things and must bring form out of definite material. He merely determines the form of his work, and can be only the cause of the form that he builds. God, however, is the universal cause of all things, and he not only creates the form but also the matter. Hence, he makes out of nothing, and thus it is said in the Creed: "the Creator of heaven and earth." We must see in this the difference between making and creating. To create is to make something out of nothing; and if everything were destroyed, he could again make all things. He, thus,

---

[56] In the Nicene Creed.
[57] Gn 1:1
[58] Jn 1:3
[59] 2 Pt 3:4
[60] In the Nicene Creed.
[61] Ps 148:5

makes the blind to see, raises up the dead, and works other similar miracles. "Thy power is at hand when thou wilt."[62]

Good Effects of Our Faith

From a consideration of all this, one is led to a fivefold benefit.

1. We are led to a knowledge of the Divine Majesty. Now, if a maker is greater than the things he makes, then God is greater than all things which he has made. "With whose beauty, if they being delighted, took them to be gods, let them know how much the Lord of them is more beautiful than they...Or if they admired their power and their effects, let them understand by them that he that made them, is mightier than they."[63] Hence, whatsoever can even be affirmed or thought of is less than God. "Behold: God is great, exceeding our knowledge."[64]

2. We are led to give thanks to God. Because God is the Creator of all things, it is certain that what we are and what we have is from God: "What hast thou that thou hast not received?"[65] "The earth is the Lord's and the fullness thereof; the world and all they that dwell therein."[66] We, therefore, must render thanks to God: "What shall I render to the Lord for all the things that he hath rendered to me?"[67]

3. We are led to bear our troubles in patience. Although every created thing is from God and is good according to its nature, yet, if something harms us or brings us pain, we believe that such comes from God, not as a fault in him, but because God permits no evil that is not for good. Affliction purifies from sin, brings low the guilty, and urges on the good to a love of God: "If we have received good things from the hand of God, why should we not receive evil?"[68]

---

[62] Ws 12:18
[63] Ws 13:3-4
[64] Jb 36:26
[65] 1 Cor 4:7
[66] Ps 23:1
[67] Ps 115:12
[68] Jb 2:10

4. We are led to a right use of created things. Thus, we ought to use created things as having been made by God for two purposes: for his glory, "since all things are made for himself"[69] (that is, for the glory of God), and finally for our profit: "Which the Lord thy God created for the service of all the nations."[70] Thus, we ought to use things for God's glory in order to please him no less than for our own profit, that is, so as to avoid sin in using them: "All things are thine, and we have given thee what we received of thy hand."[71] Whatever we have, be it learning or beauty, we must revere all and use all for the glory of God.

5. We are led also to acknowledge the great dignity of man. God made all things for man: "Thou hast subjected all things under his feet,"[72] and man is more like to God than all other creatures save the angels: "Let us make man to our image and likeness."[73] God does not say this of the heavens or of the stars, but of man; and this likeness of God in man does not refer to the body but to the human soul, which has free will and is incorruptible, and therein man resembles God more than other creatures do. We ought, therefore, to consider the nobleness of man as less than the angels but greater than all other creatures. Let us not, therefore, diminish his dignity by sin and by an inordinate desire for earthly things which are beneath us and are made for our service. Accordingly, we must rule over things of the earth and use them, and be subject to God by obeying and serving him. And thus we shall come to the enjoyment of God forever.

THE SECOND ARTICLE

"And in Jesus Christ, his only Son, our Lord."

It is not only necessary for Christians to believe in one God who is the Creator of heaven and earth and of all things; but also they must believe

---

[69] Prv 16:4
[70] Dt 4:19
[71] 1 Par 29:14
[72] Ps 8:8
[73] Gn 1:26

that God is the Father and that Christ is the true Son of God. This, as St. Peter says, is not mere fable, but is certain and proved by the word of God on the Mount of Transfiguration. "For we have not by following artificial fables made known to you the power and presence of our Lord Jesus Christ; but we were eyewitnesses of his greatness. For he received from God the Father honor and glory, this voice coming down to him from the excellent glory: 'This is my beloved Son, in whom I am well pleased. Hear ye him.' And this voice, we heard brought from heaven, when we were with him in the holy mount."[74] Christ Jesus himself in many places called God his Father, and himself the Son of God. Both the apostles and the fathers placed in the articles of faith that Christ is the Son of God by saying: "And (I believe) in Jesus Christ, his (i.e., God's) only Son."

Errors Relating to the Second Article

There were, however, certain heretics who erred in this belief.

Photinus, for instance, believed that Christ is not the Son of God but a good man who, by a good life and by doing the will of God, merited to be called the son of God by adoption; and so Christ, who lived a good life and did the will of God, merited to be called the son of God. Moreover, this error would not have Christ living before the Blessed Virgin, but would have him begin to exist only at his conception. Accordingly, there are here two errors: the first, that Christ is not the true Son of God according to his nature; and the second, that Christ in his entire being began to exist in time. Our faith, however, holds that he is the Son of God in his nature, and that he is from all eternity. Now, we have definite authority against these errors in the holy scriptures. Against the first error it is said that Christ is not only the Son, but also the only begotten Son of the Father: "The only begotten Son who is in the bosom of the Father, he hath declared him."[75] And again the second error it is said: "Before Abraham was made, I AM."[76] It is evident that Abraham lived before the Blessed Virgin. And what the

[74] 2 Pt 1:16-18
[75] Jn 1:18
[76] Jn 8:58

fathers added to the other Creed (i.e., the Nicene Creed), namely, "the only begotten Son of God," is against the first error; and "born of the Father before all ages" is against the second error.

Sabellius said that Christ indeed was before the Blessed Virgin, but he held that the Father himself became incarnate and, therefore, the Father and the Son is the same Person. This is an error because it takes away the trinity of Persons in God, and against it is this authority: "I am not alone, but I and the Father that sent me."[77] It is clear that one cannot be sent from himself. Sabellius errs therefore, and in the Symbol[78] of the fathers it is said: "God of God; light of light," that is, we are to believe in God the Son from God the Father, and the Son who is light from the Father who is light.

Arius, although he would say that Christ was before the Blessed Virgin and that the Person of the Father is other than the Person of the Son, nevertheless made a threefold attribution to Christ: 1) that the Son of God was a creature; 2) that he is not from eternity, but was formed the noblest of all creatures in time by God; 3) that God the Son is not of one nature with God the Father, and therefore that he was not true God. But this too is erroneous and contrary to the teaching of the holy scriptures. It is written: "I and the Father are one."[79] That is, in nature; and therefore, just as the Father always existed, so also the Son; and just as the Father is true God, so also is the Son. That Christ is a creature, as said by Arius, is contradicted in the Symbol by the fathers: "True God of true God;" and the assertion that Christ is not from eternity but in time is also contrary to the Symbol: "Begotten not made"; and finally, that Christ is not of the same substance as the Father is denied by the Symbol: "Consubstantial with the Father."

It is, therefore, clear we must believe that Christ is the only begotten of God, and the true Son of God, who always was with the Father, and that there is one Person of the Son and another of the Father who have

---

[77] Jn 8:16

[78] Translator's note: *Symbol* (from the Greek *symbolon*, and the late Latin *symbolum*) is a formal authoritative statement of the religious belief of the Church, referring here to the Nicene Creed. This treatise of St. Thomas is indeed called by him an "Explanation of the Symbol of the Apostles," or the Apostles' Creed.

[79] Jn 10:30

the same divine nature. All this we believe now through faith, but we shall know it with a perfect vision in the life eternal. Hence, we shall now speak somewhat of this for our own edification.

The Divine Generation

It must be known that different things have different modes of generation. The generation of God is different from that of other things. Hence, we cannot arrive at a notion of divine generation except through the generation of that created thing which more closely approaches to a likeness to God. We have seen that nothing approaches in likeness to God more than the human soul. The manner of generation in the soul is effected in the thinking process in the soul of man, which is called a conceiving of the intellect. This conception takes its rise in the soul as from a father, and its effect is called the word of the intellect or of man. In brief, the soul by its act of thinking begets the word. So also the Son of God is the Word of God, not like a word that is uttered exteriorly (for this is transitory), but as a word is interiorly conceived; and this Word of God is of the one nature as God and equal to God.[80]

The testimony of St. John concerning the Word of God destroys these three heresies, viz., that of Photinus in the words: "In the beginning was the Word";[81] that of Sabellius in saying: "And the Word was with God";[82] and that of Arius when it says: "And the Word was God."[83]

But a word in us is not the same as the Word in God. In us the word is an accident;[84] whereas in God the Word is the same as God, since there is nothing in God that is not of the essence of God. No one would say God has not a word, because such would make God wholly without knowledge; and therefore, as God always existed, so also did his Word ever exist. Just as a sculptor works from a form which he has previously thought out, which

---

[80] Translator's note: St. Thomas treats more fully the eternal generation and sonship of Christ in the *Summa Theologiae*, I, q. 27, a. 2; q. 34.

[81] Jn 1:1

[82] Ibid.

[83] Ibid.

[84] Translator's note: An accident is an attribute which is not part of the essence.

is his word; so also God makes all things by his Word, as it were through his art: "All things were made by him."[85]

Now, if the Word of God is the Son of God and all the words of God bear a certain likeness of this Word, then we ought to hear the word of God gladly; for such is a sign that we love God. We ought also believe the word of God whereby the Word of God dwells in us, who is Christ: "That Christ may dwell by faith in your hearts."[86] "And you have not his word abiding in you."[87] But we ought not only to believe that the Word of God dwells in us, but also we should meditate often upon this; for otherwise we will not be benefited to the extent that such meditation is a great help against sin: "Thy words have I hidden in my heart, that I may not sin against thee."[88] Again it is said of the just man: "On his law he shall meditate day and night."[89] And it is said of the Blessed Virgin that she "kept all these words, pondering them in her heart."[90] Then also, one should communicate the word of God to others by advising, preaching, and inflaming their hearts: "Let no evil speech proceed from your mouth; but that which is good, to the edification of faith."[91] Likewise, "Let the word of Christ dwell in you abundantly in all wisdom, teaching and admonishing one another."[92] So also: "Preach the word; be instant in season, out of season; reprove, entreat, rebuke in all patience and doctrine."[93] Finally, we ought to put the word of God into practice: "Be ye doers of the word and not hearers only, deceiving your own selves."[94]

The Blessed Virgin observed these five points when she gave birth to the Word of God. First, she heard what was said to her: "The Holy Ghost shall come upon thee."[95] Then she gave her consent through faith: "Behold

85 Jn 1:3
86 Eph 3:17
87 Jn 5:38
88 Ps 118:11
89 Ps 1:2
90 Lk 2:19
91 Eph 4:29
92 Col 3:16
93 2 Tm 4:2
94 Jas 1:22
95 Lk 1:35

the handmaid of the Lord."[96] And she also received and carried the Word in her womb. Then she brought forth the Word of God and, finally, she nourished and cared for him. And so, the Church sings: "Only a Virgin didst nourish him who is King of the angels."[97]

THE THIRD ARTICLE

"Who was conceived by the Holy Ghost, born of the Virgin Mary."

The Christian must not only believe in the Son of God, as we have seen, but also in his incarnation. St. John, after having written of things subtle and difficult to understand,[98] points out the incarnation to us when he says: "And the Word was made flesh."[99] Now, in order that we may understand something of this, I give two illustrations at the outset.

It is clear that there is nothing more like the Word of God than the word which is conceived in our mind but not spoken. Now, no one knows this interior word in our mind except the one who conceives it, and then it is known to others only when it is pronounced.[100] So also as long as the Word of God was in the heart of the Father, it was not known except by the Father himself; but when the Word assumed flesh — as a word becomes audible — then was it first made manifest and known. "Afterwards he was seen upon earth and conversed with men."[101] Another example is that, although the spoken word is known through hearing, yet it is neither seen nor touched, unless it is written on paper. So also the Word of God was made both visible and tangible when he became flesh. And as the paper upon which the word of a king is written is called the word of the king, so also man to whom the Word of God is conjoined in one *hypostasis*[102] is

96 Lk 1:38
97 Fourth Responsory, Office of the Circumcision, Dominican Breviary.
98 Cf. Jn 1:1-13
99 Jn 1:14
100 See above, under the section "Divine Generation."
101 Bar 3:38
102 Translator's note: *Hypostasis* is person distinct from nature, as in the one

called the Son of God. "Take thee a great book and write in it with a man's pen."[103] Therefore, the holy apostles affirmed: "Who was conceived by the Holy Ghost, born of the Virgin Mary."

Errors Relating to the Third Article

On this point there arose many errors; and the holy fathers at the Council of Nicaea added in that other Creed a number of things which suppress all these errors.

Origen said that Christ was born and came into the world to save even the devils, and, therefore, at the end of the world all the demons will be saved. But this is contrary to the holy scripture: "Depart from me, you cursed, into everlasting fire which was prepared for the devil and his angels."[104] Consequently, to remove this error they added in the Creed: "Who for us men (not for the devils) and for our salvation, came down from heaven." In this the love of God for us is made more apparent.

Photinus would have Christ born of the Blessed Virgin, but added that he was a mere man who by a good life in doing the will of God merited to become the son of God even as other holy men. This, too, is denied by this saying of John: "I came down from heaven, not to do my own will but the will of him that sent me."[105] Now if Christ were not in heaven, he would not have descended from heaven; and were he a mere man, he would not have been in heaven. Hence, it is said in the Nicene Creed: "He came down from heaven."

Manichaeus, however, said that Christ was always the Son of God and he descended from heaven, but he was not actually but only in appearance clothed in true flesh. But this is false, because it is not worthy of the teacher of truth to have anything to do with what is false, and just as he showed his physical body, so it was really his: "Handle, and see; for a spirit hath not

hypostasis of Christ as distinct from his two natures, human and divine; also distinct from substance, as in the three hypostases of the Godhead, which are the same in substance.

[103] Is 8:1
[104] Mt 25:41
[105] Jn 6:38

flesh and bones, as you see me to have."[106] To remove this error, therefore, they added: "And he was incarnate."

Ebion, who was a Jew, said that Christ was born of the Blessed Virgin in the ordinary human way. But this is false, for the angel said of Mary: "That which is conceived in her is of the Holy Ghost."[107] And the holy fathers to destroy this error, added: "By the Holy Ghost."

Valentinus believed that Christ was conceived by the Holy Ghost, but would have the Holy Spirit deposit a heavenly body in the Blessed Virgin, so that she contributed nothing to Christ's birth except to furnish a place for him. Thus, he said, this body appeared by means of the Blessed Virgin, as though she were a channel. This is a great error, for the angel said: "And therefore also the Holy which shall be born of thee shall be called the Son of God."[108] And the apostle adds: "But when the fullness of time was come, God sent his Son, made of a woman."[109] Hence the Creed says: "Born of the Virgin Mary."

Arius and Apollinarius held that, although Christ was the Word of God and was born of the Virgin Mary, nevertheless he did not have a soul, but in place of the soul was his divinity. This is contrary to the scripture, for Christ says: "Now is my soul troubled."[110] And again: "My soul is sorrowful even unto death."[111] For this reason the fathers added: "And was made man." Now, man is made up of body and soul. Christ had all that a true man has save sin. All the above-mentioned errors and all others that can be offered are destroyed by this: that he was made man. The error of Eutyches particularly is destroyed by it. He held that, by a commixture of the divine nature of Christ with the human, he was neither purely divine nor purely human. This is not true, because by it Christ would not be a man. And so it is said: "He was made man." This destroys also the error of Nestorius, who said that the Son of God only by an indwelling was united

---

[106] Lk 24:39
[107] Mt 1:20
[108] Lk 1:35
[109] Gal 4:4
[110] Jn 12:27
[111] Mt 26:38

to man. This, too, is false, because by this Christ would not be man but only in a man, and that he became man is clear from these words: "He was in habit found as man."[112] "But now you seek to kill me, a man who have spoken the truth to you, which I have heard of God."[113]

Good Effects of These Considerations

We can learn something from all this.

1. Our faith is strengthened. If, for instance, someone should tell us about a certain foreign land which he himself had never seen, we would not believe him to the extent we would if he had been there. Now, before Christ came into the world, the patriarchs and prophets and John the Baptist told something of God; but men did not believe them as they believed Christ, who was with God, nay more, was one with God. Hence, far more firm is our faith in what is given us by Christ himself: "No one hath seen God at any time; the only begotten Son who is in the bosom of the Father, he hath declared him."[114] Thus, many mysteries of our faith which before the coming of Christ were hidden from us, are now made clear.

2. Our hope is raised up. It is certain that the Son of Man did not come to us, assuming our flesh, for any trivial cause, but for our exceeding great advantage. For he made as it were a trade with us, assuming a living body and deigning to be born of the Virgin, in order that to us might be vouchsafed part of his divinity. And thus he became man that he might make man divine.[115]

3. Our charity is enkindled. There is no proof of divine charity so clear as that God, the Creator of all things, is made a creature; that our Lord is become our brother, and that the Son of God is made the Son of Man: "For God so loved the world as to give his only begotten Son."[116] Therefore,

[112] Phil 2:7
[113] Jn 8:40
[114] Jn 1:18
[115] "*Et sic factus est homo, ut hominem faceret Deum.*"
[116] Jn 3:16

upon consideration of this, our love for God ought to be reignited and burst into flame.

4. This induces us to keep our souls pure. Our nature was exalted and ennobled by its union with God to the extent of being assumed into union with a divine Person.

Indeed, after the incarnation, the angel would not permit St. John to adore him, although he allowed this to be done before by even the greatest patriarchs.[117] Therefore, one who reflects on this exaltation of his nature and is ever conscious of it, should scorn to cheapen and lower himself and his nature by sin. Thus, says St. Peter: "By whom he hath given us most great and precious promises; that by these you may be made partakers of the divine nature; flying the corruption of that concupiscence which is in the world."[118]

Finally, by consideration of all this, our desire to come to Christ is intensified. If a king had a brother who was away from him a long distance, that brother would desire to come to the king to see, to be with him, and to abide with him. So also Christ is our brother, and we should desire to be with him and to be united to him. "Wheresoever the body shall be, there shall the eagles also be gathered together."[119] The apostle desired "to be dissolved and be with Christ."[120] And it is this desire which grows in us as we meditate upon the incarnation of Christ.

THE FOURTH ARTICLE

"Suffered under Pontius Pilate, was crucified, died, and was buried."

It is just as necessary for the Christian to believe in the passion and death of the Son of God as it is to believe in his incarnation. For, as St. Gregory

---

[117] "And after I had heard and seen, I fell down to adore before the feet of the angel who showed me these things. And he said to me: 'See thou do it not'" (Apoc 22:8-9).
[118] 2 Pt 1:4
[119] Mt 24:28
[120] Phil 1:23

says, "there would have been no advantage in his having been born for us unless we had profited by his redemption." That Christ died for us is so tremendous a fact that our intellect can scarcely grasp it; for in no way does it fall in the natural way of our understanding. This is what the apostle says: "I work in your days, a work which you will not believe, if any man shall tell it to you."[121] The grace of God is so great and his love for us is such that we cannot understand what he has done for us. Now, we must believe that, although Christ suffered death, yet his Godhead did not die; it was the human nature in Christ that died. For he did not die as God, but as man.

This will be clear from two examples, one of which is taken from himself. Now, when a man dies, in the separation of the soul from the body the soul does not die but the body or flesh does die. So also in the death of Christ, his divinity did not die, but his human nature suffered death. But if the Jews did not slay the divinity of Christ, it would seem that their sin was not any greater than if they killed any ordinary man. In answering this we say that it is as if a king were clothed only in one garment, and if someone befouled this garment, such a one has committed as grave a crime as if he had defiled the king himself. Likewise, although the Jews could not slay God, yet in putting to death the human nature which Christ assumed, they were as severely punished as if they had put the Godhead itself to death. Another example is had from what we said before, viz., that the Son of God is the Word of God, and the Word of God made flesh is like the word of a king written on paper.[122] So if one should tear this royal paper in pieces, it would be considered that he had rent apart the word of the king. Thus, the sin of the Jews was as grievous as if they had slain the Word of God.

But what need was there that the Son of God should suffer for us? There was a great need; and indeed it can be assigned to two reasons. The first is that it was a remedy against sin, and the second is for an example of what we ought to do. It was a remedy to such an extent that in the passion of Christ we find a remedy against all the evils which we incur by our sins. And by our sins we incur five different evils.

---

[121] Acts 13:41 (quoting Hb 1:5)
[122] See above, under the section "What Is Faith?"

Evil Effects of Sin

The first evil that man incurs by sin is the defilement of his soul. Just as virtue gives the soul its beauty, so sin makes it ugly. "How happened it, O Israel, that thou art in thy enemies' land?...Thou art defiled with the dead."[123] But all this is taken away by the passion of Christ, whereby Christ poured out his blood as a laver wherein sinners are cleansed: "Who hath loved us, and washed us from our sins in his own blood."[124] So, too, the soul is washed by the blood of Christ in baptism because then a new birth is had in virtue of his blood, and hence when one defiles one's soul by sin, one offers insult to Christ and sins more gravely than before one's baptism. "A man making void the law of Moses, dieth without any mercy under two or three witnesses: How much more, do you think he deserveth worse punishments, who hath trodden underfoot the Son of God, and hath esteemed the blood of the testament unclean?"[125]

Secondly, we commit an offense against God. A sensual man loves the beauty of the flesh, but God loves spiritual beauty, which is the beauty of the soul. When, however, the soul is defiled by sin, God is offended and the sinner incurs his hatred: "To God the wicked and his wickedness are hateful alike."[126] This also is removed by the passion of Christ, which made satisfaction to God the Father for sin—a thing which man of himself could never do. The charity and obedience of Christ in his suffering were greater than the sin and disobedience of the first man: "When we were enemies, we were reconciled to God by the death of his Son."[127]

Thirdly, we have been weakened by sin. When a person sins the first time, he believes that he will thereafter keep away from sin, but what happens is the very opposite. This is because by that first sin he is weakened and made more prone to commit sins, and sin more and more has power over him. Such a one, as far as he alone is concerned, has lowered himself

---

[123] Bar 3:10-11
[124] Apoc 1:5
[125] Heb 10:28-29
[126] Ws 14:9
[127] Rom 5:10

43

to such a condition that he cannot rise up, and is like to a man who jumps into a well from which, without God's help, he would never be rescued. After the fall of man, our nature was weakened and corrupted, and we were made more prone to sin. Christ, however, lessened this sickness and weakness, although he did not entirely take it away. So now man is strengthened by the passion of Christ, and sin is not given such power over him. Moreover, he can rise clean from his sins when aided by God's grace conferred by the sacraments, which receive their efficacy from the passion of Christ: "Our old man is crucified with him, that the body of sin may be destroyed."[128] Indeed, before the passion of Christ few there were who lived without falling into mortal sin; but afterwards many have lived and are living without mortal sin.

Fourthly, we incur the punishment due to sin. For the justice of God demands that whosoever sins must be punished. This punishment, however, is in proportion to the guilt. But the guilt of mortal sin is infinite, because it is an offense against the infinite good, namely, God, whose commandments the sinner holds in contempt. Therefore, the punishment due to mortal sin is infinite. Christ, however, through his passion has taken away this punishment from us and borne it himself: "Who his own self bore our sins in his body upon the tree."[129] "Our sins (that is, the punishment due to sin) his own self bore in his body." The passion of Christ was of such value that it sufficed to expiate for all the sins of the whole world, even of a hundred thousand worlds. And so it is that, when a man is baptized, he is released from all his sins; and so also is it that the priest forgives sins; and, again, the more one conforms himself to the passion of Christ, the greater is the pardon and the grace which he gains.

Fifthly, we incur banishment from the kingdom of heaven. Those who offend kings are compelled to go into exile. Thus, man is expelled from heaven on account of sin. Adam was driven out of paradise immediately after his sin, and the gate of paradise was shut. But Christ by his sufferings and death opened this gate and recalled all the exiles to the kingdom.

---

[128] Rom 6:6
[129] 1 Pt 2:24

With the opening of the side of Christ, the gate of paradise is opened; and with the pouring out of his blood, guilt is washed away, satisfaction is made to God, infirmity is removed, punishment is expiated, and the exiles are called back to the kingdom. Hence, the thief received the immediate response: "This day thou shalt be with me in paradise."[130] Never before was this spoken to anyone, not to Adam, not to Abraham, not to David; but this day (i.e., as soon as the gate is opened) the thief, having asked for pardon, received it: "Having a confidence in the entering into the holies by the blood of Christ."[131]

Christ, Exemplar of Virtues

From all this then is seen the effect of the passion of Christ as a remedy for sin. But no less does it profit us as an example. St. Augustine says that the passion of Christ can bring about a complete reformation of our lives. Whoever wishes to live perfectly need do nothing other than despise what Christ despised on the cross, and desire what Christ desired. There is no virtue that did not have its example on the cross.

So if you seek an example of charity, then, "Greater love than this no man hath, that a man lay down his life for his friends."[132] And this Christ did upon the cross. If, therefore, he gave his life for us, we ought to endure any and all evils for him: "What shall I render to the Lord, for all the things that he hath rendered to me?"[133]

If you seek an example of patience, you will find it in its highest degree upon the cross. Great patience is exemplified in two ways: either when one suffers intensely in all patience, or when one suffers that which he could avoid if he so wished. Christ suffered greatly upon the cross: "O all ye that pass by the way, attend, and see if there be any sorrow like to my sorrow."[134] And with all patience, because, "when he suffered, he threatened

---

130 Lk 23:43
131 Heb 10:19
132 Jn 15:13
133 Ps 115:12
134 Lam 1:12

not."[135] And again: "He shall be led as a sheep to the slaughter, and shall be dumb before his shearer, and shall not open his mouth."[136] He could have avoided this suffering, but he did not: "Thinkest thou that I cannot ask my Father, and he will give me presently more than twelve legions of angels?"[137] The patience of Christ upon the cross, therefore, was of the highest degree: "Let us run by patience to the fight proposed to us; looking on Jesus, the author and finisher of faith, who having joy set before him, endured the cross, despising the shame."[138]

If you seek an example of humility, look upon him who is crucified; although he was God, he chose to be judged by Pontius Pilate and to be put to death: "Thy cause has been judged as that of the wicked."[139] Truly "that of the wicked," because: "Let us condemn him to a most shameful death."[140] The Lord chose to die for his servant; the life of the angels suffered death for man: "He humbled himself, becoming obedient unto death, even to the death of the cross."[141]

If you seek an example of obedience, imitate him who was obedient to the Father unto death: "For by the disobedience of one man, many were made sinners; so also by the obedience of one, many shall be made just."[142]

If you seek an example of contempt for earthly things, imitate him who is the King of kings, the Lord of rulers, in whom are all the treasures of wisdom; but on the cross he was stripped naked, ridiculed, spat upon, bruised, crowned with thorns, given to drink of vinegar and gall, and finally put to death. How falsely, therefore, is one attached to riches and raiment, for: "They parted my garments amongst them; and upon my vesture they cast lots";[143] how falsely to honors, since: "I was covered with lashes and insults"; how falsely to positions of power, because: "taking a

---

[135] 1 Pt 2:23
[136] Is 53:7
[137] Mt 26:53
[138] Heb 12:1-2
[139] Jb 36:17
[140] Ws 2:20
[141] Phil 2:8
[142] Rom 5:19
[143] Ps 21:19

crown of thorns, they placed it upon my brow"; how falsely to delicacies of the table, for: "in my thirst they gave me to drink of vinegar."[144] Thus, St. Augustine, in commenting on these words, "Who having joy set before him, endured the cross, despising the shame,"[145] says: "The man Christ despised all earthly things in order to teach us to despise them."

THE FIFTH ARTICLE

"He descended into hell."

The death of Christ was the separation of his soul from his body as it is with other men. But the divinity was so indissolubly conjoined to the Man-Christ that although his soul and body were disunited, his divinity was always most perfectly united to both the soul and body. This we have seen above. Therefore, in the sepulchre, his body was together with the Son of God who together with his soul descended into hell.

Reasons for Christ's Descent

There are four reasons why Christ together with his soul descended into hell.

First, he wished to take upon himself the entire punishment for our sin, and thus atone for its entire guilt. The punishment for the sin of man was not alone death of the body, but there was also a punishment of the soul, since the soul had its share in sin; and it was punished by being deprived of the beatific vision; and as yet no atonement had been offered whereby this punishment would be taken away. Therefore, before the coming of Christ all men, even the holy fathers after their death, descended into hell. Accordingly in order to take upon himself most perfectly the punishment due to sinners, Christ not only suffered death, but also his soul descended into hell. He, however, descended for a different cause than did the fathers;

144 Ps 68:22
145 Heb 12:2

for they did so out of necessity and were of necessity taken there and detained, but Christ descended there of his own power and free will: "I am counted among them that go down to the pit; I am become as a man without help, free among the dead."[146] The others were there as captives, but Christ was freely there.

The second reason is that he might perfectly deliver all his friends. Christ had his friends both in the world and in hell. The former were his friends in that they possessed charity; and the latter were they who departed this life with charity and faith in the future Redeemer, such as Abraham, Isaac, Jacob, Moses, David, and other just and good men. Therefore, since Christ had dwelt among his friends in this world and had delivered them by his death, so he wished to visit his friends who were detained in hell and deliver them also: "I will penetrate to all the lower parts of the earth, and will behold…all that hope in the Lord."[147]

The third reason is that he would completely triumph over the devil. Now, a person is perfectly vanquished when he is not only overcome in conflict, but also when the assault is carried into his very home, and the seat of his kingdom is taken away from him. Thus, Christ triumphed over the devil,[148] and on the cross he completely vanquished him: "Now is the judgment of this world: now shall the prince of this world (that is, the devil) be cast out."[149] To make this triumph complete, Christ wished to deprive the devil of the seat of his kingdom and to imprison him in his own house—which is hell. Christ, therefore, descended there, and despoiled the devil of everything and bound him, taking away his prey:[150] "And despoiling the principalities and powers, he hath exposed them confidently in open show, triumphing over them in himself."[151] Likewise, Christ, who had received the power and possession of heaven and earth, desired too

---

[146] Ps 87:5-6

[147] Ecclus 24:45

[148] Translator's note: This refers to the temptation of our Lord in the desert.

[149] Jn 12:31

[150] Translator's note: St. Thomas says that the soul of Christ descended to the hell of the just or to limbo *per suam essentiam*, but to the hell of the damned only *per suum effectum* (*Summa Theologiae*, III, q. 52, a. 2).

[151] Col 2:15

the possession of hell, as says the apostle: "That in the name of Jesus every knee should bow, of those that are in heaven, on earth, and under the earth."[152] "In my name they shall cast out devils."[153]

The fourth and final reason is that Christ might free the just who were in hell (or limbo). For as Christ wished to suffer death to deliver the living from death, so also he would descend into hell to deliver those who were there: "Thou also by the blood of thy testament, hast sent forth thy prisoners out of the pit, wherein is no water."[154] And again: "O death, I will be thy death; O hell, I will be thy bite."[155] Although Christ wholly overcame death, yet not so completely did he destroy hell, but, as it were, he bit it. He did not free all from hell, but those only who were without mortal sin. He likewise liberated those without original sin, from which they, as individuals, were freed by circumcision; or before (the institution of) circumcision, they who had been saved through their parents' faith (which refers to those who died before having the use of reason); or by the sacrifices, and by their faith in the future coming of Christ (which refers to adults). The reason they were there in hell (i.e., limbo) is original sin which they had contracted from Adam, and from which as members of the human race they could not be delivered except by Christ. Therefore, Christ left there those who had descended there with mortal sin, and the non-circumcised children. Thus, it is seen that Christ descended into hell, and for what reasons. Now we may gather four considerations from this for our own instruction.

What We May Learn from This

1. A firm hope in God. No matter how much one is afflicted, one ought always hope in the assistance of God and have trust in him. There is nothing so serious as to be in hell. If, therefore, Christ delivered those who were in hell, what great confidence ought every friend of God have that he will be

[152] Phil 2:10
[153] Mk 16:17
[154] Zac 9:11
[155] Os 13:14

delivered from all his troubles! "She (that is, wisdom) forsook not the just when he was sold, but delivered him from sinners: she went down with him into the pit. And in bonds she left him not."[156] God helps in a special manner those who serve him, and hence the servant of God should feel secure in him: "He that feareth the Lord shall tremble at nothing, and shall not be afraid for he is his hope."[157]

2. We ought to conceive a fear of God and avoid all presumption. We have already seen that Christ suffered for sinners and descended into hell for them. However, he did not deliver all sinners, but only those who were free from mortal sin. He left there those who departed this life in mortal sin. Hence, anyone who descends into hell in mortal sin has no hope of deliverance; and he will remain in hell as long as the holy fathers remain in paradise, that is, for all eternity: "And these shall go into everlasting punishment: but the just, into life everlasting."[158]

3. We ought to arouse in ourselves a mental anxiety. Since Christ descended into hell for our salvation, we ought in all care go down there in spirit by considering, for instance, its punishments as did that holy man, Hezekiah: "I said: In the midst of my days I shall go to the gates of hell."[159] Indeed, he who during this life frequently descends into hell by thinking of it, will not easily fall into hell at death; for such meditation keeps one from sin, and draws one out of it. We see how men of this world guard themselves against wrongdoing because of the temporal punishment; but with how much more care ought they avoid the punishment of hell which far exceeds all else in its duration, its severity, and its varied nature! "In all thy works remember thy last end, and thou shalt never sin."[160]

4. There comes to us in this an example of love. Christ descended into hell in order to deliver his own; and so we should go down there to rescue our own. They cannot help themselves. Therefore, let us deliver those who are in purgatory. He would be very hard-hearted who does not come to

---

[156] Ws 10:13-14
[157] Ecclus 34:16
[158] Mt 25:46
[159] Is 38:10
[160] Ecclus 7:40

the aid of a relative who is detained in an earthly prison; but much more cruel is he who will not assist a friend who is in purgatory, for there is no comparison between the pains of this world and of that: "Have pity on me, have pity on me, at least you my friends, because the hand of the Lord hath touched me."[161] "It is therefore a holy and wholesome thought to pray for the dead, that they may be loosed from their sins."[162] We may assist these souls in three ways as St. Augustine tells us, viz., through Masses, prayers, and almsgiving. St. Gregory adds a fourth, that is, fasting. All this is not so amazing, for even in this world a friend can pay a debt for his friend; but this applies only to those who are in purgatory.

THE FIFTH ARTICLE (CONTINUED)

"The third day he arose again from the dead."

We must necessarily know two things: the glory of God and the punishment of hell. For being attracted by his glory and made fearful by punishments, we take warning and withdraw ourselves from sin. But for us to appreciate these facts is very difficult. Thus, it is said of God's glory: "But the things that are in heaven, who shall search out?"[163] For those who are worldly minded this is indeed difficult, because "he that is of the earth, of the earth he is, and of the earth he speaketh";[164] but it is easier for the spiritually minded, because, "he that cometh from above is above all," as is said in the same place. Accordingly, God descended from heaven and became incarnate to teach us heavenly things. Once it was difficult to know about the punishments of hell: "no man hath been known to have returned from hell,"[165] as it is said in the person of the wicked. But this cannot be said now, for just as Christ descended from heaven to teach us heavenly

---

[161] Jb 19:21
[162] 2 Mc 12:46
[163] Ws 9:16
[164] Jn 3:31
[165] Ws 2:1

things, so also he came back from the region of hell to teach us about it. It is, therefore, necessary that we believe not only that Christ was made man, and died, but also that he arose again from the dead. Therefore, it is said in the Creed: "The third day he arose again from the dead."

We find that many arose from the dead, such as Lazarus,[166] the son of the widow,[167] and the daughter of the ruler of the synagogue.[168] But the resurrection of Christ differed from the resurrection of these and of all others in four points.

Special Character of Christ's Resurrection

1. Christ's resurrection differed from that of all others in its cause. Those others who arose did so not of their own power, but either by the power of Christ or through the prayers of some saint. Christ, on the contrary, arose by his own power, because he was not only man but also God, and the divinity of the Word was at no time separated either from his soul or from his body. Therefore, his body could, whenever he desired, take again the soul, and his soul the body: "I lay down my life, that I may take it again...And I have power to lay it down; and I have power to take it up again."[169] Christ truly died, but not because of weakness or of necessity, but rather of his own will entirely and by his own power. This is seen in that moment when he yielded up the Ghost; he cried out with a loud voice,[170] which could not be true of others at the moment of dying, because they die out of weakness. For this the centurion said: "Indeed, this was the Son of God."[171] By that same power whereby he gave up his soul, he received it again; and hence the Creed says, "He arose again," because he was not raised up as if by anyone else. "I have slept and have taken my rest; and I have risen up."[172] Nor can this be contrary to these words, "This Jesus hath

---

[166] Cf. Jn 11:1-44
[167] Cf. Lk 7:11-15
[168] Cf. Mk 5:35-43
[169] Jn 10:17-18
[170] Cf. Mt 27:50
[171] Mt 27:54
[172] Ps 3:6

God raised again,"[173] because both the Father and the Son raised him up, since one and the same power is of the Father and the Son.

2. Christ's resurrection was different as regards the life to which he arose. Christ arose again to a glorious and incorruptible life: "Christ is risen from the dead by the glory of the Father."[174] The others, however, were raised to that life which they had before, as is seen of Lazarus and the others.

3. Christ's resurrection was different also in effect and efficacy. In virtue of the resurrection of Christ all shall rise again: "And many bodies of the saints that had slept arose."[175] The apostle declares that "Christ is risen from the dead, the first fruits of them that sleep."[176] But also note that Christ by his passion arrived at glory: "Ought not Christ to have suffered these things and so to enter into his glory?"[177] And this is to teach us how we also may arrive at glory: "Through many tribulations we must enter into the kingdom of God."[178]

4. Christ's resurrection was different in point of time. Christ arose on the third day; but the resurrection of the others is put off until the end of the world. The reason for this is that the resurrection and death and nativity of Christ were "for our salvation,"[179] and thus he wished to rise again at a time when it would be of profit to us. Now, if he had risen immediately, it would not have been believed that he died; and similarly, if he had put it off until much later, the disciples would not have remained in their belief, and there would have been no benefit from his passion. He arose again, therefore, on the third day, so that it would be believed that he died, and his disciples would not lose faith in him.

[173] Acts 2:32
[174] Rom 6:4
[175] Mt 27:52
[176] 1 Cor 15:20
[177] Lk 24:26
[178] Acts 14:21
[179] From the Nicene Creed.

What We May Learn from the Resurrection

From all this we can take four things for our instruction. Firstly, let us endeavor to arise spiritually from the death of the soul, which we incur by our sins, to that life of justice which is had through penance: "Rise, thou that sleepest, and arise from the dead; and Christ shall enlighten thee."[180] This is the first resurrection: "Blessed and holy is he that hath part in the first resurrection."[181]

Secondly, let us not delay to rise until our death, but do it at once, since Christ arose on the third day: "Delay not to be converted to the Lord; and defer it not from day to day."[182] You will not be able to consider what pertains to salvation when weighed down by illness, and, moreover, by persevering in sin, you will lose part of all the good which is done in the Church, and you will incur many evils. Indeed, the longer you possess the devil, the harder it is to put him away, as St. Bede tells us.

Thirdly, let us rise up again to an incorruptible life in that we may not die again, but resolve to sin no more: "Knowing that Christ, rising again from the dead, dieth now no more. Death shall no more have dominion over him...So do you also reckon that you are dead to sin, but alive unto God, in Christ Jesus our Lord...Neither yield ye your members as instruments of iniquity unto sin; but present yourselves to God, as those that are alive from the dead."[183]

Fourthly, let us rise again to a new and glorious life by avoiding all that which formerly were the occasions and the causes of our death and sin: "As Christ is risen from the dead by the glory of the Father, so we also may walk in newness of life."[184] This new life is the life of justice which renews the soul and leads it to the life of glory.

[180] Eph 5:14
[181] Apoc 20:6
[182] Ecclus 5:8
[183] Rom 6:9, 11, 13
[184] Rom 6:4

THE SIXTH ARTICLE

"He ascended into heaven, and sitteth at the right hand of God, the Father Almighty."

Besides the resurrection of Christ, we must also believe in his ascension; for he ascended into heaven on the fortieth day. Hence, the Creed says: "He ascended into heaven." Concerning this we ought to observe three things, viz., that it was sublime, reasonable, and beneficial.

The Sublimity of the Ascension

It was certainly sublime that Christ ascended into heaven. This is expounded in three ways. Firstly, he ascended above the physical heaven: "He...ascended above all the heavens."[185] Secondly, he ascended above all the spiritual heavens, i.e., spiritual natures: "Raising (Jesus) up from the dead and setting him on his right hand in the heavenly places. Above all principality and power and virtue and dominion and every name that is named, not only in this world but also in that which is to come. And he hath subjected all things under his feet."[186] Thirdly, he ascended up to the very throne of the Father: "Lo, one like the son of man came with the clouds of heaven. And he came even to the Ancient of days."[187] "And the Lord Jesus, after he had spoken to them, was taken up into heaven and sitteth on the right hand of God."[188] Now, it is not to be taken in the literal sense, but figuratively, that Christ is at the right hand of God. Inasmuch as Christ is God, he is said to sit at the right hand of the Father, that is, in equality with the Father; and as Christ is man, he sits at the right hand of the Father, that is, in a more preferable place. The devil once feigned to do this: "I will ascend above the height of the clouds. I will be like the most High."[189] But Christ alone succeeded in this, and so it is said: "He ascended

---

[185] Eph 4:10
[186] Eph 1:20-22
[187] Dn 7:13
[188] Mk 16:19
[189] Is 14:14

into heaven, and sitteth at the right hand of the Father." "The Lord said to my Lord: Sit thou at my right hand."[190]

The Reasonableness of the Ascension

The ascension of Christ into heaven is in accord with reason.

1. Because heaven was due to Christ by his very nature. It is natural for one to return to that place from whence he takes his origin. The beginning of Christ is from God, who is above all things: "I came forth from the Father and am come into the world; again I leave the world and I go to the Father."[191] "No man hath ascended into heaven, but he that descended from heaven, the Son of man who is in heaven."[192] The just ascend into heaven, but not in the manner that Christ ascended, i.e., by his own power; for they are taken up by Christ: "Draw me, we will run after thee."[193] Or, indeed, we can say that no man but Christ has ascended into heaven, because the just do not ascend except insofar as they are the members of Christ who is the head of the Church. "Wheresoever the body shall be, there shall the eagles also be gathered together."[194]

2. Heaven is due to Christ because of his victory. For he was sent into the world to combat the devil, and he did overcome him. Therefore, Christ deserved to be exalted above all things: "I also have overcome and am set down with my Father in his throne."[195]

3. The ascension is reasonable because of the humility of Christ. There never was humility so great as that of Christ, who, although he was God, yet wished to become man; and although he was the Lord, yet wished to take the form of a servant, and, as St. Paul says: "He was made obedient unto death,"[196] and descended even into hell. For this he deserved to be exalted even to heaven and to the throne of God, for humility leads to

---

[190] Ps 109:1
[191] Jn 16:28
[192] Jn 3:13
[193] Cant 1:3
[194] Mt 24:28
[195] Apoc 3:21
[196] Phil 2:8

exaltation: "He that humbleth himself shall be exalted."[197] "He that descended is the same also that ascended above all the heavens."[198]

The Benefits of the Ascension

The ascension of Christ was very beneficial for us. This is seen in three ways. Firstly, as our leader, because he ascended in order to lead us; for we had lost the way, but he has shown it to us. "For he shall go up that shall open the way before them,"[199] and thus we may be made certain of possessing the heavenly kingdom: "I go to prepare a place for you."[200] Secondly, that he might draw our hearts to himself: "For where thy treasure is, there is thy heart also."[201] Thirdly, to let us withdraw from worldly things: "Therefore, if you be risen with Christ, seek the things that are above, where Christ is sitting at the right hand of God. Mind the things that are above, not the things that are upon the earth."[202]

THE SEVENTH ARTICLE

"From thence he shall come to judge the living and the dead."

It is of the office of the King and Lord to pronounce judgment: "The king that sitteth on the throne of judgment scattereth away all evil with his look."[203] Since Christ, therefore, ascended into heaven and sits at the right hand of God as Lord of all, it is clear that his is the office of judge. For this reason we say in the rule of Catholic faith that: "He shall come to judge the living and the dead." Indeed, the angels have said that: "This Jesus who is taken up from you into heaven shall so come as you have seen him going into heaven."[204]

[197] Lk 14:11
[198] Eph 4:10
[199] Mi 2:13
[200] Jn 14:2
[201] Mt 6:21
[202] Col 3:1-2
[203] Prv 20:8
[204] Acts 1:11

We shall consider three facts about the judgment: 1) the form of the judgment; 2) the fear of the judgment; 3) our preparation for the judgment.

The Form of the Judgment

Now, concerning the form of the judgment there is a threefold question. Who is the judge, who are to be judged, and upon what will they be judged? Christ is the judge: "It is he who is appointed by God to be judge of the living and of the dead."[205] We may here interpret *the dead* to mean sinners and *the living* to mean the just; or *the living* to refer to those who at that time were living and *the dead* to mean those who had died. Christ of a certain is judge, not only in that he is God, but also in that he is man. The first reason for this is because it is necessary that they who are to be judged may see the judge. But the Godhead is so wholly delightful that no one could behold it without great enjoyment; and hence the damned are not permitted to see the judge, nor in consequence to enjoy anything. Christ, therefore, of necessity will appear in the form of man so that he may be seen by all: "And he hath given him power to do judgment, because he is the Son of man."[206] Again, Christ deserved this office as man, for as man he was unjustly judged, and therefore God constitutes him judge of the entire world: "Thy cause hath been judged as that of the wicked. Cause and judgment thou shalt recover."[207] And, lastly, if God alone should judge men, they, being terrified, would despair; but this despair disappears from men if they are to be judged by a man: "And then they shall see the Son of man coming in a cloud."[208]

Who Are to Be Judged?

All are to be judged—those who are, who were, and who will be: "We must all be manifested before the judgment seat of Christ, that every one may receive the proper things of the body, according as he hath done, whether it

[205] Acts 10:42
[206] Jn 5:27
[207] Jb 36:17
[208] Lk 21:27

be good or evil."[209] There are, says St. Gregory, four different classes of people to be judged. The chief difference is between the good and the wicked.

Of the wicked, some will be condemned but not judged. They are the infidels whose works are not to be discussed because, as St. John says: "He that doth not believe is already judged."[210] Others will be both condemned and judged. They are those possessing the faith who departed this life in mortal sin: "For the wages of sin is death."[211] They shall not be excluded from the judgment because of the faith which they possessed.

Of the good also, some will be saved and shall not be judged, they are the poor in spirit for God's sake who rather shall judge others: "Amen, I say to you that you, who have followed me, in the regeneration, when the Son of man shall sit on the seat of his majesty, you also shall sit on twelve seats judging the twelve tribes of Israel."[212] Now, this is not to be understood only of the disciples, but of all those who are poor in spirit; for otherwise Paul, who labored more than others, would not be among this number. These words, therefore, must refer also to all the followers of the apostles and to all apostolic men: "Know you not that we shall judge angels?"[213] "The Lord will enter into judgment with the ancients of his people and its princes."[214]

Others shall both be saved and judged, that is, they who die in a state of righteousness. For although they departed this life in justice, nevertheless they fell somewhat amiss in the business of temporal matters, and hence shall be judged but saved. The judgment will be upon all their deeds good and bad: "Walk in the ways of thy heart,…and know that for all these God will bring thee into judgment."[215] "And all things that are done, God will bring into judgment for every error, whether it be good or evil."[216] Even idle words shall be judged: "But I say to you that every idle word that men

---

[209] 2 Cor 5:10
[210] Jn 3:18
[211] Rom 6:23
[212] Mt 19:28
[213] 1 Cor 6:3
[214] Is 3:14
[215] Eccles 11:9
[216] Eccles 12:14

shall speak, they shall render an account for it in the day of judgment."[217] And thoughts also: "For inquisition shall be made into the thought of the ungodly."[218] Thus, the form of the judgment is clear.

The Fear of the Judgment

The judgment ought indeed to be feared.

a) Because of the wisdom of the judge. God knows all things, our thoughts, words and deeds, and "all things are naked and open to his eyes."[219] "All the ways of men are open to his eyes."[220] He knows our words: "The ear of jealousy heareth all things."[221] Also our thoughts: "The heart is perverse above all things and unsearchable. Who can know it? I am the Lord, who search the heart and prove the reins; who give to every one according to his way and according to the fruit of his devices."[222] There will be infallible witnesses—men's own consciences: "Who show the work of the law written in their hearts, their conscience bearing witness to them; and their thoughts between themselves accusing or also defending one another, in the day when God shall judge the secrets of men."[223]

b) Because of the power of the judge, who is almighty in himself: "Behold, the Lord God will come with strength."[224] And also almighty in others: "The whole world shall fight with him against the unwise."[225] Hence, Job says: "Whereas there is no man that can deliver out of thy hand."[226] "If I ascend into heaven, thou art there; if I descend into hell, thou art present," says the psalmist.[227]

[217] Mt 12:36
[218] Ws 1:9
[219] Heb 4:13
[220] Prv 16:2
[221] Ws 1:10
[222] Jer 17:9-10
[223] Rom 2:15-16
[224] Is 40:10
[225] Ws 5:21
[226] Jb 10:7
[227] Ps 138:8

c) Because of the inflexible justice of the judge. The present is the time for mercy; but the future is the time solely for justice; and so the present is our time, but the future is God's time: "When I shall take a time, I shall judge justices."[228] "The jealousy and rage of the husband will not spare in the day of revenge. Nor will he yield to any man's prayers; nor will he accept for satisfaction ever so many gifts."[229]

d) Because of the anger of the judge. He shall appear in different ways to the just and to the wicked. To the just, he will be pleasant and gracious: "They will behold the king of beauty."[230] To the wicked he will be angry and pitiless, so that they may say to the mountains: "Fall upon us and hide us...from the wrath of the Lamb."[231] But this anger of God does not bespeak in him any perturbation of soul, but rather the effect of his anger which is the eternal punishment inflicted upon sinners.

Our Preparation for the Judgment

Now, against this fear of the judgment we ought to have four remedies. The first is good works: "Wilt thou then not be afraid of the power? Do that which is good, and thou shalt have praise from the same."[232] The second is confession and repentance for sins committed; and this ought to include sorrow in thinking of them, feeling of shame in confessing them, and all severity in making satisfaction for them. And these will take away the eternal punishment. The third is giving of alms, which makes all things clean: "Make unto you friends of the mammon of iniquity; that when you shall fail, they may receive you into everlasting dwellings."[233] The fourth is charity, viz., the love of God and our neighbor, for "charity covereth a multitude of sins."[234]

---

[228] Ps 74:3
[229] Prv 6:34-35
[230] Is 33:17
[231] Apoc 6:16
[232] Rom 13:3
[233] Lk 16:9
[234] 1 Pt 4:8

THE EIGHTH ARTICLE

"I believe in the Holy Ghost."

As we have said, the Word of God is the Son of God just as in a way the word of man is the concept of his intellect.[235] But sometimes man has a word which is dead. This is when, for instance, he conceives what he ought to do, but he has not the will to do it; or when one believes but does not practice; then his faith is said to be dead, as St. James points out.[236] The Word of God, however, is alive: "For the word of God is living."[237] It is necessary, therefore, that in God there be will and love. Thus, St. Augustine says: "The word of God which we plan to speak is knowledge with love."[238] Now, as the Word of God is the Son of God, God's love is the Holy Ghost. Hence, it is that one possesses the Holy Ghost when he loves God: "The charity of God is poured forth in our hearts, by the Holy Ghost who is given to us."[239]

Teaching of the Nicene Creed

There are some who held false opinions concerning the Holy Ghost. They said, for instance, that he was only the servant and minister of God. Hence, to remove these errors the holy fathers added five phrases concerning the Holy Ghost.[240]

"The Holy Ghost, the Lord." — The first is, that although there are other spirits, such as the angels who are ministers of God ("Art they not all ministering spirits?"[241]) nevertheless the Holy Ghost is the Lord. "God is

---

[235] See above, under the section "Divine Generation."

[236] "So faith also, if it have not works, is dead in itself" (Jas 2:17).

[237] Heb 4:12

[238] Augustine, *On the Trinity*, Bk. 9, Ch. 10

[239] Rom 5:5

[240] "And I believe in the Holy Ghost, 1) the Lord and 2) life-giver, 3) who proceeds from the Father and the Son: 4) who together with the Father and the Son is adored and glorified, 5) who spoke by the prophets" (The Nicene Creed).

[241] Heb 1:14

a spirit,"[242] and, "Now the Lord is a Spirit,"[243] and also, "Where the Spirit of the Lord is, there is liberty."[244] The reason is that he makes us love God and cease to love the world. Thus, the Creed says: "In the Holy Ghost, the Lord."

"And life-giver." — The second phrase is there because the soul's life is to be united to God, inasmuch as God is the life of the soul, and as truly as the soul is the life of the body.[245] Now, the Holy Ghost unites the soul to God through love, because he is the love of God, and therefore he gives life. "It is the spirit that quickeneth."[246] Therefore, it is said: "and life-giver."

"Who proceeds from the Father and the Son." — The third is that the Holy Ghost is one in substance with the Father and the Son; because as the Son is the Word of the Father, so the Holy Spirit is the love both of the Father and the Son, and, therefore, he proceeds from them both. Moreover, just as the Word of God is of the same substance as the Father, so also is Love (Holy Ghost) of the same substance as the Father and the Son. Hence, it is said: "Who proceedeth from the Father and the Son." From this it is seen that the Holy Spirit is not a creature.

"Who...is adored and glorified." — The fourth phrase is that the Holy Ghost as regards adoration is equal to the Father and the Son: "The true adorers shall adore the Father in spirit and truth."[247] "Teach ye all nations; baptizing them in the name of the Father and of the Son and of the Holy Ghost."[248] Hence, it is said: "Who together with the Father and the Son is adored."

"Who spoke by the prophets." — The fifth phrase, wherein the Holy Ghost is declared equal to God, is that the holy prophets spoke on behalf of God. It is clear that, if the Holy Ghost were not God, then it would not be said that the prophets had spoken of God on his behalf. Thus, says St. Peter:

---

[242] Jn 4:24
[243] 2 Cor 3:17
[244] Ibid.
[245] *"Cum ipse Deus sit vita animae, sicut anima vita corporis."*
[246] Jn 6:64
[247] Jn 4:23
[248] Mt 28:19

"The holy men of God spoke, inspired by the Holy Ghost."[249] Also: "The Lord God hath sent me, and his spirit."[250] And so it is said: "Who spoke by the prophets."

In all this, two errors are condemned. The Manicheans said that the old testament was not from God. But this is false because the Holy Spirit spoke through the prophets. Likewise, the error of Priscillian and Montanus was that they believed that the prophets did not speak by the Holy Ghost but were somewhat beside themselves.

Benefits from the Holy Ghost

Many benefits come to us from the Holy Ghost.

1. He cleanses us from our sins. The reason is that one must repair that which one has made. Now, the soul is created by the Holy Spirit, because God has made all things through him; for God, by loving his goodness, created everything: "Thou lovest all things that are, and hatest none of the things which thou hast made."[251] Thus, Dionysius says: "Divine love did not permit him to be without offspring."[252] It is necessary, therefore, that the hearts of men, destroyed by sin, be made anew by the Holy Ghost: "Thou shalt send forth thy spirit, and they shall be created; and thou shalt renew the face of the earth."[253] Nor is it any wonder that the Spirit cleanses, since all sins are taken away by love: "Many sins are forgiven her, because she hath loved much."[254] "Charity covereth all sins."[255] And likewise: "Charity covereth a multitude of sins."[256]

2. The Holy Spirit enlightens the intellect, since all that we know, we know through the Holy Ghost: "But the Paraclete, the Holy Ghost, whom the Father will send in my name, he will teach you all things and bring all

---

[249] 2 Pt 1:21
[250] Is 48:16
[251] Ws 11:25
[252] Dionysius, *On Divine Names*, Ch. 4
[253] Ps 103:30
[254] Lk 7:47
[255] Prv 10:12
[256] 1 Pt 4:8

things to your mind, whatsoever I shall have said to you."[257] Also: "His unction teacheth you all things."[258]

3. He assists us and, to a certain extent, compels us to keep the commandments. No one can keep the commandments unless he loves God: "If any one love me, he will keep my word."[259] Thus, the Holy Spirit makes us love God: "And I give you a new heart and put a new spirit within you; and I will take away the stony heart out of your flesh and will give you a heart of flesh. And I will put my spirit in the midst of you; and I will cause you to walk in my commandments and to keep my judgments and do them."[260]

4. He strengthens in us the hope of eternal life, because he is the pledge to us of this our destiny: "You were signed with the holy Spirit of promise who is the pledge of our inheritance."[261] He is, as it were, the surety of our eternal life. The reason is that eternal life is due to man inasmuch as he is become the son of God; and this is brought about in that he is made like unto Christ; and this, in turn, follows from his having the Spirit of Christ, and this is the Holy Ghost: "For you have not received the spirit of bondage again in fear; but you have received the spirit of adoption of sons, whereby we cry: Abba (Father). For the Spirit himself giveth testimony to our spirit that we are the sons of God."[262] And also: "Because you are sons, God hath sent the Spirit of his Son into your hearts, crying: Abba, Father."[263]

5. He counsels us when we are in doubt, and teaches us what is the will of God: "He that hath an ear let him hear what the Spirit saith to the churches."[264] Likewise: "I may hear him as a master."[265]

[257] Jn 14:26
[258] 1 Jn 2:27
[259] Jn 14:23
[260] Ez 36:26-27
[261] Eph 1:13
[262] Rom 8:15-16
[263] Gal 4:6
[264] Apoc 2:7
[265] Is 50:4

THE NINTH ARTICLE

"I believe in the holy Catholic Church."

We see that in a man there are one soul and one body; and of his body there are many members. So also the Catholic Church is one body and has different members. The soul which animates this body is the Holy Spirit.[266] Hence, after confessing our faith in the Holy Ghost, we are bid to believe in the holy Catholic Church. Thus, in the Symbol it is said, "the holy Catholic Church."

It must be known that *church* is the same as "assembly." So, the holy Church is the same as the assembly of the faithful, and every Christian is a member of this Church, of which it is written: "Draw near to me, ye unlearned; and gather yourselves together into the house of discipline."[267]

The Church has four essential conditions, in that she is one, holy, catholic, and strong and firm.

The Unity of the Church

Of the first, it must be known that the Church is one. Although various heretics have founded various sects, they do not belong to the Church, since they are but so many divisions. Of her it is said: "One is my dove; my perfect one is but one."[268] The unity of the Church arises from three sources.

1. *The unity of faith.* All Christians who are of the body of the Church believe the same doctrine. "I beseech you...that you all speak the same

---

[266] Translator's note: "For as the body is one and hath many members; and all the members of the body, whereas they are many, yet are one body, so also is Christ. For in one Spirit were we all baptized into one body...For the body also is not one member, but many" (1 Cor 12:12-14). For St. Paul's admirable description of the Church, Christ's mystical body, see all of this chapter.

[267] Ecclus 51:31

[268] Cant 6:8

thing and that there be no schisms among you."[269] And: "One Lord, one faith, one baptism."[270]

2. *The unity of hope.* All are strengthened in one hope of arriving at eternal life. Hence, the apostle says: "One body and one Spirit, as you are called in one hope of your calling."[271]

3. *The unity of charity.* All are joined together in the love of God, and to each other in mutual love: "And the glory which thou hast given me, I have given them; that they may be one, as we also are one."[272] It is clear that this is a true love when the members are solicitous for one another and sympathetic towards each other: "We may in all things grow up in him who is the head, Christ. From whom the whole body, being compacted, and fitly joined together, by what every joint supplieth, according to the operation in the measure of every part, maketh increase of the body unto the edifying of itself in charity."[273] This is because each one ought to make use of the grace God grants him, and be of service to his neighbor. No one ought to be indifferent to the Church, or allow himself to be cut off and expelled from it; for there is but one Church in which men are saved, just as outside of the ark of Noah no one could be saved.

The Holiness of the Church

Concerning the second mark, holiness, it must be known that there is indeed another assembly, but it consists of the wicked: "I hate the assembly of the malignant."[274] But such a one is evil; the Church of Christ, however, is holy: "For the temple of God is holy, which you are."[275] Hence, it is said: "the holy Church."

The faithful of this Church are made holy because of four things. 1) Just as a church is cleansed materially when it is consecrated, so also the

---

[269] 1 Cor 1:10
[270] Eph 4:5
[271] Eph 4:4
[272] Jn 17:22
[273] Eph 4:15-16
[274] Ps 25:5
[275] 1 Cor 3:17

faithful are washed in the blood of Christ: "Jesus Christ…who hath loved us and washed us from our sins in his own blood."[276] And: "That he might sanctify the people by his blood, suffered without the gate."[277] 2) Just as there is the anointing of the church, so also the faithful are anointed with a spiritual unction in order to be sanctified. Otherwise, they would not be Christians, for *Christ* is the same as "anointed." This anointing is the grace of the Holy Spirit: "He that confirmeth us with you in Christ and that hath anointed us, is God."[278] And: "You are sanctified…in the name of our Lord Jesus Christ."[279] 3) The faithful are made holy because of the Trinity who dwells in the Church; for wheresoever God dwells, that place is holy. "The place whereon thou standest is holy."[280] And: "Holiness becometh thy house, O Lord."[281] 4) Lastly, the faithful are sanctified because God is invoked in the Church: "But thou, O Lord, art among us, and thy name is called upon by us; forsake us not."[282] Let us, therefore, beware, seeing that we are thus sanctified, lest by sin we defile our soul which is the temple of God: "Know you not that you are the temple of God and that the Spirit of God dwelleth in you? But if any man violate the temple of God, him shall God destroy."[283]

The Catholicity or Universality of the Church

The Church is catholic, that is, universal. Firstly, it is universal in place, because it is worldwide. This is contrary to the error of the Donatists. For the Church is a congregation of the faithful; and since the faithful are in every part of the world, so also is the Church: "Your faith is spoken of in the whole world."[284] And also: "Go ye into the whole world

---

[276] Apoc 1:5
[277] Heb 13:12
[278] 2 Cor 1:21
[279] 1 Cor 6:11
[280] Jo 5:16; Cf. Gn 3:5
[281] Ps 92:5
[282] Jer 14:9
[283] 1 Cor 3:16-17
[284] Rom 1:8

and preach the gospel to every creature."[285] Long ago, indeed, God was known only in Judea; now, however, he is known throughout the entire world. The Church has three parts: one is on earth, one is in heaven, and one is in purgatory. Secondly, the Church is universal in regard to all the conditions of mankind; for no exceptions are made, neither master nor servant, neither man nor woman: "Neither bond nor free; there is neither male nor female."[286] Thirdly, it is universal in time. Some have said that the Church will exist only up to a certain time. But this is false, for the Church began to exist in the time of Abel and will endure up to the end of the world: "Behold, I am with you all days, even to the consummation of the world."[287] Nay more, even after the end of the world, it will continue to exist in heaven.

The Apostolicity of the Church

The Church is firm. A house is said to be firm if it has a solid foundation. The principal foundation of the Church is Christ: "For other foundation no men can lay but that which is laid, which is Christ Jesus."[288] The secondary foundation, however, is the apostles and their teaching. Therefore, the Church is firm. It is said in the Apocalypse that the city has "twelve foundations," and therein were "written the names of the twelve apostles."[289] From this the Church is called apostolic. Likewise, to indicate this firmness of the Church St. Peter is called the crowning head.[290]

The firmness of a house is evident if, when it is violently struck, it does not fall. The Church similarly can never be destroyed, neither by persecution nor by error. Indeed, the Church grew during the persecutions, and both those who persecuted her and those against whom she threatened completely failed: "And whosoever shall fall upon this stone, shall be

285 Mk 16:15
286 Gal 3:28
287 Mt 28:20
288 1 Cor 3:11
289 Apoc 21:14
290 Cf. Mt 16:18

broken; but on whomsoever it shall fall, it shall grind him to powder."[291] As regards errors, indeed, the more errors arise, the more surely truth is made to appear: "Men corrupt in mind, reprobate in faith; but they shall proceed no further."[292]

Nor shall the Church be destroyed by the temptations of the demons. For she is like a tower towards which all flee who war against the devil: "The name of the Lord is a strong tower."[293] The devil, therefore, is chiefly intent on destroying the Church, but he will not succeed, for the Lord has said: "The gates of hell shall not prevail against it."[294]

This is as if he said: "They shall make war against thee, but they shall not overcome thee." And thus it is that only the Church of Peter (to whom it was given to evangelize Italy when the disciples were sent to preach) was always firm in faith. On the contrary, in other parts of the world there is either no faith at all or faith mixed with many errors. The Church of Peter flourishes in faith and is free from error. This, however, is not to be wondered at, for the Lord has said to Peter: "But I have prayed for thee, that thy faith fail not; and thou, being once converted, confirm thy brethren."[295]

THE TENTH ARTICLE

"The communion of saints, the forgiveness of sins."

As in our natural body the operation of one member works for the good of the entire body, so also is it with a spiritual body, such as is the Church. Because all the faithful are one body, the good of one member is communicated to another: "And every one members, one of another."[296] So, among the points of faith which the apostles have handed down is that there is a common sharing of good in the Church. This is expressed in the words, "the communion of saints." Among the various members of the Church,

[291] Mt 21:14
[292] 2 Tm 3:8-9
[293] Prv 18:10
[294] Mt 16:18
[295] Lk 22:32
[296] Rom 12:5

the principal member is Christ, because he is the head: "He hath made him head over all the Church, which is his body."[297] Christ communicates his good, just as the power of the head is communicated to all the members.

The Seven Sacraments: A Review

This communication takes place through the sacraments of the Church in which operate the merits of the passion of Christ, which in turn operates for the conferring of grace unto the remission of sins. These sacraments of the Church are seven in number.

Baptism. — The first is baptism which is a certain spiritual regeneration. Just as there can be no physical life unless man is first born in the flesh, so spiritual life or grace cannot be had unless man is spiritually reborn. This rebirth is effected through baptism: "Unless a man be born again of water and the Holy Ghost, he cannot enter into the kingdom of God."[298] It must be known that, just as a man can be born but once, so only once is he baptized. Hence, the holy fathers put into the Nicene Creed: "I confess one baptism." The power of baptism consists in this, that it cleanses from all sins as regards both their guilt and their punishment. For this reason, no penance is imposed on those who are baptized, no matter to what extent they had been sinners. Moreover, if they should die immediately after baptism, they would without delay go to heaven. Another result is that, although only priests *ex officio* may baptize, yet anyone may baptize in case of necessity, provided that the proper form of baptism is used. This is: "I baptize thee in the name of the Father, and of the Son, and of the Holy Ghost." This sacrament receives its power from the passion of Christ. "All we who are baptized in Christ Jesus are baptized in his death."[299] Accordingly there is a threefold immersion in water after the three days in which Christ was in the sepulchre.

Confirmation. — The second sacrament is confirmation. Just as they who are physically born need certain powers to act, so those who are reborn

---

[297] Eph 1:22-23
[298] Jn 3:5
[299] Rom 6:3

spiritually must have the strength of the Holy Spirit which is imparted to them in this sacrament. In order that they might become strong, the apostles received the Holy Spirit after the ascension of Christ: "Stay you in the city till you be endowed with power from on high."[300] This power is given in the sacrament of confirmation. They, therefore, who have the care of children should be very careful to see that they be confirmed, because great grace is conferred in confirmation. He who is confirmed will, when he dies, enjoy greater glory than one not confirmed, because greater grace will be his.

Holy Eucharist. — The Eucharist is the third sacrament. In the physical life, after man is born and acquires powers, he needs food to sustain and strengthen him. Likewise in the spiritual life, after being fortified, he has need of spiritual food; this is the body of Christ: "Except you eat the flesh of the Son of man and drink his blood, you shall not have life in you."[301] According to the prescribed law of the Church, therefore, every Christian must at least once a year receive the body of Christ, and in a worthy manner and with a clean conscience: "For he that eateth and drinketh unworthily (that is, by being conscious of unconfessed mortal sin on his soul, or with no intent to abstain from it) eateth and drinketh judgment to himself."[302]

Penance. — The fourth sacrament is penance. In the physical life, one who is sick and does not have recourse to medicine, dies; so in the spiritual order, one becomes ill because of sin. Thus, medicine is necessary for recovery of health; and this is the grace which is conferred in the sacrament of penance: "Who forgiveth all thy iniquities; who healeth all thy diseases."[303] Three things must be present in the sacrament of penance: contrition, which is sorrow for sin together with a resolution not to sin again; confession of sins, as far as possible entire; and satisfaction, which is accomplished by good works.

[300] Lk 24:49
[301] Jn 6:54
[302] 1 Cor 11:29
[303] Ps 102:3

Extreme unction. — Extreme unction is the fifth sacrament. In this life there are many things which prevent one from a perfect purification from one's sins. But since no one can enter into eternal life until he is well cleansed, there is need of another sacrament which will purify man of his sins, and both free him from sickness and prepare him for entry into the heavenly kingdom. This is the sacrament of extreme unction. That this sacrament does not always restore health to the body is due to this, that perhaps to live is not to the advantage of the soul's salvation. "Is any man sick amongst you? Let him bring in the priests of the church and let them pray over him, anointing him with oil in the name of the Lord. And the prayer of faith shall save the sick man. And the Lord shall raise him up; and if he be in sins, they shall be forgiven him."[304] It is now clear that the fullness of life is had from these five sacraments.

Holy orders. — It is necessary that these sacraments be administered by chosen ministers. Therefore, the sacrament of orders is necessary, by whose powers these sacraments are dispensed. Nor need one note the life of such ministers, if here and there one fail in his office, but remember the virtue of Christ through whose merits the sacraments have their efficacy, and in whose name the ministers are but dispensers: "Let a man so account of us as of the ministers of Christ and the dispensers of the mysteries of God."[305] This then is the sixth sacrament, namely, orders.

Matrimony. — The seventh sacrament is matrimony, and in it men, if they live uprightly, are saved; and thereby they are enabled to live without mortal sin. Sometimes the partners in marriage fall into venial sin, when their concupiscence does not extend beyond the rights of matrimony; but if they do go beyond such rights, they sin mortally.[306]

---

[304] Jas 5:14-15
[305] 1 Cor 4:1
[306] See under the section "Matrimony" in the "Explanation of the Sacraments" below; and under "The Sixth Commandment" in the "Explanation of the Ten Commandments," also below.

The Forgiveness of Sins

By these seven sacraments we receive the remission of sins, and so in the Creed there follows immediately: "the forgiveness of sins." The power was given to the apostles to forgive sins. We must believe that the ministers of the Church receive this power from the apostles; and the apostles received it from Christ; and thus the priests have the power of binding and loosing. Moreover, we believe that there is the full power of forgiving sins in the Church, although it operates from the highest to the lowest, i.e., from the pope down through the prelates.

The Communion of Saints

We must also know that not only the efficacy of the passion of Christ is communicated to us, but also the merits of his life; and, moreover, all the good that all the saints have done is communicated to all who are in the state of grace, because all are one: "I am a partaker of all them that fear thee."[307] Therefore, he who lives in charity participates in all the good that is done in the entire world; but more specially does he benefit for whom some good work is done; since one man certainly can satisfy for another. Thus, through this communion we receive two benefits. One is that the merits of Christ are communicated to all; the other is that the good of one is communicated to another. Those who are excommunicated, however, because they are cut off from the Church, forfeit their part of all the good that is done, and this is a far greater loss than being bereft of all material things. There is a danger lest the devil impede this spiritual help in order to tempt one; and when one is thus cut off, the devil can easily overcome him. Thus it was in the primitive Church that, when one was excommunicated, the devil even physically attacked him.

[307] Ps 118:63

THE ELEVENTH ARTICLE

"The resurrection of the body."

Not only does the Holy Spirit sanctify the Church as regards the souls of its members, but also our bodies shall rise again by his power: "We believe in him that raised up Jesus Christ, our Lord, from the dead."[308] And: "By a man came death: and by a man the resurrection of the dead."[309] In this there occur four considerations: 1) the benefits which proceed from our faith in the resurrection; 2) the qualities of those who shall rise, taken all in general; 3) the condition of the blessed; 4) the condition of the damned.

The Benefits of the Resurrection

Concerning the first, our faith and hope in the resurrection is beneficial in four ways.

Firstly, it takes away the sorrow which we feel for the departed. It is impossible for one not to grieve over the death of a relative or friend; but the hope that such a one will rise again greatly tempers the pain of parting: "And we will not have you ignorant, brethren, concerning them that are asleep, that you be not sorrowful, even as others who have no hope."[310]

Secondly, it takes away the fear of death. If one does not hope in another and better life after death, then without doubt one is greatly in fear of death and would willingly commit any crime rather than suffer death. But because we believe in another life which will be ours after death, we do not fear death, nor would we do anything wrong through fear of it: "That, through death he might destroy him who had the empire of death, that is to say, the devil. And might deliver them who through fear of death were all their lifetime subject of servitude."[311]

Thirdly, it makes us watchful and careful to live uprightly. If, however, this life in which we live were all, we would not have this great incentive to

[308] Rom 4:24
[309] 1 Cor 15:21
[310] 1 Thes 4:12
[311] Heb 2:14-15

live well, for whatever we do would be of little importance, since it would be regulated not by eternity, but by brief, determined time. But we believe that we shall receive eternal rewards in the resurrection for whatsoever we do here. Hence, we are anxious to do good: "If in this life only we have hope in Christ, we are of all men most miserable."[312]

Finally, it withdraws us from evil. Just as the hope of reward urges us to do good, so also the fear of punishment, which we believe is reserved for wicked deeds, keeps us from evil: "But they that have done good things shall come forth unto the resurrection of life; but they that have done evil, unto the resurrection of judgment."[313]

Qualities of the Risen Bodies

There is a fourfold condition of all those who shall take part in the resurrection.

a) *The identity of the bodies of the risen.* — It will be the same body as it is now, both as regards its flesh and its bones. Some, indeed, have said that it will not be this same body which is corrupted that shall be raised up; but such view is contrary to the apostle: "For this corruptible must put on incorruption."[314] And likewise, the sacred scripture says that by the power of God this same body shall rise to life: "And I shall be clothed again with my skin; and in my flesh I shall see my God."[315]

b) *The incorruptibility of the risen bodies.* — The bodies of the risen shall be of a different quality from that of the mortal body, because they shall be incorruptible, both of the blessed, who shall be ever in glory, and of the damned, who shall be ever in punishments: "For this corruptible must put on incorruption; and this mortal must put on immortality."[316] And since the body will be incorruptible and immortal, there will no longer be the use of food or of the marriage relations: "For in the resurrection they shall

---

[312] 1 Cor 15:19
[313] Jn 5:29
[314] 1 Cor 15:53
[315] Jb 19:26
[316] 1 Cor 15:53

neither marry nor be married, but shall be as the angels of God in heaven."[317] This is directly against the Jews and Mohammedans: "Nor shall he return any more into his house."[318]

c) *The integrity of the risen bodies.* — Both the good and the wicked shall rise with all soundness of body which is natural to man. He will not be blind or deaf or bear any kind of physical defect: "The dead shall rise again incorruptible,"[319] this is to mean, wholly free from the defects of the present life.

d) *The age of the risen bodies.* — All will rise in the condition of perfect age, which is of thirty-two or thirty-three years. This is because all who were not yet arrived at this age, did not possess this perfect age, and the old had already lost it. Hence, youths and children will be given what they lack, and what the aged once had will be restored to them: "Until we all attain the unity of faith and of the knowledge of the Son of God, unto a perfect man, unto the measure of the age of the fullness of Christ."[320]

Condition of the Blessed

It must be known that the good will enjoy a special glory because the blessed will have glorified bodies which will be endowed with four gifts.

a) *Brilliance.* — "Then shall the just shine as the sun in the kingdom of their Father."[321]

b) *Impassibility (i.e., incapability of receiving action).* — "It is sown in dishonor; it shall rise in glory."[322] "And God shall wipe away all tears from their eyes; and death shall be no more. Nor mourning, nor crying, nor sorrow shall be anymore, for the former things are passed away."[323]

---

[317] Mt 22:30
[318] Jb 7:10
[319] 1 Cor 15:52
[320] Eph 4:13
[321] Mt 13:43
[322] 1 Cor 15:43
[323] Apoc 21:4

c) *Agility.* — "The just shall shine and shall run to and fro like sparks among the reeds."[324]

d) *Subtility.* — "It is sown a natural body; it shall rise a spiritual body."[325] This is in the sense of not being altogether a spirit, but that the body will be wholly subject to the spirit.

Condition of the Damned

It must also be known that the condition of the damned will be the exact contrary to that of the blessed. Theirs is the state of eternal punishment, which has a fourfold evil condition. The bodies of the damned will not be brilliant: "Their countenances shall be as faces burnt."[326] Likewise they shall be passible, because they shall never deteriorate and, although burning eternally in fire, they shall never be consumed: "Their worm shall not die and their fire shall not be quenched."[327] They will be weighed down, and the soul of the damned will be as it were chained therein: "To bind their kings with fetters, and their nobles with manacles of iron."[328] Finally, they will be in a certain manner fleshly both in soul and body: "The beasts have rotted in their dung."[329]

THE TWELFTH ARTICLE

"Life everlasting. Amen."

The end of all our desires, eternal life, is fittingly placed last among those things to be believed; and the Creed says: "life everlasting. Amen." They wrote this to stand against those who believe that the soul perishes with the body. If this were indeed true, then the condition of man would be just the same as that of the beasts. This agrees with what the psalmist says: "Man

---

[324] Ws 3:7
[325] 1 Cor 15:44
[326] Is 13:8
[327] Is 66:24
[328] Ps 149:8
[329] Jl 1:17

when he was in honor did not understand; he hath been compared to senseless beasts, and made like to them."[330] The human soul, however, is in its immortality made like unto God, and in its sensuality alone is it like the brutes. He, then, who believes that the soul dies with the body withdraws it from this similarity to God and likens it to the brutes. Against such it is said: "They knew not the secrets of God, nor hoped for the wages of justice, nor esteemed the honor of holy souls. For God created man incorruptible, and to the image of his own likeness he made him."[331]

What Is Everlasting Life?

We must first consider in this article what is everlasting life. And in this we must know that in everlasting life man is united to God. God himself is the reward and the end of all our labors: "I am thy protector, and thy reward exceeding great."[332] This union with God consists, firstly, in a perfect vision: "We see now through a glass in a dark manner; but then face to face."[333] Secondly, in a most fervent love; for the better one is known, the more perfectly is one loved: "The Lord hath said it, whose fire is in Sion, and his furnace in Jerusalem."[334] Thirdly, in the highest praise: "We shall see, we shall love, and we shall praise," as says St. Augustine.[335] "Joy and gladness shall be found therein, thanksgiving and the voice of praise."[336]

Then, too, in everlasting life is the full and perfect satisfying of every desire; for there every blessed soul will have to overflowing what he hoped for and desired. The reason is that in this life no one can fulfill all his desires, nor can any created thing fully satisfy the craving of man. God

---

[330] Ps 48:21

[331] Ws 2:22-23; Translator's note: Also: "And though in the sight of men they suffer torments their hope is full of immortality" (Ws 3:4).

[332] Gn 15:1

[333] 1 Cor 13:12

[334] Is 31:9; Translator's note: This second consideration is found in the Vives edition, Chapter 15.

[335] *"Ibi vacabimus, et videbimus: videbimus, et amabimus: amabimus, et laudabimus"* ["There we shall rest and we shall see; we shall see and we shall love; we shall love and we shall praise," (Augustine, *City of God*, Bk. 22, Ch. 30)].

[336] Is 51:3

only satisfies and infinitely exceeds man's desires; and, therefore, perfect satiety is found in God alone. As St. Augustine says: "Thou hast made us for thee, O Lord, and our heart is restless until it rests in thee."[337] Because the blessed in the fatherland will possess God perfectly, it is evident that their desires will be abundantly filled, and their glory will exceed their hopes. The Lord has said: "Enter thou into the joy of the Lord."[338] And as St. Augustine says: "Complete joy will not enter into those who rejoice, but all those who rejoice will enter into joy." "I shall be satisfied when thy glory shall appear."[339] And again: "Who satisfieth thy desire with good things."[340]

The Fullness of Desires

Whatever is delightful will be there in abundant fullness. Thus, if pleasures are desired, there will be the highest and most perfect pleasure, for it derives from the highest good, namely, God: "Then shalt thou abound in delights in the Almighty."[341] "At the right hand are delights even to the end."[342] Likewise, if honors are desired, there too will be all honor. Men wish particularly to be kings, if they be laymen; and to be bishops, if they be clerics. Both these honors will be there: "And hath made us a kingdom and priests."[343] "Behold how they are numbered among the children of God."[344] If knowledge is desired, it will be there most perfectly, because we shall possess in the life everlasting knowledge of all the natures of things and all truth, and whatever we desire we shall know. And whatever we desire to possess, that we shall have, even life eternal: "Now, all good things come to me together with her."[345] "To the just their desire shall be given."[346]

---

[337] Augustine, *Confessions*, Bk. 1, Ch. 1
[338] Mt 25:21
[339] Ps 16:15
[340] Ps 102:5
[341] Jb 22:26
[342] Ps 15:11
[343] Apoc 5:10
[344] Ws 5:5
[345] Ws 7:11
[346] Prv 10:24

Again, most perfect security is there. In this world there is no perfect security; for insofar as one has many things, and the higher one's position, the more one has to fear and the more one wants. But in the life everlasting there is no anxiety, no labor, no fear. "And my people shall sit in the beauty of peace,"[347] and "shall enjoy abundance, without fear of evils."[348]

Finally, in heaven there will be the happy society of all the blessed, and this society will be especially delightful. Since each one will possess all good together with the blessed, and they will love one another as themselves, and they will rejoice in the others' good as their own. It will also happen that, as the pleasure and enjoyment of one increases, so will it be for all: "The dwelling in thee is as it were of all rejoicing."[349]

What Is Everlasting Death?

The perfect will enjoy all this in the life everlasting, and much more that surpasses description. But the wicked, on the other hand, will be in eternal death suffering pain and punishment as great as will be the happiness and glory of the good. The punishment of the damned will be increased, firstly, by their separation from God and from all good. This is the pain of loss which corresponds to aversion, and is a greater punishment than that of sense: "And the unprofitable servant, cast ye out into the exterior darkness."[350] The wicked in this life have interior darkness, namely sin; but then they shall also have exterior darkness.

Secondly, the damned shall suffer from remorse of conscience: "I will reprove thee, and set before thy face."[351] "Groaning for anguish of spirit."[352] Nevertheless, their repentance and groaning will be of no avail, because it rises not from hatred of evil, but from fear and the enormity of their punishments. Thirdly, there is the great pain of sense. It is the fire of hell which tortures the soul and the body; and this, as the saints tell us, is the

---

[347] Is 32:18; Translator's note: This is in the Vives edition, Chapter 15.
[348] Prv 1:33
[349] Ps 86:7
[350] Mt 25:30
[351] Ps 49:21
[352] Ws 5:3

sharpest of all punishments. They shall be ever dying, and yet never die; hence it is called eternal death, for as dying is the bitterest of pains, such will be the lot of those in hell: "They are laid in hell like sheep; death shall feed upon them."[353] Fourthly, there is the despair of their salvation. If some hope of delivery from their punishments would be given them, their punishment would be somewhat lessened; but since all hope is withdrawn from them, their sufferings are made most intense: "Their worm shall not die, and their fire shall not be quenched."[354]

We thus see the difference between doing good and doing evil. Good works lead to life, evil drags us to death. For this reason, men ought frequently to recall these things to mind, since they will incite one to do good and withdraw one from evil. Therefore, very significantly, at the end of the Creed is placed "life everlasting," so that it would be more and more deeply impressed on the memory. To this life everlasting may the Lord Jesus Christ, blessed God forever, bring us! Amen.

[353] Ps 48:15
[354] Is 66:24

Explanation of the Ten Commandments

THE TEN COMMANDMENTS

1. I am the Lord thy God, who brought thee out of the land of Egypt, out of the house of bondage. Thou shalt not have strange gods before me. Thou shalt not make to thyself a graven thing, nor the likeness of any thing that is in heaven above, or in the earth beneath, nor of those things that are in the waters under the earth. Thou shalt not adore them, nor serve them. I am the Lord thy God, mighty, jealous, visiting the iniquity of the fathers upon the children, unto the third and fourth generation of them that hate me; and showing mercy unto thousands of them that love me, and keep my commandments.
2. Thou shalt not take the name of the Lord thy God in vain.
3. Remember that thou keep holy the sabbath-day.
4. Honor thy father and thy mother.
5. Thou shalt not kill.
6. Thou shalt not commit adultery.
7. Thou shalt not steal.
8. Thou shalt not bear false witness against thy neighbor.
9. Thou shalt not covet thy neighbor's wife.
10. Thou shalt not covet thy neighbor's house, nor his field, nor his servant, nor his handmaid, nor his ox, nor his ass, nor anything that is his.[355]

---

[355] Ex 20:2-17; Dt 5:6-21

THE FIRST COMMANDMENT

"Thou shalt not have strange gods before me."

The entire law of Christ depends upon charity. And charity depends on two precepts, one of which concerns loving God and the other concerns loving our neighbor.

Now God, in delivering the law to Moses, gave him ten commandments written upon two tablets of stone. Three of these commandments, that were written on the first tablet, referred to the love of God; and the seven commandments, written on the other tablet, related to the love of our neighbor. The whole law, therefore, is founded on these two precepts.[356]

The first commandment which relates to the love of God is: "Thou shalt not have strange gods." For an understanding of this commandment, one must know how of old it was violated. Some worshipped demons. "All the gods of the Gentiles are devils."[357] This is the greatest and most detestable of all sins. Even now there are many who transgress this commandment: all such as practice divinations and fortune-telling. Such things, according to St. Augustine, cannot be done without some kind of pact with the devil. "I would not that you should be made partakers with devils."[358]

Some worshipped the heavenly bodies, believing the stars to be gods: "They have imagined...the sun and the moon to be the gods that rule the world."[359] For this reason Moses forbade the Jews to raise their eyes, or adore the sun and moon and stars: "Keep therefore your souls carefully... lest perhaps lifting up thy eyes to heaven, thou see the sun and the moon, and all the stars of heaven, and being deceived by error thou adore and serve them, which the Lord thy God created for the service of all the nations."[360] The astrologers sin against this commandment in that they say

---

[356] Translator's note: "The decalogue is the summary and epitome of the entire law of God," is the opinion of St. Augustine (*Quaestiones in Heptateuchum*, Bk. 2, q. 140).

[357] Ps 95:5

[358] 1 Cor 10:20

[359] Ws 13:2

[360] Dt 4:15, 19

that these bodies are the rulers of souls, when in truth they were made for the use of man whose sole ruler is God.

Others worshipped the lower elements: "They imagined the fire or the wind...to be gods."[361] Into this error also fall those who wrongly use the things of this earth and love them too much: "Or covetous person (who is a server of idols)."[362]

Some men have erred in worshipping their ancestors. This arose from three causes.

1. *From their carnal nature.* — "For a father being afflicted with a bitter grief, made to himself the image of his son who was quickly taken away; and him who then had died as a man, he began now to worship as a god, and appointed him rites and sacrifices among his servants."[363]

2. *Because of flattery.* — Thus being unable to worship certain men in their presence, they, bowing down, honored them in their absence by making statues of them and worshipping one for the other: "Whom they had a mind to honor...they made an image...that they might honor as present him that was absent."[364] Of such also are those men who love and honor other men more than God: "He that loveth his father and mother more than me, is not worthy of me."[365] "Put your trust not in princes; in the children of man, in whom there is no salvation."[366]

3. *From presumption.* — Some, because of their presumption, made themselves be called gods; such, for example, was Nabuchodonosor.[367] "Thy heart is lifted up and thou hast said: I am God."[368] Such are also those who believe more in their own pleasures than in the precepts of God. They worship themselves as gods, for by seeking the pleasures of the flesh, they

---

[361] Ws 13:2
[362] Eph 5:5
[363] Ws 14:15
[364] Ws 14:17
[365] Mt 10:37
[366] Ps 145:2-3
[367] Cf. Jdt 3:13
[368] Ez 28:2

worship their own bodies instead of God: "Their god is their belly."[369] We must, therefore, avoid all these things.

Why We Should Adore One God

"Thou shalt not have strange gods before me." As we have already said, the first commandment forbids us to worship other than the one God. We shall now consider five reasons for this.

God's dignity. — The first reason is the dignity of God which, were it belittled in any way, would be an injury to God. We see something similar to this in the customs of men. Reverence is due to every degree of dignity. Thus, a traitor to the king is he who robs him of what he ought to maintain. Such, too, is the conduct of some towards God: "They changed the glory of the incorruptible God into the likeness of the image of a corruptible man."[370] This is highly displeasing to God: "I will not give my glory to another, nor my praise to graven things."[371] For it must be known that the dignity of God consists in his omniscience, since the name of God, *Deus*, is from "seeing," and this is one of the signs of divinity: "Show the things that are to come hereafter, and we shall know that ye are gods."[372] "All things are naked and open to his eyes."[373] But this dignity of God is denied him by practitioners of divination, and of them it is said: "Should not the people seek of their God, for the living and the dead?"[374]

God's bounty. — We receive every good from God; and this also is of the dignity of God, that he is the Maker and giver of all good things: "When thou openest thy hand, they shall all be filled with good."[375] And this is implied in the name of God, namely, *Deus*, which is said to be distributor, that is, *dator* of all things, because he fills all things with his goodness. You are, indeed, ungrateful if you do not appreciate what you have received

---

[369] Phil 3:19
[370] Rom 1:23
[371] Is 42:8
[372] Is 41:23
[373] Heb 4:13
[374] Is 8:19
[375] Ps 103:28

from him, and, furthermore, you make for yourself another god; just as the sons of Israel made an idol after they had been brought out of Egypt: "I will go after my lovers."[376] One does this also when one puts too much trust in someone other than God, and this occurs when one seeks help from another: "Blessed is the man whose hope is in the name of the Lord."[377] Thus, the apostle says: "Now that you have known God...how turn you again to the weak and needy elements?...You observe days and months and times and years."[378]

The strength of our promise. — The third reason is taken from our solemn promise. For we have renounced the devil, and we have promised fidelity to God alone. This is a promise which we cannot break: "A man making void the law of Moses dieth without mercy under two or three witnesses. How much more think ye he deserveth punishment who hath trodden under foot the Son of God, and hath esteemed the blood of the testament unclean, by which he was sanctified, and hath offered an affront to the Spirit of grace?"[379] "Whilst her husband liveth, she shall be called an adulteress, if she be with another man."[380] Woe, then, to the sinner who enters the land by two ways, and who "halts between two sides."[381]

Against service of the devil. — The fourth reason is because of the great burden imposed by service to the devil: "You shall serve strange gods day and night, who will give you no rest."[382] The devil is not satisfied with leading to one sin, but tries to lead on to others: "Whosoever sins shall be a slave of sin."[383] It is, therefore, not easy for one to escape from the habit of sin. Thus, St. Gregory says: "The sin which is not remitted by penance soon draws man into another sin."[384] The very opposite of all this is true of service to God; for his commandments are not a heavy burden: "My

---

[376] Os 2:5
[377] Ps 39:5
[378] Gal 4:9-10
[379] Heb 10:28-29
[380] Rom 7:3
[381] 3 Kgs 18:21
[382] Jer 16:13
[383] Jn 8:34
[384] Gregory, *Super Ezech.*, xi.

yoke is sweet and my burden light."[385] A person is considered to have done enough if he does for God as much as what he has done for the sake of sin: "For as you have yielded your members to serve uncleanness and iniquity, unto iniquity; so now yield your members to serve justice unto sanctification."[386] But on the contrary, it is written of those who serve the devil: "We wearied ourselves in the way of iniquity and destruction, and have walked through hard ways."[387] And again: "They have labored to commit iniquity."[388]

Greatness of the reward. — The fifth reason is taken from the greatness of the reward or prize. In no law are such rewards promised as in the law of Christ. Rivers flowing with milk and honey are promised to the Mohammedans, to the Jews the land of promise, but to Christians the glory of the angels: "They shall be as the angels of God in heaven."[389] It was with this in mind that St. Peter asked: "Lord, to whom shall we go? Thou hast the words of eternal life."[390]

SECOND COMMANDMENT

"Thou shalt not take the name of the Lord thy God in vain."

This is the second commandment of the law. Just as there is but one God whom we must worship, so there is only one God whom we should reverence in a special manner. This, first of all, has reference to the name of God. "Thou shalt not take the name of the Lord thy God in vain."[391]

---

[385] Mt 11:30
[386] Rom 6:19
[387] Ws 5:7
[388] Jer 9:5
[389] Mt 22:30
[390] Jn 6:69
[391] Translator's note: See also the teaching of St. Thomas in *Summa Theologiae*, II-II, q. 89, a. 3, 5, 6.

The Meaning of "In Vain"

In vain has a threefold meaning. Sometimes it is said of that which is false: "They have spoken vain things every one to his neighbor."[392] One, therefore, takes the name of God in vain when one uses it to confirm that which is not true: "Love not a false oath."[393] "Thou shalt not live because thou hast spoken a lie in the name of the Lord."[394] Anyone so doing does injury to God, to himself, and to all men.

It is an insult to God because, when you swear by God, it is nothing other than to call him to witness; and when you swear falsely, you either believe God to be ignorant of the truth and thus place ignorance in God, whereas "all things are naked and open to his eyes,"[395] or you think that God loves a lie, whereas he hates it: "Thou wilt destroy all that speak a lie."[396] Or, again, you detract from his power, as if he were not able to punish a lie.

Likewise, such a one does an injury to himself, for he binds himself to the judgment of God. It is the same thing to say, "By God this is so," as to say, "May God punish me if it is not so!"

He, finally, does an injury to other men. For there can be no lasting society unless men believe one another. Matters that are doubtful may be confirmed by oaths: "An oath in confirmation puts an end to all controversy."[397] Therefore, he who violates this precept does injury to God, is cruel to himself, and harmful to other men.

Sometimes *vain* signifies useless: "The Lord knoweth the thoughts of men, that they are vain."[398] God's name, therefore, is taken in vain when it is used to confirm vain things.

[392] Ps 11:3
[393] Zac 8:17
[394] Zac 13:3
[395] Heb 4:13
[396] Ps 5:7
[397] Heb 6:16
[398] Ps 93:11

In the old law it was forbidden to swear falsely: "Thou shalt not take the name of the Lord thy God in vain."[399] And Christ forbade the taking of oaths except in case of necessity: "You have heard that it was said to them of old: Thou shalt not forswear thyself...But I say to you not to swear at all."[400] And the reason for this is that in no part of our body are we so weak as in the tongue, for "the tongue no man can tame."[401] And thus even in light matter one can perjure himself. "Let your speech be: Yea, yea; No, no...But I say to you not to swear at all."[402]

Note well that an oath is like medicine, which is never taken continually but only in times of necessity. Hence, the Lord adds: "And that which is over and above these is evil."[403] "Let not the mouth be accustomed to swearing, for in it there are many falls. And let not the name of God be usual in thy mouth, and meddle not with the names of saints. For thou shalt not escape free from them."[404]

Sometimes *in vain* means sin or injustice: "O ye sons of men, how long will you be dull of heart? Why do you love vanity?"[405] Therefore, he who swears to commit a sin, takes the name of his God in vain. Justice consists in doing good and avoiding evil. Therefore, if you take an oath to steal or commit some crime of this sort, you sin against justice. And although you must not keep this oath, you are still guilty of perjury. Herod did this against John.[406] It is likewise against justice when one swears not to do some good act, as not to enter a church or a religious community. And although this oath, too, is not binding, yet, despite this, the person himself is a perjurer.

[399] Dt 5:11
[400] Mt 5:33-34
[401] Jas 3:8
[402] Mt 5:37, 34
[403] Mt 5:37
[404] Ecclus 23:9-10
[405] Ps 4:3
[406] Cf. Mk 6:17-28

Conditions of a Lawful Oath

One cannot, therefore, swear to a falsehood, or without good reason, or in any way against justice: "And thou shalt swear: As the Lord liveth, in truth, and in judgment and in justice."[407]

Sometimes *vain* also means foolish: "All men are vain, in whom there is not the knowledge of God."[408] Accordingly, he who takes the name of God foolishly, by blasphemy, takes the name of God in vain: "And he that blasphemeth the name of the Lord, dying let him die."[409]

Taking God's Name Justly

"Thou shalt not take the name of the Lord thy God in vain." However, the name of God may be taken for six purposes.

First, to confirm something that is said, as in an oath. In this we show God alone is the first truth, and also we show due reverence to God. For this reason it was commanded in the old law that one must not swear except by God.[410] They who swore otherwise violated this order: "By the name of strange gods you shall not swear."[411] Although at times one swears by creatures, nevertheless, it must be known that such is the same as swearing by God. When you swear by your soul or your head, it is as if you bind yourself to be punished by God. Thus: "But I call God to witness upon my soul."[412] And when you swear by the gospel, you swear by God who gave the gospel. But they sin who swear either by God or by the gospel for any trivial reason.

The second purpose is that of sanctification. Thus, baptism sanctifies, for as St. Paul says: "But you are washed, but you are sanctified, but you are justified in the name of our Lord Jesus Christ, and the Spirit of God."[413] Baptism, however, does not have power except through the invocation of

---

[407] Jer 4:2
[408] Ws 13:1
[409] Lv 24:16
[410] Cf. Dt 6:13
[411] Ex 23:13
[412] 2 Cor 1:23
[413] 1 Cor 6:11

the Trinity: "But thou, O Lord, art among us, and thy name is called upon by us."[414]

The third purpose is the expulsion of our adversary; hence, before baptism we renounce the devil: "Only let thy name be called upon us; take away our reproach."[415] Wherefore, if one return to his sins, the name of God has been taken in vain.

Fourthly, God's name is taken in order to confess it: "How then shall they call on him, in whom they have not believed?"[416] And again: "Whosoever shall call upon the name of the Lord, shall be saved."[417] First of all, we confess by word of mouth that we may show forth the glory of God: "And every one that calleth upon my name, I have created him for my glory."[418] Accordingly, if one says anything against the glory of God, he takes the name of God in vain. Secondly, we confess God's name by our works, when our very actions show forth God's glory: "That they may see your good works, and may glorify your Father who is in heaven."[419] "Through you the name of God is blasphemed among the Gentiles."[420]

Fifthly it is taken for our defense: "The name of the Lord is a strong tower; the just runneth to it and shall be exalted."[421] "In my name they shall cast out devils."[422] "There is no other name under heaven given to men, whereby we must be saved."[423]

Lastly, it is taken in order to make our works complete. Thus says the apostle: "All whatsoever you do in word or work, do all in the name of the Lord Jesus Christ."[424] The reason is because "our help is in the name of the Lord."[425] Sometimes it happens that one begins a work imprudently

---

[414] Jer 14:9
[415] Is 4:1
[416] Rom 10:14
[417] Rom 10:13
[418] Is 43:7
[419] Mt 5:16
[420] Rom 2:24
[421] Prv 18:10
[422] Mk 16:17
[423] Acts 4:12
[424] Col 3:17
[425] Ps 123:8

by starting with a vow, for instance, and then not completing either the work or the vow. And this again is taking God's name in vain. "If thou hast vowed anything to God, defer not to pay it."[426] "Vow and pay to the Lord your God; all ye that are round about him bring presents."[427] "For an unfaithful and foolish promise displeaseth him."[428]

THE THIRD COMMANDMENT

"Remember that you keep holy the sabbath-day."

This is the third commandment of the law, and very suitably is it so. For we are first commanded to adore God in our hearts, and the commandment is to worship one God: "Thou shalt not have strange gods before me." In the second commandment we are told to reverence God by word: "Thou shalt not take the name of the Lord thy God in vain." The third commands us to reverence God by act. It is: "Remember that thou keep holy the sabbath-day."[429] God wished that a certain day be set aside on which men direct their minds to the service of the Lord.

Reasons for This Commandment

There are five reasons for this commandment.

The first reason was to put aside error, for the Holy Spirit saw that in the future some men would say that the world had always existed. "In the last days there shall come deceitful scoffers, walking after their own lusts, saying: Where is his promise or his coming? For since the time that the fathers slept, all things continue as they were from the beginning of creation. For this they are willfully ignorant of, that the heavens were before, and the earth out of water, and through water, created by the word of God."[430]

---

[426] Eccles 5:3

[427] Ps 75:12

[428] Eccles 5:3

[429] Translator's note: St. Thomas also treats of this commandment in the *Summa Theologiae*, I-II, q. 102, a. 4, rep. 10; II-II, q. 122, a. 4.

[430] 2 Pt 3:3-5

God, therefore, wished that one day should be set aside in memory of the fact that he created all things in six days, and that on the seventh day he rested from the creation of new creatures. This is why the Lord placed this commandment in the law, saying: "Remember that thou keep holy the sabbath-day."

The Jews kept holy the sabbath in memory of the first creation; but Christ at his coming brought about a new creation. For by the first creation an earthly man was created, and by the second a heavenly man was formed: "For in Christ Jesus neither circumcision availeth any thing, nor uncircumcision, but a new creature."[431] This new creation is through grace, which came by the resurrection: "That as Christ is risen from the dead by the glory of the Father, so we also may walk in newness of life. For if we have been planted together in the likeness of his death, so shall we also be in the likeness of his resurrection."[432] And thus, because the resurrection took place on Sunday, we celebrate that day, even as the Jews observed the sabbath on account of the first creation.

The second reason for this commandment is to instruct us in our faith in the Redeemer. For the flesh of Christ was not corrupted in the sepulchre, and thus it is said: "Moreover my flesh also shall rest in hope."[433] "Nor wilt thou give thy holy one to see corruption."[434] Wherefore, God wished that the sabbath should be observed, and that just as the sacrifices of the old law signified the death of Christ, so should the quiet of the sabbath signify the rest of his body in the sepulchre. But we do not now observe these sacrifices, because with the advent of the reality and the truth, figures of it must cease, just as the darkness is dispelled with the rising of the sun. Nevertheless, we keep the Saturdays in veneration of the Blessed Virgin, in whom remained a firm faith on that Saturday while Christ was dead.

The third reason is that this commandment was given to strengthen and foreshadow the fulfillment of the promise of rest. For rest indeed was promised to us: "And it shall come to pass on that day, that when God

[431] Gal 6:15
[432] Rom 6:4-5
[433] Ps 15:9
[434] Ps 15:10

shall give thee rest from thy labor, and from thy vexation, and from the hard bondage, wherewith thou didst serve before."[435] "My people shall sit in the beauty of peace, and in the tabernacle of confidence, and in wealthy rest."[436]

We hope for rest from three things: from the labors of the present life, from the struggles of temptations, and from the servitude of the devil. Christ promised this rest to all those who will come to him: "Come to me, all ye that labor and are burdened, and I will refresh you. Take up my yoke upon you, and learn of me, because I am meek and humble of heart; and you shall find rest to your souls. For my yoke is sweet and my burden light."[437]

However, the Lord, as we know, worked for six days and on the seventh he rested, because it is necessary to do a perfect work: "Behold with your eyes how I have labored a little, and have found much rest to myself."[438] For the period of eternity exceeds the present time incomparably more than a thousand years exceeds one day.

Fourthly, this commandment was given for the increase of our love: "For the corruptible body is a load upon the soul."[439] And man always tends downwards towards earthly things unless he takes means to raise himself above them. It is indeed necessary to have a certain time for this; in fact, some do this continually: "I will bless the Lord at all times, his praise shall ever be in my mouth."[440] And again: "Pray without ceasing."[441] These shall enjoy the everlasting sabbath. There are others who do this (i.e., excite love for God) during a certain portion of the day: "Seven times a day I have given praise to thee."[442] And some, in order to avoid being entirely apart from God, find it necessary to have a fixed day, lest they become too lukewarm in their love of God: "If you…call the sabbath delightful…then

---

[435] Is 14:3
[436] Is 32:18
[437] Mt 11:28-30
[438] Ecclus 51:35
[439] Ws 9:15
[440] Ps 33:2
[441] 1 Thes 5:17
[442] Ps 118:164

shalt thou be delighted in the Lord."[443] Again: "Then shalt thou abound in delights of the Almighty, and shalt lift up thy face to God."[444] And accordingly this day is not set aside for the sole exercise of games, but to praise and pray to the Lord God. Wherefore, St. Augustine says that it is a lesser evil to plough than to play on this day.[445]

Lastly, we are given this commandment in order to exercise works of kindliness to those who are subject to us. For some are so cruel to themselves and to others that they labor ceaselessly all on account of money. This is true especially of the Jews, who are most avaricious. "Observe the day of the sabbath to sanctify it...that thy manservant and thy maidservant may rest, even as thyself."[446] This commandment, therefore, was given for all these reasons.

From What We Should Abstain on the Sabbath

"Remember that you keep holy (sanctify) the sabbath-day." We have already said that, as the Jews celebrated the sabbath, so do we Christians observe the Sunday and all principal feasts. Let us now see in what way we should keep these days. We ought to know that God did not say to "keep" the sabbath, but to remember to keep it holy. The word *holy* may be taken in two ways. Sometimes *holy* (sanctified) is the same as pure: "But you are washed, but you are sanctified,"[447] (that is, made holy). Then again at times *holy* is said of a thing consecrated to the worship of God, as, for instance, a place, a season, vestments, and the holy vessels. Therefore, in these two ways we ought to celebrate the feasts, that is, both purely and by giving ourselves over to divine service.

We shall consider two things regarding this commandment. First, what should be avoided on a feast day, and secondly, what we should do. We ought to avoid three things. The first is servile work.

---

[443] Is 58:13-14
[444] Jb 22:26
[445] Translator's note: This is a reference to the great public spectacles and games.
[446] Dt 5:12, 14
[447] 1 Cor 6:11

Avoidance of servile work. — "Neither do ye any work; sanctify the sabbath day."[448] And so also it is said in the law: "You shall do no servile work therein."[449] Now, servile work is bodily work; whereas "free work" (i.e., non-servile work) is done by the mind, for instance, the exercise of the intellect and such like. And one cannot be servilely bound to do this kind of work.

When servile work is lawful. — We ought to know, however, that servile work can be done on the sabbath for four reasons. The first reason is necessity. Wherefore, the Lord excused the disciples plucking the ears of corn on the sabbath, as we read in St. Matthew.[450] The second reason is when the work is done for the service of the Church; as we see in the same gospel how the priests did all things necessary in the Temple on the sabbath-day.[451] The third reason is for the good of our neighbor; for on the sabbath the Savior cured one having a withered hand, and he refuted the Jews who reprimanded him, by citing the example of the sheep in a pit.[452] And the fourth reason is the authority of our superiors. Thus, God commanded the Jews to circumcise on the sabbath.[453]

Avoidance of sin and negligence on the sabbath. — Another thing to be avoided on the sabbath is sin: "Take heed to your souls, and carry no burdens on the sabbath day."[454] This weight and burden on the soul is sin: "My iniquities…as a heavy burden are become heavy upon me."[455] Now, sin is a servile work because "whosoever committeth sin is the servant of sin."[456] Therefore, when it is said, "You shall do no servile work therein,"[457] it can be understood of sin. Thus, one violates this commandment as often as one commits sin on the sabbath; and so, both by working and by sin God

---

448 Jer 17:22
449 Lv 23:25
450 Cf. Mt 12:1-5
451 Cf. Mt 12:5
452 Cf. Mt 12:10-13
453 Cf. Jn 7:22-23
454 Jer 17:21
455 Ps 37:5
456 Jn 8:34
457 Lv 23:25

is offended. "The sabbaths and other festivals I will not abide." And why? "Because your assemblies are wicked. My soul hateth your new moon and your solemnities; they are become troublesome to me."[458]

Another thing to avoid on the sabbath is idleness: "For idleness hath taught much evil."[459] St. Jerome says: "Always do some good work, and the devil will always find you occupied."[460] Hence, it is not good for one to keep only the principal feasts, if on the others one would remain idle. "The king's honor loveth judgment,"[461] that is to say, discretion. Wherefore, we read that certain of the Jews were in hiding, and their enemies fell upon them; but they, believing that they were not able to defend themselves on the sabbath, were overcome and killed.[462] The same thing happens to many who are idle on the feast days: "The enemies have seen her, and have mocked at her sabbaths."[463] But all such should do as those Jews did, of whom it is said: "Whosoever shall come up against us to fight on the sabbath day, we will fight against him."[464]

With What the Sabbath and Feasts Should Be Occupied

"Remember that thou keep holy the sabbath day." We have already said that man must keep the feast days holy; and that *holy* is considered in two ways, namely, "pure" and "consecrated to God." Moreover, we have indicated what things we should abstain from on these days. Now it must be shown with what we should occupy ourselves, and they are three in number.

The offering of sacrifice. — The first is the offering of sacrifices. In the book of Numbers it is written how God ordered that on each day there be offered one lamb in the morning and another in the evening, but on

---

[458] Is 1:13-14
[459] Ecclus 33:29
[460] Jerome, *Letter 125 to Rusticus*, n. 11
[461] Ps 98:4
[462] Cf. 1 Mc 2:31-38
[463] Lam 1:7
[464] 1 Mc 2:41

the sabbath day the number should be doubled.[465] And this showed that on the sabbath we should offer sacrifice to God from all that we possess: "All things are thine; and we have given thee what we received from thy hand."[466] We should offer, first of all, our soul to God, being sorry for our sins: "A sacrifice to God is an afflicted spirit";[467] and also pray for his blessings: "Let my prayer be directed as incense in thy sight."[468] Feast days were instituted for that spiritual joy which is the effect of prayer. Therefore, on such days our prayers should be multiplied.

Secondly, we should offer our body, by mortifying it with fasting:[469] "I beseech you therefore, brethren, by the mercy of God, that you present your bodies a living sacrifice,"[470] and also by praising God: "The sacrifice of praise shall honor me."[471] And thus on these days our hymns should be more numerous. Thirdly, we should sacrifice our possessions by giving alms: "And do not forget to do good, and to impart; for by such sacrifice God's favor is obtained."[472] And this alms ought to be more than on other days because the sabbath is a day of common joys: "Send portions to them that have not prepared for themselves, because it is the holy day of the Lord."[473]

Hearing of God's word. — Our second duty on the sabbath is to be eager to hear the word of God. This the Jews did daily: "The voices of the prophets which are read every sabbath."[474] Therefore Christians, whose justice should be more perfect, ought to come together on the sabbath to hear sermons and participate in the services of the Church! "He that is of

---

[465] Cf. Nm 28

[466] 1 Par 29:14

[467] Ps 50:19

[468] Ps 140:2

[469] Translator's note: St. Thomas here refers not to the "fast of affliction" (*jejunium afflictionis*) but to the "fast of joy" (*jejunium exultationis*), which is a joyful lifting of the mind to higher things and proceeds from the Holy Ghost who is the Spirit of liberty (cf. *Summa Theologiae*, III, q. 147, a. 5, rep. 3).

[470] Rom 12:1

[471] Ps 49:23

[472] Heb 13:16

[473] 2 Esd 8:10

[474] Acts 13:27

God, heareth the words of God."[475] We likewise ought to speak with profit to others: "Let no evil speech proceed from your mouth; but that which is good unto sanctification."[476] These two practices are good for the soul of the sinner, because they change his heart for the better: "Are not my words as a fire, saith the Lord, and as a hammer that breaketh the rock in pieces?"[477] The opposite effect is had on those, even the perfect, who neither speak nor hear profitable things: "Evil communications corrupt good manners. Awake, ye just, and sin not."[478] "Thy words have I hidden in my heart."[479] God's word enlightens the ignorant: "Thy word is a lamp to my feet."[480] It inflames the lukewarm: "The word of the Lord inflamed him."[481]

The Spiritual Sabbath

The contemplation of divine things may be exercised on the sabbath. However, this is for the more perfect. "O taste, and see that the Lord is sweet,"[482] and this is because of the quiet of the soul. For just as the tired body desires rest, so also does the soul. But the soul's proper rest is in God: "Be thou unto me a God, a protector, and a house of refuge."[483] "There remaineth therefore a day of rest for the people of God. For he that is entered into his rest, the same also hath rested from his works, as God did from his."[484] "When I go into my house, I shall repose myself with her" (i.e., wisdom).[485]

However, before the soul arrives at this rest, three other rests must precede. The first is the rest from the turmoil of sin: "But the wicked are like

---

[475] Jn 8:47
[476] Eph 4:29
[477] Jer 23:29
[478] 1 Cor 15:33-34
[479] Ps 118:11
[480] Ps 118:105
[481] Ps 104:19
[482] Ps 33:9
[483] Ps 30:3
[484] Heb 4:9-10
[485] Ws 8:16

the raging sea which cannot rest."[486] The second rest is from the passions of the flesh, because "the flesh lusteth against the spirit, and the spirit against the flesh."[487] The third is rest from the occupations of the world: "Martha, Martha, thou art careful and art troubled about many things."[488]

The Heavenly Sabbath

And then after all these things the soul rests peacefully in God: "If thou... call the sabbath delightful...then shalt thou be delighted in the Lord."[489] The saints gave up everything to possess this rest, for it is a "pearl of great price...which a man having found, hid it, and for joy thereof goeth and selleth all that he hath, and buyeth that field."[490] This rest in truth is eternal life and heavenly joy: "This is my rest for ever and ever; here will I dwell, for I have chosen it."[491] And to this rest may the Lord bring us all!

THE FOURTH COMMANDMENT

"Honor thy father and thy mother, that thou mayest be long-lived upon the land which the Lord thy God will give thee."[492]

Perfection for man consists in the love of God and of neighbor. Now, the three commandments which were written on the first tablet pertain to the love of God; for the love of neighbor there were the seven commandments on the second tablet. But we must "love, not in word nor in tongue, but in deed and in truth."[493] For a man to love thus, he must do two things, namely, avoid evil and do good. Certain of the commandments prescribe good acts, while others forbid evil deeds. And we must also know that to avoid evil is in our power; but we are incapable of doing good to everyone. Thus, St.

---

[486] Is 57:20
[487] Gal 5:17
[488] Lk 10:41
[489] Is 58:13-14
[490] Mt 13:46, 44
[491] Ps 131:14
[492] Ex 20:12; Cf. Dt 5:16
[493] 1 Jn 3:18

Augustine says that we should love all, but we are not bound to do good to all. But among those to whom we are bound to do good are those in some way united to us. Thus, "if any man have not care of his own and especially of those of his house, he hath denied the faith."[494] Now, amongst all our relatives there are none closer than our father and mother. "We ought to love God first," says St. Ambrose, "then our father and mother." Hence, God has given us the commandment: "Honor thy father and thy mother."[495]

The philosopher also gives another reason for this honor to parents, in that we cannot make an equal return to our parents for the great benefits they have granted to us; and, therefore, an offended parent has the right to send his son away, but the son has no such right.[496] Parents, indeed, give their children three things. The first is that they brought them into being: "Honor thy father, and forget not the groanings of thy mother; remember that thou hadst not been born but through them."[497] Secondly, they furnished nourishment and the support necessary for life. For a child comes naked into the world, as Job relates,[498] but he is provided for by his parents. The third is instruction: "We have had fathers of our flesh for instructors."[499] "Hast thou children? Instruct them."[500]

Parents, therefore, should give instruction without delay to their children, because "a young man according to his way, even when he is old will not depart from it."[501] And again: "It is good for a man when he hath borne the yoke from his youth."[502] Now, the instruction which Tobias gave his son[503] was this: to fear the Lord and to abstain from sin. This is indeed contrary to those parents who approve of the misdeeds of their children. Children, therefore, receive from their parents birth, nourishment, and instruction.

---

[494] 1 Tm 5:8

[495] Translator's note: St. Thomas also treats of the fourth commandment in *Summa Theologiae*, II-II, q. 122 and 101.

[496] Cf. Aristotle, *Ethics*, Bk. 8, Ch. 14

[497] Ecclus 7:29-30

[498] Cf. Jb 1:21

[499] Heb 12:9

[500] Ecclus 7:25

[501] Prv 22:6

[502] Lam 3:27

[503] Cf. Tb 4

What Children Owe Parents

Now, because we owe our birth to our parents, we ought to honor them more than any other superiors, because from such we receive only temporal things: "He that feareth the Lord honoreth his parents, and will serve them as his masters that brought him into the world. Honor thy father in work and word and all patience, that a blessing may come upon thee from him."[504] And in doing this you shall also honor thyself, because "the glory of a man is from honor of his father, and a father without honor is the disgrace of his son."[505]

Again, since we receive nourishment from our parents in our childhood, we must support them in their old age: "Son, support the old age of thy father, and grieve him not in his life. And if his understanding fail, have patience with him; and despise him not when thou art in thy strength...Of what an evil fame is he that forsaketh his father! And he is cursed of God that angereth his mother."[506] For the humiliation of those who act contrary to this, Cassiodorus relates how young storks, when the parents have lost their feathers by approaching old age and are unable to find suitable food, make the parent storks comfortable with their own feathers, and bring back food for their worn-out bodies. Thus, by this affectionate exchange the young ones repay the parents for what they received when they were young.[507]

We must obey our parents, for they have instructed us. "Children, obey your parents in all things."[508] This excepts, of course, those things which are contrary to God. St. Jerome says that the only loyalty in such cases is to be cruel:[509] "If any man...hate not his father and mother...he cannot be my disciple."[510] This is to say that God is in the truest sense our Father: "Is not he thy Father who hath possessed thee, and hath made thee, and created thee?"[511]

---

[504] Ecclus 3:8-10
[505] Ecclus 3:13
[506] Ecclus 3:14-15, 18
[507] Cf. Cassiodorus, *Letters of Cassiodorus*, Bk. 2, Letter 14
[508] Col 3:20
[509] Cf. Jerome, *Letter 14 to Heliodorus*, n. 2
[510] Lk 14:26
[511] Dt 32:6

Rewards for Keeping This Commandment

"Honor thy father and thy mother." Among all the commandments, this one only has the additional words: "that thou mayest be long-lived upon the land."[512] The reason for this is lest it be thought that there is no reward for those who honor their parents, seeing that it is a natural obligation. Hence it must be known that five most desirable rewards are promised those who honor their parents.

Grace and glory. — The first reward is grace for the present life, and glory in the life to come, which surely are greatly to be desired: "Honor thy father...that a blessing may come upon thee from God, and his blessing may remain in the latter end."[513] The very opposite comes upon those who dishonor their parents; indeed, they are cursed in the law by God.[514] It is also written: "He that is unjust in that which is little, is unjust also in that which is greater."[515] But this our natural life is as nothing compared with the life of grace. And so, therefore, if you do not acknowledge the blessing of the natural life which you owe to your parents, then you are unworthy of the life of grace, which is greater, and all the more so for the life of glory, which is the greatest of all blessings.

A long life. — The second reward is a long life: "That thou mayest be long-lived upon the land." For "he that honoreth his father shall enjoy a long life."[516] Now, that is a long life which is a full life, and it is not observed in time but in activity, as the philosopher observes. Life, however, is full inasmuch as it is a life of virtue; so a man who is virtuous and holy enjoys a long life even if in body he dies young: "Being perfect in a short space, he fulfilled a long time; for his soul pleased God."[517] Thus, for example, he is a good merchant who does as much business in one day as another would do in a year. And note well that it sometimes happens that a long life may lead up to a spiritual as well as a bodily death, as was the

---

[512] Ex 20:12; Eph 6:3
[513] Ecclus 3:9-10
[514] Cf. Dt 27:16
[515] Lk 16:10
[516] Ecclus 3:7
[517] Ws 4:13-14

case with Judas. Therefore, the reward for keeping this commandment is a long life for the body. But the very opposite, namely death, is the fate of those who dishonor their parents. We receive our life from them; and just as the soldiers owe fealty to the king, and lose their rights in case of any treachery, so also they who dishonor their parents deserve to forfeit their lives: "The eye that mocketh at his father and that despiseth the labor of his mother in bearing him, let the ravens…pick it out, and the young eagles eat it."[518] Here *the ravens* signify officials of kings and princes, who in turn are the *young eagles*. But if it happens that such are not bodily punished, they nevertheless cannot escape death of the soul. It is not well, therefore, for a father to give too much power to his children: "Give not to son or wife, brother or friend, power over thee while thou livest; and give not thy estate to another, lest thou repent."[519]

The third reward is to have in turn grateful and pleasing children. For a father naturally treasures his children, but the contrary is not always the case: "He that honoreth his father shall have joy in his own children."[520] Again: "With what measure you mete, it shall be measured to you again."[521]

The fourth reward is a praiseworthy reputation: "For the glory of a man is from the honor of his father."[522] And again: "Of what an evil fame is he that forsaketh his father?"[523] A fifth reward is riches: "The father's blessing establisheth the houses of his children, but the mother's curse rooteth up the foundation."[524]

The Different Applications of "Father"

"Honor thy father and thy mother." A man is called father not only by reason of generation, but also for other reasons, and to each of these is due a certain reverence. Thus, the apostles and the saints are called

[518] Prv 30:17
[519] Ecclus 33:20
[520] Ecclus 3:6
[521] Mt 7:2
[522] Ecclus 3:13
[523] Ecclus 3:18
[524] Ecclus 3:11

fathers because of their doctrine and their exemplification of faith: "For if you have ten thousand instructors in Christ, yet not many fathers. For in Christ Jesus, by the gospel, I have begotten you."[525] And again: "Let us now praise men of renown and our fathers in their generation."[526] However, let us praise them not in word only, but by imitating them; and we do this if nothing is found in us contrary to what we praise in them.

Our superiors in the Church are also called fathers; and they too are to be respected as the ministers of God: "Remember your prelates,…whose faith follow, considering the end of their conversation."[527] And again: "He that heareth you, heareth me; and he that despiseth you, despiseth me."[528] We honor them by showing them obedience: "Obey your prelates, and be subject to them."[529] And also by paying them tithes: "Honor the Lord with thy substance, and give him of the first of thy fruits."[530]

Rulers and kings are called fathers: "Father, if the prophet had bid thee do some great thing, surely thou shouldst have done it."[531] We call them fathers because their whole care is the good of their people. And we honor them by being subject to them: "Let every soul be subject to higher powers."[532] We should be subject to them not merely through fear, but through love; and not merely because it is reasonable, but because of the dictates of our conscience. Because "there is no power but from God."[533] And so to all such we must render what we owe them: "Tribute, to whom tribute is due; custom, to whom custom; fear, to whom fear; honor, to whom honor."[534] And again: "My son, fear the Lord and the king."[535]

[525] 1 Cor 4:15
[526] Ecclus 44:1
[527] Heb 13:7
[528] Lk 10:16
[529] Heb 13:17
[530] Prv 3:9
[531] 4 Kgs 5:13
[532] Rom 13:1
[533] Ibid.
[534] Rom 13:7
[535] Prv 24:21

Our benefactors also are called fathers: "Be merciful to the fatherless as a father."[536] He, too, is like a father (who gives his bond) of whom it is said: "Forget not the kindness of thy surety."[537] On the other hand, the thankless shall receive a punishment such as is written: "The hope of the unthankful shall melt away as the winter's ice."[538] Old men also are called fathers: "Ask thy father, and he will declare to thee; thy elders and they will tell thee."[539] And again: "Rise up before the hoary head, and honor the person of the aged man."[540] "In the company of great men take not upon thee to speak; and when the ancients are present, speak not much."[541] "Hear in silence, and for thy reverence good grace shall come to thee."[542] Now, all these fathers must be honored, because they all resemble to some degree our Father who is in heaven; and of all of them it is said: "He that despiseth you, despiseth me."[543]

THE FIFTH COMMANDMENT

"Thou shalt not kill."

The sin of killing. —In the divine law which tells us we must love God and our neighbor, it is commanded that we not only do good but also avoid evil. The greatest evil that can be done to one's neighbor is to take his life. This is prohibited in the commandment: "Thou shalt not kill."[544]

Killing of animals is lawful. —In connection with this commandment there are three errors. Some have said that it is not permitted to kill even brute animals. But this is false, because it is not a sin to use that which is subordinate to the power of man. It is in the natural order that plants be

---

[536] Ecclus 4:10
[537] Ecclus 29:19
[538] Ws 16:29
[539] Dt 32:7
[540] Lv 19:32
[541] Ecclus 32:13
[542] Ecclus 32:9
[543] Lk 10:16
[544] Translator's note: St. Thomas also treats of this commandment in *Summa Theologiae*, II-II, q. 69; q. 122, a. 6.

the nourishment of animals, certain animals nourish others, and all for the nourishment of man: "Even the green herbs have I delivered them all to you."[545] The philosopher says that hunting is like a just war.[546] And St. Paul says: "Whatsoever is sold in the shambles eat; asking no questions for conscience' sake."[547] Therefore, the sense of the commandment is: "Thou shalt not kill men."

The execution of criminals. — Some have held that the killing of man is prohibited altogether. They believe that judges in the civil courts are murderers, who condemn men to death according to the laws. Against this St. Augustine says that God by this commandment does not take away from himself the right to kill. Thus, we read: "I will kill and I will make to live."[548] It is, therefore, lawful for a judge to kill according to a mandate from God, since in this God operates, and every law is a command of God: "By me kings reign, and lawgivers decree just things."[549] And again: "For if thou dost that which is evil, fear; for he beareth not the sword in vain. Because he is God's minister."[550] To Moses also it was said: "Wizards thou shalt not suffer to live."[551] And thus that which is lawful to God is lawful for his ministers when they act by his mandate. It is evident that God who is the author of laws, has every right to inflict death on account of sin. For "the wages of sin is death."[552] Neither does his minister sin in inflicting that punishment. The sense, therefore, of "Thou shalt not kill" is that one shall not kill by one's own authority.

Suicide is prohibited. — There are those who held that although this commandment forbids one to kill another, yet it is lawful to kill oneself. Thus, there are the examples of Samson[553] and Cato and certain virgins who threw themselves into the flames, as St. Augustine relates in *The City*

---

[545] Gn 9:3
[546] Cf. Aristotle, *Politics*, Bk. 1
[547] 1 Cor 10:25
[548] Dt 32:39
[549] Prv 8:15
[550] Rom 13:4
[551] Ex 22:18
[552] Rom 6:23
[553] Cf. Jgs 16

of God.[554] But he also explains this in the words: "He who kills himself, certainly kills a man."[555] If it is not lawful to kill except by the authority of God, then it is not lawful to kill oneself except either upon the authority of God or instructed by the Holy Ghost, as was the case of Samson. Therefore, "Thou shalt not kill."

Other meanings of "to kill." — It ought to be known that to kill a man may happen in several ways. Firstly, by one's own hand: "Your hands are full of blood."[556] This is not only against charity, which tells us to love our neighbor as ourself: "No murderer hath eternal life abiding in himself."[557] But also it is against nature, for "every beast loveth its like."[558] And so it is said: "He that striketh a man with a will to kill him, shall be put to death."[559] He who does this is more cruel than the wolf, of which Aristotle says that one wolf will not eat of the flesh of another wolf.[560]

Secondly, one kills another by word of mouth. This is done by giving counsel to anyone against another by provocation, accusation, or detraction: "The sons of men whose teeth are weapons and arrows, and their tongue a sharp sword."[561] Thirdly, by lending aid, as it is written: "My son, walk not thou with them…for their feet run to evil, and they make haste to shed blood."[562] Fourthly, by consent: "They are worthy of death, not only they that do them, but they also that consent to them that do them."[563] Lastly, one kills another by giving a partial consent when the act could be completely prevented: "Deliver them that are led to death";[564] or, if one can prevent it, yet does not do so through negligence or avarice. Thus, St.

---

[554] Cf. Augustine, *City of God*, Bk. 1, Ch. 17, 23-27
[555] Augustine, *City of God*, Bk. 1, Ch. 17
[556] Is 1:15
[557] 1 Jn 3:15
[558] Ecclus 13:19
[559] Ex 21:12
[560] Cf. Aristotle, *De Animal.*, Bk. 8
[561] Ps 56:5
[562] Prv 1:15-16
[563] Rom 1:32
[564] Prv 24:11

Ambrose says: "Give food to him that is dying of hunger; if you do not, you are his murderer."[565]

We have already considered the killing of the body, but some kill the soul also by drawing it away from the life of grace, namely, by inducing it to commit mortal sin: "He was a murderer from the beginning,"[566] that is, insofar as he drew men into sin. Others, however, slay both body and soul. This is possible in two ways: first, by the murder of one with child, whereby the child is killed both in body and soul; and, secondly, by committing suicide.

The Sin of Anger

Why we are forbidden to be angry. — In the gospel of St. Matthew,[567] Christ taught that our justice should be greater than the justice of the old law. This means that Christians should observe the commandments of the law more perfectly than the Jews observed them. The reason is that greater effort deserves a better reward: "He who soweth sparingly, shall also reap sparingly."[568] The old law promised a temporary and earthly reward: "If you be willing and will hearken to me, you shall eat the good things of the land."[569] But in the new law heavenly and eternal things are promised. Therefore, justice, which is the observance of the commandments, should be more generous because a greater reward is expected.

The Lord mentioned this commandment in particular among the others when he said: "You have heard that it was said to them of old: Thou shalt not kill...But I say to you that anyone who is angry with his brother, shall be in danger of the judgment."[570] By this is meant the penalty which the law prescribes: "If any man kill his neighbor on set

---

[565] Editor's note: In the *Summa Theologiae* (II-II, q. 32, a. 7, obj. 3), Thomas quotes Ambrose as saying, "Feed him that dies of hunger, if thou hast not fed him, thou hast slain him."

[566] Jn 8:44

[567] Cf. Mt 5

[568] 2 Cor 9:6

[569] Is 1:19

[570] Mt 5:21-22

purpose, and by lying in wait for him; thou shalt take him away from my altar, that he may die."[571]

Ways of avoiding anger. — Now, there are five ways to avoid being angry. The first is that one be not quickly provoked to anger: "Let every man be swift to hear, but slow to speak and slow to anger."[572] The reason is that anger is a sin, and is punished by God. But is all anger contrary to virtue? There are two opinions about this. The Stoics said that the wise man is free from all passions; even more, they maintained that true virtue consisted in perfect quiet of soul. The Peripatetics, on the other hand, held that the wise man is subject to anger, but in a moderate degree. This is the more accurate opinion. It is proved firstly by authority, in that the gospel shows us that these passions were attributed to Christ, in whom was the full fountainhead of wisdom. Then, secondly, it is proved from reason. If all the passions were opposed to virtue, then there would be some powers of the soul which would be without good purpose; indeed, they would be positively harmful to man, since they would have no acts in keeping with them. Thus, the irascible and concupiscible powers would be given to man to no purpose. It must, therefore, be concluded that sometimes anger is virtuous, and sometimes it is not.

Three considerations of anger. — We see this if we consider anger in three different ways. First, as it exists solely in the judgment of reason, without any perturbation of soul; and this is more properly not anger but judgment. Thus, the Lord punishing the wicked is said to be angry: "I will bear the wrath of the Lord because I have sinned against him."[573]

Secondly, anger is considered as a passion. This is in the sensitive appetite, and is twofold. Sometimes it is ordered by reason or it is restrained within proper limits by reason, as when one is angry because it is justly fitting to be angry and within proper limits. This is an act of virtue and is called righteous anger. Thus, the philosopher says that meekness is in no way opposed to anger. This kind of anger then is not a sin.

---

[571] Ex 21:14
[572] Jas 1:19
[573] Mi 7:9

There is a third kind of anger which overthrows the judgment of reason and is always sinful, sometimes mortally and sometimes venially. And whether it is one or the other will depend on that object to which the anger incites, which is sometimes mortal, sometimes venial. This may be mortal in two ways: either in its genus or by reason of the circumstances. For example, murder would seem to be a mortal sin in its genus, because it is directly opposite to a divine commandment. Thus, consent to murder is a mortal sin in its genus, because if the act is a mortal sin, then the consent to the act will be also a mortal sin. Sometimes, however, the act itself is mortal in its genus, but, nevertheless, the impulse is not mortal, because it is without consent. This is the same as if one is moved by the impulse of concupiscence to fornication, and yet does not consent; one does not commit a sin. The same holds true of anger. For anger is really the impulse to avenge an injury which one has suffered. Now, if this impulse of the passion is so great that reason is weakened, then it is a mortal sin; if, however, reason is not so perverted by the passion as to give its full consent, then it will be a venial sin. On the other hand, if up to the moment of consent, the reason is not perverted by the passion, and consent is given without this perversion of reason, then there is no mortal sin. "Whosoever is angry with his brother, shall be in danger of the judgment,"[574] must be understood of that impulse of passion tending to do injury to the extent that reason is perverted—and this impulse, inasmuch as it is consented to, is a mortal sin.

Why we should not get angry easily. — The second reason why we should not be easily provoked to anger is because every man loves liberty and hates restraint. But he who is filled with anger is not master of himself: "Who can bear the violence of one provoked?"[575] And again: "A stone is heavy, and sand weighty, but the anger of a fool is heavier than both."[576]

One should also take care that one does not remain angry overlong: "Be ye angry, and sin not."[577] And: "Let not the sun go down upon your

[574] Mt 5:22
[575] Prv 27:4
[576] Prv 27:3
[577] Ps 4:5

anger."[578] The reason for this is given in the gospel by our Lord: "Be at agreement with thy adversary betimes whilst thou art in the way with him; lest perhaps the adversary deliver thee to the judge, and the judge deliver thee to the officer, and thou be cast into prison. Amen, I say to thee, thou shalt not go out from hence till thou repay the last farthing."[579]

We should beware lest our anger grow in intensity, having its beginning in the heart, and finally leading on to hatred. For there is this difference between anger and hatred, that anger is sudden, but hatred is long-lived and, thus, is a mortal sin: "Whosoever hateth his brother is a murderer."[580] And the reason is because he kills both himself (by destroying charity) and another. Thus, St. Augustine in his *Rule* says: "Let there be no quarrels among you; or if they do arise, then let them end quickly, lest anger should grow into hatred, the mote becomes a beam, and the soul becomes a murderer."[581] Again: "A passionate man stirreth up strifes."[582] "Cursed be their fury, because it was stubborn, and their wrath, because it was cruel."[583]

We must take care lest our wrath explode in angry words: "A fool immediately showeth his anger."[584] Now, angry words are twofold in effect; either they injure another, or they express one's own pride in oneself. Our Lord has reference to the first when he said: "And whosoever shall say to his brother...'Thou fool,' shall be in danger of hell fire."[585] And he has reference to the latter in the words: "And he that shall say: 'Raca,' shall be in danger of the council."[586] Moreover: "A mild answer breaketh wrath, but a harsh word stirreth up fury."[587]

Finally, we must beware lest anger provoke us to deeds. In all our dealings we should observe two things, namely, justice and mercy; but anger

---

[578] Eph 4:26
[579] Mt 5:25-26
[580] 1 Jn 3:15
[581] Augustine, *Rule*, Ch. 6, n. 1
[582] Prv 15:18
[583] Gn 49:7
[584] Prv 12:16
[585] Mt 5:22
[586] Ibid.
[587] Prv 15:1

hinders us in both: "For the anger of a man worketh not the justice of God."[588] For such a one may indeed be willing but his anger prevents him. A certain philosopher once said to a man who had offended him: "I would punish you, were I not angry." "Anger hath no mercy, nor fury when it breaketh forth."[589] And: "In their fury they slew a man."[590]

It is for all this that Christ taught us not only to beware of murder but also of anger. The good physician removes the external symptoms of a malady; and, furthermore, he even removes the very root of the illness, so that there will be no relapse. So also the Lord wishes us to avoid the beginnings of sins; and anger is thus to be avoided because it is the beginning of murder.

THE SIXTH COMMANDMENT

"Thou shalt not commit adultery."

After the prohibition of murder, adultery is forbidden. This is fitting, since husband and wife are as one body. "They shall be," says the Lord, "two in one flesh."[591] Therefore, after an injury inflicted upon a man in his own person, none is so grave as that which is inflicted upon a person with whom one is joined.[592]

Adultery is forbidden both to the wife and the husband. We shall first consider the adultery of the wife, since in this seems to lie the greater sin, for a wife who commits adultery is guilty of three grave sins, which are implied in the following words: "So every woman that leaveth her husband,… first, she hath been unfaithful to the law of the most High; and secondly, she hath offended against her husband; thirdly, she hath fornicated in adultery, and hath gotten her children of another man."[593]

---

[588] Jas 1:20
[589] Prv 27:4
[590] Gn 49:6
[591] Gn 2:24
[592] Translator's note: St. Thomas treats of this commandment also in the *Summa Theologiae*, II-II, q. 122, a. 6; q. 154.
[593] Ecclus 23:32-33

First, therefore, she has sinned by lack of faith, since she is unfaithful to the law wherein God has forbidden adultery. Moreover, she has spurned the ordinance of God: "What therefore God has joined together, let no man put asunder."[594] And also she has sinned against the institution or sacrament. Because marriage is contracted before the eyes of the Church, and thereupon God is called, as it were, to witness a bond of fidelity which must be kept: "The Lord hath been witness between thee and the wife of thy youth whom thou hast despised."[595] Therefore, she has sinned against the law of God, against a precept of the Church, and against a sacrament of God.

Secondly, she sins by infidelity because she has betrayed her husband: "The wife hath not power of her own body: but the husband."[596] In fact, without the consent of the husband she cannot observe chastity. If adultery is committed, then, an act of treachery is perpetrated in that the wife gives herself to another, just as if a servant gave himself to another master: "She forsaketh the guide of her youth, and hath forgotten the covenant of her God."[597]

Thirdly, the adulteress commits the sin of theft in that she brings forth children from a man not her husband; and this is a most grave theft in that she expends her heredity upon children not her husband's. Let it be noted that such a one should encourage her children to enter religion, or upon such a walk of life that they do not succeed in the property of her husband. Therefore, an adulteress is guilty of sacrilege, treachery, and theft.

Husbands, however, do not sin any less than wives, although they sometimes may salve themselves to the contrary. This is clear for three reasons. First, because of the equality which holds between husband and wife, for "the husband also hath not power of his own body, but the wife."[598] Therefore, as far as the rights of matrimony are concerned, one cannot act without the consent of the other. As an indication of this, God did not

[594] Mt 19:6
[595] Mal 2:14
[596] 1 Cor 7:4
[597] Prv 2:17-18
[598] 1 Cor 7:4

form woman from the foot or from the head, but from the rib of the man. Now, marriage was at no time a perfect state until the law of Christ came, because the Jew could have many wives, but a wife could not have many husbands; hence, equality did not exist.

The second reason is because strength is a special quality of the man, while the passion proper to the woman is concupiscence: "Ye husbands, likewise dwelling with them according to knowledge, giving honor to the female as to the weaker vessel."[599] Therefore, if you ask from your wife what you do not keep yourself, then you are unfaithful. The third reason is from the authority of the husband. For the husband is head of the wife, and as it is said: "Women may not speak in the church,…if they would learn anything, let them ask their husbands at home."[600] The husband is the teacher of his wife, and God, therefore, gave the commandment to the husband. Now, as regards fulfillment of their duties, a priest who fails is more guilty than a layman, and a bishop more than a priest, because it is especially incumbent upon them to teach others. In like manner, the husband that commits adultery breaks faith by not obeying that which he ought.

Why Adultery and Fornication Must Be Avoided

Thus, God forbids adultery both to men and women. Now, it must be known that, although some believe that adultery is a sin, yet they do not believe that simple fornication is a mortal sin. Against them stand the words of St. Paul: "For fornicators and adulterers God will judge."[601] And: "Do not err: neither fornicators,…nor adulterers, nor the effeminate, nor liers with mankind…shall possess the kingdom of God."[602] But one is not excluded from the kingdom of God except by mortal sin; therefore, fornication is a mortal sin.

---

[599] 1 Pt 3:7
[600] 1 Cor 14:34-35
[601] Heb 13:4
[602] 1 Cor 6:9-10

But one might say that there is no reason why fornication should be a mortal sin, since the body of the wife is not given, as in adultery. I say, however, if the body of the wife is not given, nevertheless, there is given the body of Christ which was given to the husband when he was sanctified in baptism. If, then, one must not betray his wife, with much more reason must he not be unfaithful to Christ: "Know you not that your bodies are the members of Christ? Shall I then take the members of Christ and make them the members of a harlot? God forbid!"[603] It is heretical to say that fornication is not a mortal sin.

Moreover, it must be known that the commandment, "Thou shalt not commit adultery," not only forbids adultery but also every form of immodesty and impurity. There are some who say that intercourse between married persons is not devoid of sin. But this is heretical, for the apostle says: "Let marriage be honorable in all and the bed undefiled."[604] Not only is it devoid of sin, but for those in the state of grace it is meritorious for eternal life. Sometimes, however, it may be a venial sin, sometimes a mortal sin. When it is had with the intention of bringing forth offspring, it is an act of virtue. When it is had with the intent of rendering mutual comfort, it is an act of justice. When it is a cause of exciting lust, although within the limits of marriage, it is a venial sin; and when it goes beyond these limits, so as to intend intercourse with another if possible, it would be a mortal sin.

Adultery and fornication are forbidden for a number of reasons. First of all, because they destroy the soul: "He that is an adulterer, for the folly of his heart shall destroy his own soul."[605] It says: "for the folly of his heart," which is whenever the flesh dominates the spirit. Secondly, they deprive one of life; for one guilty of such should die according to the law, as we read in Leviticus and Deuteronomy.[606] Sometimes the guilty one is not punished now bodily, which is to his disadvantage since punishment of the body may be borne with patience and is conducive to the remission of sins; but nevertheless he shall be punished in the future life. Thirdly,

[603] 1 Cor 6:15
[604] Heb 13:4
[605] Prv 6:32
[606] Cf. Lv 20:10; Dt 22:22

these sins consume his substance, just as happened to the prodigal son in that "he wasted his substance living riotously."[607] "Give not thy soul to harlots in any point; lest thou destroy thyself and thy inheritance."[608] Fourthly, they defile the offspring: "The children of adulterers shall not come to perfection, and the seed of the unlawful bed shall be rooted out. And if they live long they shall be nothing regarded, and their last old age shall be without honor."[609] And again: "Otherwise your children should be unclean; but now they are holy."[610] Thus, they are never honored in the Church, but if they be clerics their dishonor may go without shame. Fifthly, these sins take away one's honor, and this especially is applicable to women: "Every woman that is a harlot shall be trodden upon as dung in the way."[611] And of the husband it is said: "He gathereth to himself shame and dishonor, and his reproach shall not be blotted out."[612]

St. Gregory says that sins of the flesh are more shameful and less blameful than those of the spirit, and the reason is because they are common to the beasts: "Man when he was in honor did not understand; and he hath been compared to senseless beasts, and made like to them."[613]

THE SEVENTH COMMANDMENT

"Thou shalt not steal."

The Lord specifically forbids injury to our neighbor in the commandments. Thus, "Thou shalt not kill" forbids us to injure our neighbor in his own person; "Thou shalt not commit adultery" forbids injury to the person to whom one is bound in marriage; and now the commandment, "Thou shalt not steal," forbids us to injure our neighbor in his goods. This

---

[607] Lk 15:13
[608] Ecclus 9:6
[609] Ws 3:16-17
[610] 1 Cor 7:14
[611] Ecclus 9:10
[612] Prv 6:33
[613] Ps 48:21

commandment forbids any worldly goods whatsoever to be taken away wrongfully.[614]

Theft is committed in a number of ways. First, by taking stealthily: "If the goodman of the house knew at what hour the thief would come."[615] This is an act wholly blameworthy because it is a form of treachery. "Confusion...is upon the thief."[616]

Secondly, by taking with violence, and this is an even greater injury: "They have violently robbed the fatherless."[617] Among such that do such things are wicked kings and rulers: "Her princes are in the midst of her as roaring lions; her judges are evening wolves, they left nothing for the morning."[618] They act contrary to God's will who wishes a rule according to justice: "By me kings reign and lawgivers decree just things."[619] Sometimes they do such things stealthily and sometimes with violence: "Thy princes are faithless companions of thieves, they all love bribes, they run after rewards."[620] At times they steal by enacting laws and enforcing them for profit only: "Woe to them that make wicked laws."[621] And St. Augustine says that every wrongful usurpation is theft when he asks: "What are thrones but forms of thievery?"[622]

Thirdly, theft is committed by not paying wages that are due: "The wages of him that hath been hired by thee shall not abide by thee until the morning."[623] This means that a man must pay everyone his due, whether he be prince, prelate, or cleric, etc.: "Render therefore to all men their dues. Tribute, to whom tribute is due, custom, to whom custom."[624] Hence, we are bound to give a return to rulers who guard our safety.

---

[614] Translator's note: St. Thomas also treats of this commandment in the *Summa Theologiae*, II-II, q. 122, a. 6.

[615] Mt 24:43

[616] Ecclus 5:17

[617] Jb 24:9

[618] Soph 3:3

[619] Prv 8:15

[620] Is 1:23

[621] Is 10:1

[622] Augustine, *City of God*, Bk. 4, Ch. 4

[623] Lv 19:13

[624] Rom 13:7

The fourth kind of theft is fraud in buying and selling: "Thou shalt not have divers weights in thy bag, a greater and a less."[625] And again: "Do not any unjust thing in judgment, in rule, in weight, or in measure."[626] All this is directed against the keepers of wine-shops who mix water with the wine. Usury is also forbidden: "Who shall dwell in thy tabernacle, or who shall rest in thy holy hill?...He that hath not put his money out to usury."[627] This is also against money-changers who commit many frauds, and against the sellers of cloth and other goods.

Fifthly, theft is committed by those who buy promotions to positions of temporal or spiritual honor. "The riches which he hath swallowed, he shall vomit up, and God shall draw them out of his belly,"[628] has reference to temporal position. Thus, all tyrants who hold a kingdom or province or land by force are thieves, and are held to restitution. Concerning spiritual dignities: "Amen, amen, I say to you, he that entereth not by the door into the sheepfold but climbeth up another way is a thief and a robber."[629] Therefore, they who commit simony are thieves.

Why Stealing Must Be Avoided

"Thou shalt not steal." This commandment, as has been said, forbids taking things wrongfully, and we can bring forth many reasons why it is given. The first is because of the gravity of this sin, which is likened to murder: "The bread of the needy is the life of the poor; he that defraudeth them thereof is a man of blood."[630] And again: "He that sheddeth blood and he that defraudeth the laborer of his hire are brothers."[631]

The second reason is the peculiar danger involved in theft, for no sin is so dangerous. After committing other sins a person may quickly repent, for instance, of murder when his anger cools, or of fornication when his

[625] Dt 25:13
[626] Lv 19:35
[627] Ps 14:1, 5
[628] Jb 20:15
[629] Jn 10:1
[630] Ecclus 34:25
[631] Ecclus 34:27

passion subsides, and so on for others; but even if one repents of this sin, one does not easily make the necessary satisfaction for it. This is owing to the obligation of restitution and the duty to make up for what loss is incurred by the rightful owner. And all this is above and beyond the obligation to repent for the sin itself: "Woe to him that heapeth together that which is not his own, how long doth he load himself with thick clay!"[632] For thick clay is that from which one cannot easily extricate himself.

The third reason is the uselessness of stolen goods in that they are of no spiritual value: "Treasures of wickedness shall profit nothing."[633] Wealth can indeed be useful for almsgiving and offering of sacrifices, for "the ransom of a man's life are his riches."[634] But it is said of stolen goods: "I am the Lord that love judgment, and hate robbery in a holocaust."[635] And again: "He that offereth sacrifice of the goods of the poor is as one that sacrificeth the son in the presence of his father."[636]

The fourth reason is that the results of theft are peculiarly harmful to the thief in that they lead to his loss of other goods. It is not unlike the mixture of fire and straw: "Fire shall devour their tabernacles, who love to take bribes."[637] And it ought to be known that a thief may lose not only his own soul, but also the souls of his children, since they are bound to make restitution.

THE EIGHTH COMMANDMENT

"Thou shalt not bear false witness against thy neighbor."

The Lord has forbidden anyone to injure his neighbor by deed; now he forbids us to injure him by word. "Thou shalt not bear false witness against

---

[632] Hb 2:6
[633] Prv 10:2
[634] Prv 13:8
[635] Is 61:8
[636] Ecclus 34:24
[637] Jb 15:34

thy neighbor."[638] This may occur in two ways, either in a court of justice or in ordinary conversation.

In the court of justice, it may happen in three ways, according to the three persons who may violate this commandment in court.

The first person is the plaintiff who makes a false accusation: "Thou shalt not be a detractor nor a whisperer among the people."[639] And note well that it is not only wrong to speak falsely, but also to conceal the truth: "If thy brother shall offend against thee, go and rebuke him."[640]

The second person is the witness who testifies by lying: "A false witness shall not be unpunished."[641] For this commandment includes all the preceding ones, inasmuch as the false witness may himself be the murderer or the thief, etc. And such should be punished according to the law. "When after most diligent inquisition, they shall find that the false witness hath told a lie against his brother, they shall render to him as he meant to do to his brother...Thou shalt not pity him, but shalt require life for life, eye for eye, tooth for tooth, hand for hand, foot for foot."[642] And again: "A man that beareth false witness against his neighbor is like a dart and a sword and a sharp arrow."[643]

The third person is the judge who sins by giving an unjust sentence: "Thou shalt not...judge unjustly. Respect not the person of the poor, nor honor the countenance of the mighty. But judge thy neighbor according to justice."[644]

Ways of Violating This Commandment

In ordinary conversation one may violate this commandment in five ways.[645]

---

[638] Translator's note: St. Thomas also treats of this commandment in the *Summa Theologiae*, II-II, q. 122, a. 6.

[639] Lv 19:16

[640] Mt 18:15

[641] Prv 19:5

[642] Dt 19:18-19, 21

[643] Prv 25:18

[644] Lv 19:15

[645] Editor's note: A portion of Aquinas' original text is missing in Collins'

The first is by detraction: "Detractors, hateful to God."[646] "Hateful to God" here indicates that nothing is so dear to a man as his good name: "A good name is better than great riches."[647] But detractors take away this good name: "If a serpent bite in silence, he is no better that backbiteth secretly."[648] Therefore, if detractors do not restore this reputation, they cannot be saved.

Secondly, one may break this precept by listening to detractors willingly: "Hedge in thy ears with thorns, hear not a wicked tongue, and make doors and bars to thy mouth."[649] One should not listen deliberately to such things, but ought to turn away, showing a sad and stern countenance: "The north wind driveth away rain as doth a sad countenance a backbiting tongue."[650]

Thirdly, gossipers break this precept when they repeat whatever they hear: "Six things there are which the Lord hateth, and the seventh his soul detesteth...him that soweth discord among brethren."[651]

Fourthly, those who speak honied words, the flatterers: "The sinner is praised in the desires of his soul, and the unjust man is blessed."[652] And again: "O my people, they that call thee blessed, the same shall deceive thee."[653] Again: "The just man shall correct me in mercy and shall reprove me; but let not the oil of the sinner fatten my head."[654]

Fifthly, there are murmurers. This sin is chiefly found in those who are under authority. St. Paul says, "Neither do you murmur, as some of them murmured, and were destroyed by the destroyer."[655] So it is said,

---

translation, supplied here from H. A. Rawes, trans., *St. Thomas Aquinas on the Two Commandments of Charity and the Ten Commandments of the Law* (London: Burns and Oates, 1880), 206-207.

[646] Rom 1:30
[647] Prv 22:1
[648] Eccles 10:11
[649] Ecclus 28:28
[650] Prv 25:23
[651] Prv 6:16, 19
[652] Ps 10:3
[653] Is 3:12
[654] Ps 140:5
[655] 1 Cor 10:10

"Keep yourselves therefore from murmuring, which profiteth nothing."[656] Again: "By patience a prince shall be appeased; and a soft tongue shall break hardness."[657]

Special Effects of Telling Lies

The prohibition of this commandment includes every form of falsehood: "Be not willing to make any manner of lie; for the custom thereof is no good."[658] There are four reasons for this.

The first is that lying likens one to the devil, because a liar is as the son of the devil. Now, we know that a man's speech betrays from what region and country he comes from, thus: "Even thy speech doth discover thee."[659] Even so, some men are of the devil's kind, and are called sons of the devil because they are liars, since the devil is "a liar and the father of lies."[660] Thus, when the devil said, "No, you shall not die the death,"[661] he lied. But, on the contrary, others are the children of God, who is truth, and they are those who speak the truth.

The second reason is that lying induces the ruin of society. Men live together in society, and this is soon rendered impossible if they do not speak the truth to one another. "Wherefore putting away lying, speak ye the truth, every man with his neighbor; for we are members one of another."[662]

The third reason is that the liar loses his reputation for the truth. He who is accustomed to telling lies is not believed even when he speaks the truth: "What can be made clean by the unclean? And what truth can come from that which is false?"[663]

The fourth reason is because a liar kills his soul, for "the mouth that belieth killeth the soul."[664] And again: "Thou wilt destroy all that speak a

[656] Ws 1:11
[657] Prv 25:15
[658] Ecclus 7:14
[659] Mt 26:73
[660] Jn 8:44
[661] Gn 3:4
[662] Eph 4:25
[663] Ecclus 34:4
[664] Ws 1:11

lie."[665] Accordingly, it is clear that lying is a mortal sin; although it must be known that some lies may be venial.

It is a mortal sin, for instance, to lie in matters of faith. This concerns professors, prelates, and preachers, and is the gravest of all other kinds of lies: "There shall be among you lying teachers, who shall bring in sects of perdition."[666] Then there are those who lie to wrong their neighbor: "Lie not to one another."[667] These two kinds of lies, therefore, are mortal sins.

There are some who lie for their own advantage, and this in a variety of ways. Sometimes it is out of humility. This may be the case in confession, about which St. Augustine says: "Just as one must avoid concealing what he has committed, so also he must not mention what he has not committed." "Hath God any need of your lie?"[668] And again: "There is one that humbleth himself wickedly, and his interior is full of deceit; and there is one that humbleth himself exceedingly with a great lowness."[669]

There are others who tell lies out of shame, namely, when one tells a falsehood believing that he is telling the truth, and on becoming aware of it he is ashamed to retract: "In no wise speak against the truth, but be ashamed of the lie of thy ignorance."[670] Other some lie for desired results as when they wish to gain or avoid something: "We have placed our hope in lies, and by falsehood we are protected."[671] And again: "He that trusteth in lies feedeth the winds."[672]

Finally, there are some who lie to benefit another, that is, when they wish to free someone from death, or danger, or some other loss. This must be avoided, as St. Augustine tells us:[673] "Accept no person against thy own person, nor against thy soul a lie."[674] But others lie only out of vanity, and

[665] Ps 5:7
[666] 2 Pt 2:1
[667] Col 3:9
[668] Jb 13:7
[669] Ecclus 19:23-24
[670] Ecclus 4:30
[671] Is 28:15
[672] Prv 10:4
[673] Cf. Augustine, *On Lying*, n. 9, 42
[674] Ecclus 4:26

this, too, must never be done, lest the habit of such lead us to mortal sin: "For the bewitching of vanity obscureth good things."[675]

THE NINTH (TENTH) COMMANDMENT[676]

"Thou shalt not covet thy neighbor's goods."

"Thou shalt not covet thy neighbor's goods." There is this difference between the divine and the human laws: that human law judges only deeds and words, whereas the divine law judges also thoughts. The reason is because human laws are made by men who see things only exteriorly, but the divine law is from God, who sees both external things and the very interior of men. "Thou art the God of my heart."[677] And again: "Man seeth those things that appear, but the Lord beholdeth the heart."[678] Therefore, having considered those commandments which concern words and deeds, we now treat of the commandments about thoughts. For with God the intention is taken for the deed, and thus the words, "Thou shalt not covet," mean to include not only the taking by act, but also the intention to take. Therefore, it says: "Thou shalt not even covet thy neighbor's goods." There are a number of reasons for this.

The first reason for the commandment is that man's desire has no limits, because desire itself is boundless. But he who is wise will aim at some particular end, for no one should have aimless desires: "A covetous man shall not be satisfied with money."[679] But the desires of man are never satisfied, because the heart of man is made for God. Thus, says St. Augustine: "Thou hast made us for thee, O Lord, and our heart is restless until it rests

[675] Ws 4:12
[676] Translator's note: St. Thomas places the tenth commandment (in the present traditional enumeration) before the ninth. The tenth commandment is wider in extension than the ninth, which is specific.
[677] Ps 72:26
[678] 1 Kgs 16:7
[679] Eccles 5:9

126

in thee."[680] Nothing, therefore, less than God can satisfy the human heart: "Who satisfieth thy desire with good things."[681]

The second reason is that covetousness destroys peace of heart, which is indeed highly delightful. The covetous man is ever solicitous to acquire what he lacks, and to hold that which he has: "The fullness of the rich will not suffer him to sleep."[682] "For where thy treasure is, there is thy heart also."[683] It was for this, says St. Gregory, that Christ compared riches to thorns.[684]

Thirdly, covetousness in a man of wealth renders his riches useless both to himself and to others, because he desires only to hold on to them: "Riches are not comely for a covetous man and a niggard."[685] The fourth reason is that it destroys the equality of justice: "Neither shalt thou take bribes, which even blind the wise, and pervert the words of the just."[686] And again: "He that loveth gold shall not be justified."[687] The fifth reason is that it destroys the love of God and neighbor, for says St. Augustine: "The more one loves, the less one covets," and also the more one covets, the less one loves. "Nor despise thy dear brother for the sake of gold."[688] And just as "no man can serve two masters," so neither can he serve "God and mammon."[689]

Finally, covetousness produces all kinds of wickedness. It is "the root of all evil," says St. Paul, and when this root is implanted in the heart it brings forth murder and theft and all kinds of evil: "They that will become rich, fall into temptation, and into the snare of the devil, and into many unprofitable and hurtful desires which drown men in destruction and perdition. For the desire of money is the root of all evil."[690] And note, furthermore,

---

[680] Augustine, *Confessions*, Bk. 1, Ch. 1
[681] Ps 102:5
[682] Eccles 5:11
[683] Mt 6:21
[684] Cf. Lk 8:14
[685] Ecclus 14:3
[686] Ex 23:8
[687] Ecclus 31:5
[688] Ecclus 7:20
[689] Mt 6:24
[690] 1 Tm 6:9-10

that covetousness is a mortal sin when one covets one's neighbor's goods without reason; and even if there be a reason, it is a venial sin.

THE TENTH (NINTH) COMMANDMENT

"Thou shalt not covet thy neighbor's wife."

St. John says in his first epistle that "all that is in the world is the concupiscence of the flesh, the concupiscence of the eyes, and the pride of life."[691] Now, all that is desirable is included in these three, two of which are forbidden by the precept: "Thou shalt not covet thy neighbor's house." Here *house*, signifying height, refers to avarice, for "glory and wealth shall be in his house."[692] This means that he who desires the house, desires honors and riches. And thus, after the precept forbidding desire for the house of one's neighbor comes the commandment prohibiting concupiscence of the flesh: "Thou shalt not covet thy neighbor's wife."

Because of the corruption which resulted from the fall, none has been free from concupiscence except Christ and the glorious Virgin. And wherever there is concupiscence, there is either venial or mortal sin, provided that it is allowed to dominate the reason. Hence the precept is not, let sin not be; for it is written: "I know that there dwelleth not in me (that is to say, in my flesh) that which is good."[693]

First of all, sin rules in the flesh when, by giving consent to it, concupiscence reigns in the heart. And, therefore, St. Paul adds "so as to obey the lusts thereof" to the words: "Let not sin reign in your mortal body."[694] Accordingly, the Lord says: "Whosoever shall look on a woman to lust after her, hath already committed adultery with her in his heart."[695] For with God the intention is taken for the act.

---

[691] 1 Jn 2:16
[692] Ps 111:3
[693] Rom 7:18
[694] Rom 6:12
[695] Mt 5:28

Secondly, sin rules in the flesh when the concupiscence of our heart is expressed in words: "Out of the abundance of the heart the mouth speaketh."[696] And again: "Let no evil speech proceed from your mouth."[697] Therefore, one is not without sin who composes frivolous songs. Even the philosophers so thought, and poets who wrote amatory verses were sent into exile.

Lastly, sin rules in the flesh when at the behest of desire the members are made to serve iniquity: "As you have yielded your members to serve uncleanness and iniquity unto iniquity."[698] These, therefore, are the progressive steps of concupiscence.

Ways to Overcome Concupiscence

We must realize that the avoidance of concupiscence demands much labor, for it is based on something within us. It is as hard as trying to capture an enemy in one's own household. However, this desire can be overcome in four ways.

Firstly, by fleeing the external occasions such as, for instance, bad company; and in fact whatever may be an occasion for this sin: "Gaze not upon a maiden lest her beauty be a stumbling-block to thee...Look not around about thee in the ways of the city, nor wander up and down in the streets thereof. Turn away thy face from a woman dressed up, and gaze not about upon another's beauty. For many have perished by the beauty of a woman, and hereby lust is enkindled as a fire."[699] And again: "Can a man hide fire in his bosom, and his garments not burn?"[700] And thus Lot was commanded to flee, "neither stay thou in all the country about."[701]

The second way is by not giving an opening to thoughts which of themselves are the occasion of lustful desires. And this must be done

[696] Mt 12:34
[697] Eph 4:29
[698] Rom 6:19
[699] Ecclus 9:5, 7-9
[700] Prv 6:27
[701] Gn 19:17

by mortification of the flesh: "I chastise my body, and bring it into subjection."[702]

The third way is perseverance in prayer: "Unless the Lord build the house, they labor in vain who build it."[703] And also: "I knew that I could not otherwise be continent, except God gave it."[704] Again: "This kind is not cast out save by prayer and fasting."[705] All this is not unlike to a fight between two persons, one of whom you desire to win, the other to lose. You must sustain the one and withdraw all support from the other. So also between the spirit and the flesh there is a continual combat. Now, if you wish the spirit to win, you must assist it by prayer, and likewise you must resist the flesh by such means as fasting; for by fasting the flesh is weakened.

The fourth way is to keep oneself busy with wholesome occupations: "Idleness hath taught much evil."[706] Again: "This was the iniquity of Sodom thy sister, pride, fullness of bread, and abundance, and the idleness of her."[707] St. Jerome says: "Be always busy in doing something good, so that the devil may find you ever occupied."[708] Now, study of the scriptures is the best of all occupations, as St. Jerome tells us: "Love to study the scriptures and you will not love the vices of the flesh."[709]

Summary of the Ten Commandments

These are the ten precepts to which our Lord referred when he said: "If thou wilt enter into life, keep the commandments."[710] There are two main principles of all the commandments, namely, love of God and love of neighbor.

The man that loves God must necessarily do three things. 1) He must have no other God. And in support of this is the commandment: "Thou

---

[702] 1 Cor 9:27
[703] Ps 126:1
[704] Ws 8:21
[705] Mt 17:20
[706] Ecclus 33:29
[707] Ez 16:49
[708] Jerome, *Letter 125 to Rusticus*, n. 11
[709] Ibid.
[710] Mt 19:17

shalt not have strange gods." 2) He must give God all honor. And so it is commanded: "Thou shalt not take the name of God in vain." 3) He must freely take his rest in God. Hence: "Remember that thou keep holy the sabbath day."

But to love God worthily, one must first of all love one's neighbor. And so: "Honor thy father and mother." Then, one must avoid doing harm to one's neighbor in act: "Thou shalt not kill" refers to our neighbor's person; "Thou shalt not commit adultery" refers to the person united in marriage to our neighbor; "Thou shalt not steal" refers to our neighbor's external goods. We must also avoid injury to our neighbor both by word, "Thou shalt not bear false witness," and by thought, "Thou shalt not covet thy neighbor's goods" and "Thou shalt not covet thy neighbor's wife."

Explanation of the Sacraments

THE SACRAMENTS OF THE CHURCH

We shall now consider the sacraments of the Church. We shall treat them under one heading, since they all pertain to the effect of grace. First of all, that must be known which St. Augustine wrote in the tenth book of *The City of God*: "a sacrament is a sacred thing" or "the sign of a sacred thing."[711] Even in the old law there were certain sacraments, that is, signs of a sacred thing—for example, the paschal lamb and other legal sacred signs or "sacraments" which, however, did not cause grace but only signified or indicated the grace of Christ. The apostle calls these "sacraments," "weak and needy elements."[712] They were needy because they did not contain grace, and they were weak because they could not confer grace. In them, as St. Augustine says, the merits of Christ brought about salvation in a

---

[711] Translator's note: *Sacrementum est sacrum signum.* This is slightly different in the passage quoted in *The City of God*, Bk. 10, Ch. 5. See also *Epist. ii.*

[712] Gal 4:9

more hidden manner under the cover of visible things. The sacraments of the new law, on the other hand, both contain grace and confer it. A sacrament of the new law is a visible form of invisible grace. Thus, the exterior washing which takes place when the water is poured in baptism represents that interior cleansing which takes away sin by virtue of the sacrament of baptism.

There are seven sacraments of the new law: baptism, confirmation, the Eucharist, penance, extreme unction, orders, and matrimony. The first five of these sacraments are intended to bring about the perfection of the individual man in himself; whereas the other two, orders and matrimony, are so constituted that they perfect and multiply the entire Church.

The Spiritual and the Physical Life: An Analogy

The spiritual life conforms to the physical life. In the physical life man is perfected in three chief ways: first, by generation, in that he is born into this world; secondly, by growth, through which he is brought up into stature and perfect strength; thirdly, by food, which sustains man's life and powers. This would suffice were it not that man is attacked by illnesses, and hence, fourthly, he needs something which will bring him back to health.

This also holds true in the spiritual life. First, man needs regeneration or rebirth which is brought through the sacrament of baptism: "Unless a man be born again of water and the Holy Ghost, he cannot enter into the kingdom of God."[713] Secondly, it is necessary that man develop perfect strength, which is, as it were, a spiritual growth, and this indeed comes to him in the sacrament of confirmation. This is like the strengthening which the apostles received when the Holy Ghost came upon them and confirmed them. The Lord had said to them: "But stay you in the city (of Jerusalem) till you be endued with power from on high."[714] The third similarity is that man must be fed with spiritual food: "Unless you eat the flesh of the Son of man, and drink his blood, you shall not have life in you."[715] Fourthly,

[713] Jn 3:5
[714] Lk 24:49
[715] Jn 6:54

man must be healed spiritually through the sacrament of penance: "Heal, O Lord, my soul, for I have sinned against thee."[716] Lastly, one is healed both in soul and in body in the sacrament of extreme unction: "Is any man sick among you? Let him bring in the priests of the church, and let them pray over him, anointing him with oil in the name of the Lord. And the prayer of faith shall save the sick man, and the Lord shall raise him up, and if he be in sins, they shall be forgiven him."[717] Two of the sacraments, orders and matrimony, are instituted for the common good of the Church. Through the sacrament of orders the Church is ruled and is spiritually multiplied; and through matrimony it is increased physically in numbers.

The Seven Sacraments in General

The seven sacraments have some things which they all hold in common, and some things which are proper to each one. That which is common to all the sacraments is that they confer grace. It is also common to all the sacraments that a sacrament is made up of words and physical acts. And so also Christ, who is the author of the sacraments, is the Word made flesh. And just as the flesh of Christ was sanctified, and has the power of sanctifying because of the Word united to itself, so also the sacraments are made holy and have the power of sanctifying through the words which accompany the action. Thus, St. Augustine says: "The word is joined to the element, and the sacrament is made."[718] Now, the words by which the sacraments are sanctified are called the form of the sacraments; and the things which are sanctified are called the matter of the sacraments. Water, for example, is the matter of baptism, and the holy chrism is the matter of confirmation.

In each sacrament there is required a minister, who confers the sacrament with the intention of doing that which the Church intends. If any one of these three requirements is lacking, the sacrament is not brought

---

[716] Ps 40:5
[717] Jas 5:14-15
[718] Augustine, *Tractate 80 on John*, n. 3

into being, viz., if there is lacking the due form of the words, or if the matter is not present, or if the minister does not intend to confer the sacrament.

The effect of the sacrament is likewise impeded through the fault of the recipient, for example, if one feigns to receive it and with a heart unprepared to receive worthily. Such a one, although he actually receives the sacrament, does not receive the effect of the sacrament, that is, the grace of the Holy Spirit. "For the Holy Spirit of discipline will flee from the deceitful."[719] On the other hand, however, there are some who never even receive sacramentally, yet who receive the effect of the sacrament because of their devotion towards the sacrament, which they may have in desire or in a vow.

There are some things which are characteristic of each individual sacrament. Certain ones impress a character on the soul which is a certain spiritual sign distinct from the other sacraments. Such are the sacraments of orders, baptism, and confirmation. The sacraments which give a character are never repeated in the same person who has once received it. Thus, he who is baptized need never again receive this sacrament; neither can he who has been confirmed receive confirmation again; and one who has been ordained need never repeat his ordination. The reason is that the character which each of these sacraments impresses is indelible.

In the other sacraments, however, a character is not impressed on the recipient, and hence they can be repeated as far as the person is concerned, not however as far as the matter is concerned. Thus, one can frequently receive penance, frequently receive the Eucharist, and can be anointed more than once with extreme unction, and likewise he can be married more than once. Yet, regarding the matter, the same host cannot be frequently consecrated, nor ought the oil of the sick be frequently blessed.

BAPTISM

Having considered the sacraments in general, it is now necessary to say something about each one in particular. First, we consider baptism, of

---

[719] Ws 1:5

which it must be known that the matter of this sacrament is natural water, and it makes no difference whether it is cold or warm. In artificial waters, however, such as rose water, one cannot baptize. The form of baptism is: "I baptize thee in the name of the Father and of the Son and of the Holy Ghost." The minister of baptism ordinarily is the priest, whose office it is to baptize. In case of necessity, however, not only a deacon but also any lay person, even a pagan or a heretic, can baptize as long as he observes the form specified by the Church, and intends to act according to the intention of the Church. If a person is baptized by these not in a case of necessity, he received the sacrament and must not again be baptized; but the grace of the sacrament is not received, because such persons are not truly deputed to baptize outside of cases of necessity, and, hence, they act contrary to the law of the Church regulating reception of the sacraments.

The Effect of Baptism

The effect of baptism is to remit both original and actual sin as well as all guilt and punishment which they incur. No kind of punishment must be enjoined for past sins upon those just newly baptized. Hence, those who die immediately after baptism are admitted to the glory of God without delay. The effect, therefore, of baptism is the opening of the gates of paradise.

Errors Concerning Baptism

There have been certain errors concerning this sacrament. The first was that of the Solentiani, who received a baptism not of water but of the spirit. Against them the Lord says: "Unless a man be born again of water and the Holy Spirit, he cannot enter into the kingdom of God."[720] The second error was that of the Donatists, who re-baptized those who had been baptized by the Catholics. Against them it is written: "One faith, one baptism."[721] They also err in holding that a man in the state of sin cannot baptize. Against them it is said: "He upon whom thou shalt see the Spirit

[720] Jn 3:5
[721] Eph 4:5

descending, and remaining upon him, he it is that baptizeth."[722] It is thus seen that a minister who is himself evil does not invalidate either this or any of the other sacraments, because it is Christ who, by the merits of his passion, gives to each sacrament its efficacy; and he is good. The fourth error is that of the Pelagians, who say that children must be baptized because by their regeneration they, as adopted children of God, are admitted into the kingdom, but by this regeneration they are not freed from original sin.

CONFIRMATION

The second sacrament is confirmation. The matter of this sacrament is chrism made from oil, which signifies the bright lustre of conscience, and from balsam, which signifies the odor of a good name; both of which are blessed by the bishop. The form of this sacrament is: "I sign thee with the sign of the cross, and I confirm thee with the chrism of salvation, in the name of the Father, and of the Son, and of the Holy Ghost. Amen." The minister of this sacrament is solely the bishop. It is not licit for a priest to anoint on the forehead with chrism those who are to be confirmed.

The Effect of Confirmation

The effect of confirmation is that the Holy Spirit is imparted to give strength, just as he was given to the apostles on the day of Pentecost. Thus, the Christian must boldly confess the name of Christ. The one who is confirmed is anointed on the forehead wherein is the seat of fear; so that he will not blush to confess either the name of Christ or especially the cross of Christ, which to the Jews was a scandal and to the pagans foolishness. For this reason he is signed with the sign of the cross.

Errors Concerning Confirmation

Certain of the Greeks erred concerning this sacrament in saying that it could be administered by one who is only a priest. Against this it is said

---

[722] Jn 1:33

that the apostles sent the apostles Peter and John to impose hands upon those who had been baptized by Philip the deacon, and they received the Holy Spirit.[723] Now, the bishops of the Church are in the places of the apostles, and in their place also do they impose hands when the sacrament of confirmation is administered.

THE HOLY EUCHARIST

The third sacrament is the Holy Eucharist. Its matter is wheaten bread and wine from the grape mixed with a little water so that the water becomes part of the wine. The water signifies the faithful who are incorporated into Christ. Other than wheaten bread and wine from the grape cannot be the matter for this sacrament. The form of this sacrament is the very words of Christ, "This is my body," and "This is the chalice of my blood of the new and eternal testament; the mystery of faith; which shall be shed for you and for many, to the remission of sins." These words spoken by the priest in the person of Christ brings into being this sacrament. The minister of this sacrament is the priest; and no one else can consecrate this matter into the body of Christ.

The Effect of the Eucharist

The effect of this sacrament is twofold: first, in the very consecration of the sacrament, since in virtue of the above words bread is changed into the body of Christ, and wine into his blood; so that Christ is entirely contained under the appearances of bread which remain without a subject; and Christ is entirely contained under the appearances of wine. And, moreover, under each part of the consecrated host and of the consecrated wine, Christ is totally present even after the separation is made. The second effect of this sacrament brought about in the soul of one who worthily receives is the union of man with Christ, as he himself says: "He that eateth my flesh, and drinketh my blood, abideth in me, and I

[723] Cf. Acts 8:12-17

in him."[724] And since man is incorporated with Christ and united to his members through grace, it follows that through this sacrament grace is increased in those who receive it worthily. Thus, therefore, in this sacrament there is that which is the sacrament alone (*sacramentum tantum*), that is, the species of bread and wine; and that which is known as the *res et sacramentum*, that is, the true body of Christ; and that which is the *res tantum*, that is the unity of the mystical body, that is, the Church which this sacrament both signifies and causes.

Errors Concerning the Eucharist

There have been many errors regarding this sacrament. The first error is of those who say that in this sacrament is not the true body of Christ but only a sign of it. The author of this error is said to be Berengarius against whom it is written: "For my flesh is meat indeed; and my blood is drink indeed."[725] The second is the error of the Arrodinici, who offer in their sacrament bread and cheese because they say men at first made offerings of the fruits of the earth and of their flocks. Against this, however, stands the fact that the Lord who is the institutor of this sacrament gave to his disciples bread and wine. The third is the error of the Cataphrygae and the Praeputiati, who drew the blood of an infant from tiny punctures in its body, and mixing this with flour made a bread of it; and thus asserted that they consecrated the sacrament. This is more like the sacrifices of demons than that of Christ: "And they shed innocent blood...which they sacrificed to the idols of Chanaan."[726] The fourth is the error of the Aquarii, who offer water only in their sacrifices. But against this are the words from the mouth of wisdom, which is Christ: "Drink the wine which I have mingled for you."[727] Another error is that of the Poor People of Lyons who hold that any just man can consecrate this sacrament. Against such errors is the fact that the Lord gave to the apostles the power to celebrate this

[724] Jn 6:57
[725] Jn 6:56
[726] Ps 105:38
[727] Prv 9:5

sacrament; and hence only those who receive this power in a certain succession from the apostles can consecrate this sacrament.

PENANCE

The fourth sacrament is penance. The matter,[728] as it were, of this sacrament is the acts of the penitent, which are called the three parts of penance. The first part is a heartfelt contrition, by which one is sorry for the sins one has committed, and determines not to sin again. The second part is confession, which consists in this: that the sinner confesses all the sins of which he is mindful to the priest; and all of them at one time to one priest, not dividing them to a number of priests. The third part is satisfaction, which is enjoined according to the judgment of the priest; and consists especially in fasting and prayer and almsgiving.

The form of this sacrament is the words of absolution which the priest speaks when he says: "I absolve thee" (*Ego te absolvo*). The minister of this sacrament is the priest having authority to absolve, which is either ordinary or by commission of his superior. The effect of this sacrament is absolution from sin.

Concerning this sacrament is the error of the Novati, who say that anyone who has sinned after having been baptized cannot receive pardon through the sacrament of penance. Against this are the words: "Be mindful therefore from whence thou art fallen; and do penance, and do the first works."[729]

EXTREME UNCTION

The fifth sacrament is extreme unction. Its matter is olive oil blessed by the bishop. This sacrament should only be received by those who are in danger of death through sickness. They are to be anointed in the places of the five senses: that is, on the eyes, because it is the organ of the sense of sight; on the ears, because of hearing; on the nostrils,

---

[728] Translator's note: St. Thomas uses here the words: *quasi materia.*
[729] Apoc 2:5

because of smell; on the lips, because of taste or speech; and on the hands because of touch, and on the feet because of walking. The form of this sacrament is this: "Through this anointing and through his most divine mercy, may the Lord forgive thee whatever thou hast committed through sight" (and so on for the other senses). The minister of this sacrament is the priest. The effect of this sacrament is a medicine for both mind and body.

Concerning this sacrament is the error of the Elaeonitae, who are said to anoint their dying with oil and balsam and water and to accompany the anointing with invocations in Hebrew pronounced over the head of the sick. This is, however, contrary to the form handed down by St. James, as given above.

HOLY ORDERS

The sixth sacrament is holy orders. There are seven orders: priesthood, deaconate, subdeaconate, acolyte, exorcist, lector, and porter. Tonsure (clerk-ship, *clericatus*) is not an order, but a formal profession of giving one's life to the divine ministry. The episcopate is rather a dignity than an order. The matter of this sacrament is that matter which is handed over to the candidate at the conferring of the order. Thus, priesthood is conferred by the handing over of the chalice, and so each order is conferred by the handing over of that matter which in a special way pertains to the ministry of that particular order.[730] The form of this sacrament is this: "Receive the power to offer sacrifice in the Church for the living and the dead." And similarly, power is conferred in the other orders. The minister of this sacrament is the bishop who confers the orders. The effect of this sacrament is an increase of grace for the performance of the duties of a worthy minister of Christ.

---

[730] Editor's note: The essential matter required for valid sacramental ordination was given further precision under Pope Pius XII (cf. *Sacramentum Ordinis*, 1947) as being specifically the *impositio manus* (laying on of hands), long occurring in the Roman Rite amid the conferral of liturgical instruments (*traditio instrumentorum*) as described here.

Concerning this sacrament was the error of Arius, who taught that the priesthood could not be distinguished from the episcopate.

MATRIMONY

Matrimony is the seventh sacrament. It is a sign of the union between Christ and the Church. The efficient cause of matrimony is the mutual consent expressed in words effective in the present by the parties.

Matrimony has a threefold good. The first is the birth of children and the educating of them to the worship of God. The second is that fidelity which one must render to the other. And the third is that it is a sacrament, or, in other words, the indivisibility of matrimony which shows forth the indivisible union of Christ and his Church.

Concerning matrimony there are a number of errors. The first is that of Tatian, who condemned marriage, and against such it is written: "If thou take a wife, thou hast not sinned."[731] The second error is that of Jovinian, who made marriage equal to virginity. The third is that of the Nicolaitae, who mutually exchange their wives. There were also many other heretics who taught and worked impurities, and against which are the words of St. Paul: "Marriage honorable in all, and the bed undefiled."[732]

Seven Gifts of Eternal Glory

By the reception of these sacraments, man is led to future eternal glory which consists in seven gifts, three of the soul and four of the body.

The first gift given to the soul is the vision of God in his essence, according to the words: "We shall see him as he is."[733] The second gift is comprehension, or that understanding of God as the reward of our merits: "So run that you may obtain."[734] The third is perfect enjoyment, wherein

---

[731] 1 Cor 7:28
[732] Heb 13:4
[733] 1 Jn 3:2
[734] I Cor 9:24

we shall have full happiness in God: "Then shalt thou abound in delights of the Almighty, and shalt lift up thy face to God."[735]

The first gift which shall be enjoyed by the body is that of impassibility,[736] for "this corruptible must put on incorruption."[737] The second gift is brilliancy: "Then shall the just shine as the sun, in the kingdom of their Father."[738] The third is agility, through which they can instantly be present wheresoever they wish: "They shall run to and fro like sparks among the reeds."[739] The fourth is the gift of subtility, whereby they can penetrate wherever they desire: "It is sown a natural body, it shall rise a spiritual body."[740] To all of which may he lead us, who liveth and reigneth forever and ever! Amen.

Explanation of the Lord's Prayer

FIVE QUALITIES OF PRAYER

"Our Father who art in heaven." Among all other prayers, the Lord's Prayer holds the chief place. It has five excellent qualities which are required in all prayer. A prayer must be confident, ordered, suitable, devout and humble.

It must be confident: "Let us, therefore, go with confidence to the throne of grace."[741] It must not be wanting in faith, as it is said: "But let him ask in faith, nothing wavering."[742] That this is a most trustworthy prayer is reasonable, since it was formed by him who is our advocate and the most

---

[735] Jb 22:26

[736] Translator's note: For another description of these gifts, see St. Thomas' *opusculum* on the Apostles' Creed above, in particular, his subsection under the eleventh article, titled, "Condition of the Blessed."

[737] 1 Cor 15:53

[738] Mt 13:43

[739] Ws 3:7

[740] 1 Cor 15:44

[741] Heb 4:16

[742] Jas 1:6

wise petitioner for us: "In whom are hid all the treasures of wisdom and knowledge";[743] and of whom it is said: "For we have an advocate with the Father, Jesus Christ the just one."[744] Hence, St. Cyprian says: "Since we have Christ as our advocate with the Father for our sins, when we pray on account of our faults, we use the very words of our advocate."[745]

Furthermore, this prayer is even more worthy of confidence in that he who taught us how to pray, graciously hears our prayer, together with the Father, as it is said in the psalm: "He shall cry to me, and I will hear him."[746] Thus writes St. Cyprian: "It is a friendly, familiar, and devout prayer to ask of the Lord in his own words."[747] And so no one goes away from this prayer without fruit. St. Augustine says that through it our venial sins are remitted.[748]

Moreover, our prayer must be suitable, so that a person asks of God in prayer what is good for him. St. John Damascene says: "Prayer is the asking of what is right and fitting from God."[749] Many times our prayer is not heard because we seek that which is not good for us: "You ask and you do not receive, because you ask amiss."[750] To know, indeed, what one ought to pray for is most difficult; for it is not easy to know what one ought to desire. Those things which we rightly seek in prayer are rightly desired; hence the apostle says: "For we know not what we should pray for as we ought."[751] Christ himself is our teacher; it is he who teaches us what we ought to pray for, and it was to him that the disciples said: "Lord, teach us to pray."[752] Those things, therefore, which he has taught us to pray for, we most properly ask for. "Whatsoever words we use in prayer," says St. Augustine, "we cannot but utter that which is contained in our Lord's Prayer, if we pray in a suitable and worthy manner."[753]

---

[743] Col 2:3
[744] 1 Jn 2:1
[745] Cyprian, *Treatise 4, On the Lord's Prayer*
[746] Ps 90:15
[747] Cyprian, *Treatise 4, On the Lord's Prayer*
[748] Cf. Augustine, *Enchiridion*, Ch. 7-8
[749] John Damascene, *An Exposition of the Orthodox Faith*, Bk. 3, Ch. 24
[750] Jas 4:3
[751] Rom 8:26
[752] Lk 11:1
[753] Augustine, *Letter 130 to Proba*, Ch. 12

Our prayer ought also to be ordered as our desires should be ordered, for prayer is but the expression of desire. Now, it is the correct order that we prefer spiritual to bodily things, and heavenly things to those merely earthly. This is according to what is written: "Seek ye first therefore the kingdom of God and his justice, and all these things shall be added unto you."[754] Here our Lord shows that heavenly things must be sought first, and then things material.

Our prayer must be devout, because a rich measure of piety makes the sacrifice of prayer acceptable to God: "In thy name I will lift up my hands. Let my soul be filled with marrow and fatness."[755] Many times because of the length of our prayers our devotion grows cool; hence our Lord taught us to avoid wordiness in our prayers: "When you are praying, speak not much."[756] And St. Augustine says: "Let much talking be absent from prayer; but as long as fervor continues, let prayer likewise go on."[757] For this reason the Lord made his prayer short. Devotion in prayer rises from charity which is our love of God and neighbor, both of which are evident in this prayer. Our love for God is seen in that we call God "our Father"; and our love for our neighbor when we say: "Our Father...forgive us our trespasses," and this leads us to love of neighbor.

Prayer ought to be humble: "He hath had regard for the prayer of the humble."[758] This is seen in the parable of the Pharisee and the publican,[759] and also in the words of Judith: "The prayer of the humble and the meek hath always pleased thee."[760] This same humility is observed in this prayer, for true humility is had when a person does not presume upon his own powers, but from the divine strength expects all that he asks for.

It must be noted that prayer brings about three good effects. First, prayer is an efficacious and useful remedy against evils. Thus, it delivers us from the sins we have committed: "Thou hast forgiven the wickedness of my sin. For

---

[754] Mt 6:33
[755] Ps 62:5-6
[756] Mt 6:7
[757] Augustine, *Letter 130 to Proba*, Ch. 10
[758] Ps 101:18
[759] Cf. Lk 18:9-15
[760] Jdt 9:16

this shall every one that is holy pray to thee in a seasonable time."[761] The thief on the cross prayed and received forgiveness: "This day thou shalt be with me in paradise."[762] Thus also prayed the publican, and "went down to his home justified."[763] Prayer also frees one from the fear of future sin, and from trials and sadness of soul: "Is any one of you sad? Let him pray."[764] Again it delivers one from persecutors and enemies: "Instead of making me a return of love, they detracted me, but I gave myself to prayer."[765]

In the second place, prayer is efficacious and useful to obtain all that one desires: "All things whatsoever you ask when you pray, believe that you shall receive."[766] When our prayers are not heard, either we do not persevere in prayer, whereas "we ought always to pray, and not to faint,"[767] or we do not ask for that which is more conducive to our salvation. "Our good Lord often does not give us what we wish," says St. Augustine, "because it would really be what we do not wish for."[768] St. Paul gives us an example of this in that he thrice prayed that the sting of his flesh be removed from him, and his prayer was not heard.[769] Thirdly, prayer is profitable because it makes us friends of God: "Let my prayer be directed as incense in thy sight."[770]

THE OPENING WORDS OF THE LORD'S PRAYER

Preparation for the Petitions

Our FATHER. —Note here two things, namely, that God is our Father, and what we owe to him because he is our Father. God is our Father by reason of our special creation, in that he created us in his image and likeness, and did not so create all inferior creatures: "Is not he thy Father,

---

[761] Ps 31:5-6
[762] Lk 23:43
[763] Lk 18:14
[764] Jas 5:13
[765] Ps 108:4
[766] Mk 11:24
[767] Lk 18:1
[768] Augustine, *Letter 31 to Paulinus and Therasia*, n. 1
[769] Cf. 2 Cor 12:7-8
[770] Ps 140:2

that made thee, and created thee?"[771] Likewise God is our Father in that he governs us, yet treats us as masters, and not servants, as is the case with all other things. "For thy providence, Father, governeth all things";[772] and "with great favor disposest of us."[773] God is our Father also by reason of adoption. To other creatures he has given but a small gift, but to us an heredity — indeed, "if sons, heirs also."[774] "For you have not received the spirit of bondage again in fear; but you have received the spirit of adoption of sons, whereby we cry, Abba (Father)."[775]

We owe God, our Father, four things. First, honor: "If then I be a Father, where is my honor?"[776] Now, honor consists in three qualities. 1) It consists in giving praise to God: "The sacrifice of praise shall glorify me."[777] This ought not merely come from the lips, but also from the heart, for: "This people draw near me with their mouth, and with their lips glorify me, but their heart is far from me."[778] 2) Honor, again, consists in purity of body towards oneself: "Glorify and bear God in your body."[779] 3) Honor also consists in just estimate of one's neighbor, for: "The king's honor loveth judgment."[780]

Secondly, since God is our Father, we ought to imitate him: "Thou shalt call me Father, and shalt not cease to walk after me."[781] This imitation of our Father consists of three things. 1) It consists in love: "Be ye therefore followers of God, as most dear children; and walk in love."[782] This love of God must be from the heart. 2) It consists in mercy: "Be ye merciful."[783] This mercy must likewise come from the heart, and it must be in deed. 3)

---

[771] Dt 32:6
[772] Ws 14:3
[773] Ws 12:18
[774] Rom 8:17
[775] Rom 8:15
[776] Mal 1:6
[777] Ps 49:23
[778] Is 29:13
[779] 1 Cor 6:20
[780] Ps 98:4
[781] Jer 3:19
[782] Eph 5:1-2
[783] Lk 6:36

Finally, imitation of God consists in being perfect, since love and mercy should be perfect: "Be ye therefore perfect, as also your heavenly Father is perfect."[784]

Thirdly, we owe God obedience: "Shall we not much more obey the Father of spirits?"[785] We must obey God for three reasons. First, because he is our Lord: "All things that the Lord has spoken we will do, we will be obedient."[786] Secondly, because he has given us the example of obedience, for the true Son of God "became obedient (to his Father) even unto death."[787] Thirdly, because it is for our good: I will play before the Lord who hath chosen me.[788]

Fourthly, we owe God patience when we are chastised by him: "Reject not the correction of the Lord; and do not faint when thou art chastised by him. For whom the Lord loveth he chastises; and as a father in the son he pleaseth himself."[789]

OUR Father. — From this we see that we owe our neighbor both love and reverence. We must love our neighbor because we are all brothers, and all men are sons of God, our Father: "For he that loveth not his brother whom he seeth, how can he love God whom he seeth not?"[790] We owe reverence to our neighbor because he is also a child of God: "Have we not all one Father? Hath not one God created us? Why then does every one of us despise his brother?"[791] And again: "With honor preventing one another."[792] We do this because of the fruit we receive, for "He became to all that obey the cause of eternal salvation."[793]

[784] Mt 5:48
[785] Heb 12:9
[786] Ex 24:7
[787] Phil 2:8
[788] Cf. 2 Kgs 6:21-22
[789] Prv 3:11-12
[790] 1 Jn 4:20
[791] Mal 2:10
[792] Rom 12:10
[793] Heb 5:9

The Preeminence of God

Who art in heaven. — Among all that is necessary for one who prays, faith is above all important: "Let him ask in faith, nothing wavering."[794] Hence, the Lord, teaching us to pray, first mentions that which causes faith to spring up, namely, the kindness of a father. So, he says "Our Father," in the meaning which is had in the following: "If you then being evil know how to give good gifts to your children, how much more will your Father from heaven give the good Spirit to them that ask him!"[795] Then, he says "who art in heaven" because of the greatness of his power: "To thee have I lifted up my eyes, who dwellest in heaven."[796]

The words, "who art in heaven," signify three things. First, it serves as a preparation for him who utters the prayer, for, as it is said: "Before prayer prepare thy soul."[797] Thus, *in heaven* is understood for the glory of heaven: "For your reward is very great in heaven."[798] And this preparation ought to be in the form of an imitation of heavenly things, since the son ought to imitate his Father: "Therefore, as we have borne the image of the earthly, let us bear also the image of the heavenly."[799] So also this preparation ought to be through contemplation of heavenly things, because men are wont to direct their thoughts to where they have a Father and others whom they love, as it is written: "For where thy treasure is, there is thy heart also."[800] The apostle wrote: "Our conversation is in heaven."[801] Likewise, we prepare through attention to heavenly things, so that we may then seek only spiritual things from him who is in heaven: "Seek things that are above, where Christ is."[802]

[794] Jas 1:6
[795] Lk 11:13
[796] Ps 122:1
[797] Ecclus 18:23
[798] Mt 5:12
[799] 1 Cor 15:49
[800] Mt 6:21
[801] Phil 3:20
[802] Col 3:1

"Who art in heaven" can also pertain to him who hears us, who is nearest to us; and then the *in heaven* is understood to mean "in devout persons" in whom God dwells, as it is written: "Thou, O Lord, art among us."[803] For holy persons are called *the heavens* in the psalm: "The heavens show forth the glory of God,"[804] since God dwells in the devout through faith. "That Christ may dwell by faith in your hearts."[805] God also dwells in us through love: "He that abideth in charity, abideth in God and God in him."[806] And also through the keeping of the commandments: "If any one love me, he will keep my word, and my Father will love him, and we will come to him, and will make our abode with him."[807]

In the third place, "who art in heaven" can pertain to him who is in heaven, he who cannot be included in the physical heavens, for "the heaven and the heaven of heavens cannot contain thee."[808] And so it can mean that God is all-seeing in his survey of us, in that he sees us from above, that is, from heaven: "Because he hath looked forth from his high sanctuary; from heaven the Lord hath looked upon the earth."[809] It also signifies how sublime is God in his power: "The Lord hath prepared his throne in heaven";[810] and that he lives without change through eternity: "But thou, O Lord, endurest forever."[811] And again: "Thy years shall not fail."[812] And so of Christ was it written: "His throne as the days of heaven."[813]

The philosopher says that on account of the incorruptibility of the heavens all have considered them as the abode of spirits.[814] And so "who art in heaven" tends to give us confidence in our prayer which arises from

---

[803] Jer 14:9
[804] Ps 18:2
[805] Eph 3:17
[806] 1 Jn 4:16
[807] Jn 14:23; Translator's note: "And...with him" in Vives ed., omitted in Parma ed.
[808] 3 Kgs 8:27
[809] Ps 101:20
[810] Ps 102:19
[811] Ps 101:13
[812] Ps 101:28
[813] Ps 88:30
[814] Cf. Aristotle, *On the Heavens*, Bk. 1

a threefold consideration: of God's power, of our familiarity with him, and of the fitness of our requests.

The power of him to whom we pray is implied if we consider *heaven* as the corporeal heavens. God is not limited by any physical bounds: "Do not I fill heaven and earth? saith the Lord."[815] Nevertheless, he is said to be in the corporeal heavens to indicate two things: the extent of his power and the greatness of his nature. The former of these attributes is contrary to the view that all things happen out of necessity, by a fate regulated by the celestial bodies; and thus all prayer would be vain and useless. But such is absurd, since God dwells in the heavens as their Lord: "The Lord has prepared his throne in heaven."[816] The latter attribute, viz., his sublime nature, is against those who in praying propose or build up any corporeal images of God. Therefore, God is stated to be "in heaven" in that he exceeds all corporeal things, and even the desires and intellects of men; so that whatsoever man thinks or desires is far less than God. Thus, it is said: "Behold, God is great, exceeding our knowledge."[817] And again: "The Lord is high above all nations."[818] And finally: "To whom then have you likened God? Or what image will you make for him?"[819]

Familiar intercourse with God is shown through this *in heaven*. Some indeed have said that because of his great distance from us God does not care for men, and they cite these words: "He walketh about the poles of heaven, and he doth not consider our things."[820] Against this is the fact that God is nearer to us than we are to ourselves. This brings confidence to one who prays. First, because of the nearness of God: "The Lord is nigh unto all them that call upon him."[821] Hence, it is written: "But thou when thou shalt pray, enter into thy chamber,"[822] that is, into thy heart. Second, because of the intercession of all the saints among whom God

---

[815] Jer 23:24
[816] Ps 102:19
[817] Jb 36:26
[818] Ps 112:4
[819] Is 40:18
[820] Jb 22:14
[821] Ps 144:18
[822] Mt 6:6

dwells; for from this arises faith to ask through their merits for what we desire: "Turn to some of the saints,"[823] and, "Pray one for another, that you may be saved."[824]

This part of the prayer — that is, *in heaven* — is appropriate and fitting also, if *in heaven* is taken to mean that spiritual and eternal good in which true happiness consists. Because of it our desires are lifted up towards heavenly things; since our desires ought to tend towards where we have our Father, because there is our true home: "Seek the things that are above."[825] And again: "Unto an inheritance incorruptible, and undefiled, and that cannot fade, reserved in heaven for you."[826] Moreover, from it we are told that, if our life is to be in heaven, then we ought to be conformed to our heavenly Father: "Such as is the heavenly, such also are they that are heavenly."[827] From all this the words *in heaven* are most appropriate in prayer in that they signify both a heavenly desire and heavenly life.

THE FIRST PETITION

"Hallowed be thy name."

This is the first petition, and in it we ask that God's name be manifested and declared in us. The name of God, first of all, is wonderful because it works wonders in all creatures. Thus said our Lord: "In my name they shall cast out devils, they shall speak new tongues. They shall take up serpents; and if they shall drink any deadly thing, it shall not hurt them."[828]

---

[823] Jb 5:1
[824] Jas 5:16
[825] Col 3:1
[826] 1 Pt 1:4
[827] 1 Cor 15:48
[828] Mk 16:17-18

God's Name Is Loveable

This name is lovable: "There is no other name under heaven given to men, whereby we must be saved."[829] We all should desire to be saved. We have an example in blessed Ignatius, who had such great love for the name of Christ that, when Trajan ordered him to deny it, he affirmed that it could not be dragged from his mouth. Then, the emperor threatened to have him beheaded, and thus take the name of Christ out of the mouth of the saint. But Ignatius replied: "Even though you take it from my mouth, you will never snatch it from my heart. I have this name written in my heart and there I never cease to invoke it." Trajan heard this and wished to put it to the test. He had the servant of God beheaded and then commanded that his heart be taken out, and there upon the heart was found the name of Christ inscribed in letters of gold. This name had been engraved on the heart as a seal.

God's Name Is Venerable

The name of God is venerable: "In the name of Jesus every knee should bow, of those that are in heaven, on earth, and under the earth."[830] "Those that are in heaven" refers to the angels and the blessed; "those that are on earth" to people living in this world, who do so for love of heaven which they wish to gain; "those under the earth" to the damned, who do so out of fear.

God's Name Is Ineffable

This name is ineffable, for in the telling of it every tongue is wholly inadequate. Accordingly, it is sometimes compared to created things as, for instance, it is likened to a rock because of its firmness: "Upon this rock I will build my church."[831] It is likened to a fire because of its purifying

[829] Acts 4:12
[830] Phil 2:10
[831] Mt 16:18

power; for as fire purifies metal, so does God purify the hearts of sinners: "Thy God is a consuming fire."[832] It is compared to light because of its power of enlightening; for as light illumines the darkness, so does the name of God overcome the darkness of the mind: "O my God, enlighten my darkness."[833]

Meaning of "Hallowed"

We pray that this name may be manifested in us, that it be known and revered as holy. Now *holy* (or *hallowed*) may have a threefold meaning.

First, it is the same as "firm." Thus, those who are firmly established in eternal happiness are all the blessed in heaven, the saints. In this sense, none is a "saint" on earth because here all is continually changeable. As St. Augustine says: "I sank away from thee, O Lord, and I wandered too much astray from thee who art my firm support."[834]

Secondly, *holy* may be understood as "unearthly." The holy ones who are in heaven have naught earthly about them: "I count (all things) but as dung, that I may gain Christ."[835] Earth may signify sinners. This would arise as reference to production. For if the earth is not cultivated, it will produce thorns and thistles. Similarly, if the soul of the sinner is not cultivated by grace, it will produce only thistles and thorns of sins: "Thorns and thistles shall it bring forth to thee."[836] Again, earth may signify sinners as regards its darkness. The earth is dark and opaque; and so also is the sinner dark and obstructive to light: "Darkness was on the face of the deep."[837] And, finally, earth is a dry element which will fall to pieces unless it is mixed with the moisture of water. So God placed earth just above water: "Who established the earth above the waters."[838] So also the soul

---

[832] Dt 4:24
[833] Ps 17:29
[834] Augustine, *Confessions*, Bk. 2, Ch. 10
[835] Phil 3:8
[836] Gn 3:18
[837] Gn 1:2
[838] Ps 135:6

of the sinner is dry and without moisture as it is said: "My soul is as earth without water unto thee."[839]

Holy may, finally, be understood as "laved in blood," since the saints in heaven are called saints because they have been washed in blood: "These are they who are come out of great tribulation, and have washed their robes, and have made them white in the blood of the Lamb."[840] And again: "He hath washed us from our sins in his blood."[841]

THE SECOND PETITION

"Thy kingdom come."

The Holy Spirit makes us love, desire and pray rightly; and instills in us, first of all, a fear whereby we ask that the name of God be sanctified. He gives us another gift, that of piety. This is a devout and loving affection for our Father and for all men who are in trouble. Now, since God is our Father, we ought not only reverence and fear him, but also have towards him a sweet and pious affection. This love makes us pray that the kingdom of God may come: "We should live soberly and justly...in this world, looking for the blessed hope and coming of the glory of the great God."[842]

It may be asked of us: "Why, since the kingdom of God always was, do we then ask that it may come?" This, however, can be understood in three ways. First, a king sometimes has only the right to a kingdom or dominion, and yet his rule has not been declared because the men in his kingdom are not as yet subject to him. His rule or dominion will come only when the men of his kingdom are his subjects. Now, God is by his very essence and nature the Lord of all things; and Christ being God and man is the Lord over all things: "And he gave him power and glory and a kingdom."[843] It is, therefore, necessary that all things be subject to him. This is not yet the

---

[839] Ps 142:6
[840] Apoc 7:14
[841] Apoc 1:5
[842] Ti 2:12
[843] Dn 7:14

case, but will be so at the end of the world: "For he must reign, until he hath put all his enemies under his feet."[844] Hence it is for this we pray when we say: "Thy kingdom come."

Why We Pray Thus

In so doing we pray for a threefold purpose: that the just may be strengthened, that sinners may be punished, and that death be destroyed. Now, the reason is that men are subject to Christ in two ways, either willingly or unwillingly. Again, the will of God is so efficacious that it must be fully complied with; and God does wish that all things be subject to Christ. Hence, two things are necessary: either man will do the will of God by subjecting himself to his commands, as do the just; or God shall exert his will and punish those who are sinners and his enemies; and this will take place at the end of the world: "Until I make thy enemies thy footstool."[845]

It is enjoined upon the faithful to pray that the kingdom of God may come, namely, that they subject themselves completely to him. But it is a terrible thing for sinners, because for them to ask the coming of God's kingdom is nothing else than to ask that they be subjected to punishment: "Woe to them that desire the day of the Lord!"[846] By this prayer, too, we ask that death be destroyed. Since Christ is life, death cannot exist in his kingdom,[847] because death is the opposite of life: "And the enemy, death, shall be destroyed last."[848] "He shall cast death down headlong forever."[849] And this shall take place at the last resurrection: "Who will reform the body of our lowness, made like to the body of his glory."[850]

In a second sense, the kingdom of heaven signifies the glory of paradise. Nor is this to be wondered at, for a kingdom (regnum) is nothing other than a government (regimen). That will be the best government where nothing is

---

[844] 1 Cor 15:25
[845] Ps 109:1
[846] Am 5:18
[847] Translator's note: "Since…kingdom" in Vives edition; not in Parma.
[848] 1 Cor 15:26
[849] Is 25:8; Translator's note: This is in Vives edition; not in Parma.
[850] Phil 3:21

found contrary to the will of the governor. Now, the will of God is the very salvation of men, for he "will have all men to be saved";[851] and this especially shall come to pass in paradise where there will be nothing contrary to man's salvation. "They shall gather out of his kingdom all scandals."[852] In this world, however, there are many things contrary to the salvation of men. Hence, when we pray, "Thy kingdom come," we pray that we might participate in the heavenly kingdom and in the glory of paradise.

Why We Desire This Kingdom

This kingdom is greatly to be desired for three reasons. 1) It is to be greatly desired because of the perfect justice that obtains there: "Thy people shall be all just."[853] In this world the bad are mingled with the good, but in heaven there will be no wicked and no sinners. 2) The heavenly kingdom is to be desired because of its perfect liberty. Here below there is no liberty, although all men naturally desire it; but above, there will be perfect liberty without any form of oppression: "Because the creature also shall be delivered from the servitude of corruption."[854] Not only will men then be free, but indeed they will all be kings: "And thou hast made us to our God a kingdom."[855] This is because all shall be of one will with God, and God shall will what the saints will, and the saints shall will whatsoever God wills; hence, in the will of God shall their will be done. All, therefore, shall reign, because the will of all shall be done, and the Lord shall be their crown: "In that day, the Lord of hosts shall be a crown of glory and a garland of joy to the residue of his people."[856] 3) The kingdom of God is to be desired because of the marvelous riches of heaven: "The eye hath not

---

[851] 1 Tm 2:4
[852] Mt 13:41
[853] Is 60:21
[854] Rom 8:21
[855] Apoc 5:10
[856] Is 28:5

seen O God, besides thee, what things thou hast prepared for them that wait for thee."[857] And also: "Who satisfieth thy desire with good things."[858]

Note that man will find everything that he seeks for in this world more excellently and more perfectly in God alone. Thus, if it is pleasure you seek, then in God you will find the highest pleasure: "You shall see and your heart shall rejoice."[859] "And everlasting joy shall be upon their heads."[860] If it is riches, there you will find it in abundance: "When the soul strays from thee, she looks for things apart from thee, but she finds all things impure and useless until she returns to thee," says St. Augustine.[861]

Lastly, *Thy kingdom come* is understood in another sense because sometimes sin reigns in this world. This occurs when man is so disposed that he follows at once the enticement of sin. "Let not sin reign in your mortal body,"[862] but let God reign in your heart; and this will be when thou art prepared to obey God and keep all his commandments. Therefore, when we pray to God that his kingdom may come, we pray that God and not sin may reign in us.

May we through this petition arrive at that happiness of which the Lord speaks: "Blessed are the meek!"[863] Now, according to what we have first explained above, viz., that man desires that God be the Lord of all things, then let him not avenge injuries that are done him, but let him leave that for the Lord. If you avenge yourself, you do not really desire that the kingdom of God may come. According to our second explanation (i.e., regarding the glory of paradise), if you await the coming of this kingdom which is the glory of paradise, you need not worry about losing earthly things. Likewise, if according to the third explanation, you pray that God

---

[857] Is 64:4

[858] Ps 102:5

[859] Is 66:14

[860] Is 35:10; Translator's note: These two citations in Vives edition are omitted in Parma.

[861] Augustine, *Confessions*, Bk. 2, Ch. 6

[862] Rom 6:12

[863] Mt 5:4

may reign within you, then you must be humble, for he is himself most humble: "Learn of me because I am meek and humble of heart."[864]

THE THIRD PETITION

"Thy will be done on earth as it is in heaven."

The third gift which the Holy Spirit works in us is called the gift of knowledge. The Holy Spirit not only gives us the gift of fear and the gift of piety (which is a sweet affection for God, as we have said); but he also makes man wise. It was this for which David prayed: "Teach me goodness and discipline and knowledge."[865] This knowledge which the Holy Spirit teaches us is that whereby man lives justly. Among all that goes to make up knowledge and wisdom in man, the principal wisdom is that man should not depend solely upon his own opinion: "Lean not upon thy own prudence."[866] Those who put all their trust in their own judgment so that they do not trust others, but only themselves, are always found to be stupid and are so adjudged by others: "Hast thou seen a man wise in his own conceit? There shall be more hope of a fool than of him."[867]

The Will of God

Out of humility one does not trust one's own knowledge: "Where humility is, there is also wisdom."[868] The proud trust only themselves. Now, the Holy Spirit, through the gift of wisdom, teaches us that we do not our own will but the will of God. It is through this gift that we pray of God that his "will be done on earth as it is in heaven." And in this is seen the gift of knowledge. Thus, one says to God "let thy will be done," in the same way as one who is sick desires something from the physician; and his will is not precisely his own, because it is the will of the physician. Otherwise,

---

[864] Mt 11:29
[865] Ps 118:66
[866] Prv 3:5
[867] Prv 26:12
[868] Prv 11:2

if his desire were purely from his own will, he would be indeed foolish. So we ought not to pray other than that in us God's will may be done; that is, that his will be accomplished in us. The heart of man is only right when it is in accord with the will of God. This did Christ: "Because I came down from heaven, not to do my own will but the will of him that sent me."[869] Christ, as God, has the same will with the Father; but as a man he has a distinct will from the Father's, and it was according to this that he says he does not do his will but the Father's. Hence, he teaches us to pray and to ask: "Thy will be done."

What Does God Will?

But what is this that is asked? Does not the psalm say: "Whatsoever the Lord pleased (has willed), he hath done"?[870] Now, if he has done all that he has willed both in heaven and on earth, what then is the meaning of this "Thy will be done on earth as it is in heaven"? To understand this we must know that God wills of us three things, and we pray that these be accomplished.

The first thing that God wills is that we may have eternal life. Whoever makes something for a certain purpose, has a will regarding it which is in accord with the purpose for which he made it. In like manner, God made man, but it was not for no purpose, as it is written: "Remember what my substance is; for hast thou made all the children of men in vain?"[871]

Hence, God made men for a purpose; but this purpose was not for their mere pleasures, for also the brutes have these, but it was that they might have eternal life. The Lord, therefore, wills that men have eternal life. Now, when that for which a thing is made is accomplished, it is said to be saved; and when this is not accomplished, it is said to be lost. So when man gains eternal life, he is said to be saved, and it is this that the Lord wills: "Now, this is the will of my Father that sent me, that every one who seeth the

---

[869] Jn 6:38
[870] Ps 134:6
[871] Ps 88:48

Son and believeth in him may have life everlasting."[872] This will of God is already fulfilled for the angels and for the saints in the fatherland, for they see God and know and enjoy him. We, however, desire that, as the will of God is done for the blessed who are in heaven, it likewise be done for us who are on earth. For this we pray when we say "Thy will be done" for us who are on earth, as it is for the saints who are in heaven.

The Commandments: God's Will

In the second place, the will of God for us is that we keep his commandments. When a person desires something, he not only wills that which he desires, but also everything which will bring that about. Thus, in order to bring about a healthy condition which he desires, a physician also wills to put into effect diet, medicine, and other needs. We arrive at eternal life through observance of the commandments, and, accordingly, God wills that we observe them: "But if thou wilt enter into life, keep the commandments."[873] "Your reasonable service…that you may prove what is the good and the acceptable and the perfect will of God."[874] That is, *good* because it is profitable: "I am the Lord thy God that teach thee profitable things."[875] And *acceptable*, that is, pleasing: "Light is risen to the just; and joy to the right heart."[876] And *perfect*, because noble: "Be you therefore perfect, as your heavenly Father is perfect."[877] When we say "Thy will be done," we pray that we may fulfill the commandments of God. This will of God is done by the just, but it is not yet done by sinners. *In heaven* here signifies the just; while *on earth* refers to sinners. We, therefore, pray that the will of God may be done "on earth," that is, by sinners, "as it is in heaven," that is, by the just.

[872] Jn 6:40
[873] Mt 19:17
[874] Rom 12:1-2
[875] Is 48:17
[876] Ps 96:11
[877] Mt 5:48

Let Thy Will Be Done

It must be noted that the very words used in this petition teach us a lesson. It does not say "Do" or "Let us do," but it says, "[Let] thy will be done," because two things are necessary for eternal life: the grace of God and the will of man. Although God has made man without man, he cannot save man without his cooperation. Thus, says St. Augustine: "Who created thee without thyself, cannot save thee without thyself,"[878] because God wills that man cooperate with him or at least put no obstacle in his way: "Turn ye to me, saith the Lord of hosts, and I will turn to you."[879] "By the grace of God, I am what I am. And his grace in me hath not been void."[880] Do not, therefore, presume on your own strength, but trust in God's grace; and be not negligent, but use the zeal you have. It does not say, therefore, "Let us do," lest it would seem that the grace of God were left out; nor does it say, "Do," lest it would appear that our will and our zeal do not matter. He does say "Let it be done" through the grace of God at the same time using our desire and our own efforts.

Thirdly, the will of God in our regard is that men be restored to that state and dignity in which the first man was created. This was a condition in which the spirit and soul felt no resistance from sensuality and the flesh. As long as the soul was subject to God, the flesh was in such subjection to the spirit that no corruption of death, or weakness, or any of the passions were felt. When, however, the spirit and the soul, which were between God and the flesh, rebelled against God by sin, then the body rebelled against the soul. From that time death and weaknesses began to be felt together with continual rebellion of sensuality against the spirit: "I see another law in my members, fighting against the law of my mind."[881] "The flesh lusteth against the spirit, and the spirit against the flesh."[882]

---

[878] Augustine, *Epistle 169*
[879] Zac 1:3
[880] 1 Cor 15:10
[881] Rom 7:23
[882] Gal 5:17

Thus, there is an endless strife between the flesh and the spirit, and man is continually being brought lower by sin. The will of God, therefore, is that man be restored to his primal state so that no more would the flesh rebel against the spirit: "For this is the will of God, your sanctification."[883] Now, this will of God cannot be fulfilled in this life, but it will be fulfilled in the resurrection of the just, when glorified bodies shall arise incorrupt and most perfect: "It is sown a natural body; it shall rise a spiritual body."[884] In the just the will of God is fulfilled relative to the spirit, which abides injustice and knowledge and perfect life. Therefore, when we say "Thy will be done," let us pray that his will also may be done regarding the flesh. Thus, the sense of "Thy will be done on earth" is that it may be done "for our flesh," and "as it is in heaven" means "in our spirit." Thus, we take *in heaven* for our spirit, and *on earth* as our flesh.

By means of this petition we arrive at the happiness of those who mourn, as it is written: "Blessed are they that mourn; for they shall be comforted."[885] This can be applied to each of the threefold explanations we have given above. According to the first we desire eternal life. And in this very desire we are brought to a mourning of soul: "Woe is me, that my sojourning is prolonged."[886] This desire in the saints is so vehement that because of it they wish for death, which in itself is something naturally to be avoided: "But we are confident and have a good will to be absent rather from the body and to be present with the Lord."[887] Likewise, according to our second explanation — viz., that we will to keep the commandments — they who do so are in sorrow. For although such be sweet for the soul, it is bitter indeed for the flesh which is continually kept in discipline. "Going, they went and wept," which refers to the flesh, "But coming, they shall come with joyfulness," which pertains to the soul.[888] Again, from our third explanation (that is, concerning the struggle which is ever going on

---

[883] 1 Thes 4:3
[884] 1 Cor 15:44
[885] Mt 5:5
[886] Ps 119:5
[887] 2 Cor 5:8
[888] Ps 125:7

between the flesh and the spirit), we see that this too causes sorrow. For it cannot but happen that the soul be wounded by the venial faults of the flesh; and so in expiating for these the soul is in mourning. "Every night," that is, the darkness of sin, "I will wash my bed (that is, my conscience) with my tears."[889] Those who thus sorrow will arrive at the fatherland, where may God bring us also!

THE FOURTH PETITION

"Give us this day our daily bread."

Sometimes it happens that one of great learning and wisdom becomes fearful and timid; and, therefore, it is necessary that he have fortitude of heart lest he lack necessities: "It is he that giveth strength to the weary, and increaseth force and might to them that are not."[890] The Holy Spirit gives this fortitude: "And the spirit entered into me,…and he set me upon my feet."[891] This fortitude which is given by the Holy Ghost so strengthens the heart of man that he does not fear for the things that are necessary for him, but he trusts that God will provide for all his needs. The Holy Spirit who gives us this strength teaches us to pray to God: "Give us this day our daily bread." And thus he is called the Spirit of fortitude.

It must be noted that in the first three petitions of this prayer only things spiritual are asked for—those which indeed begin to be in this world but are only brought to fruition in the life eternal. Thus, when we pray that the name of God be hallowed, we really ask that the name of God be known; when we pray that the kingdom of God may come, we ask that we may participate in God's kingdom; and when we pray that the will of God be done, we ask that his will be accomplished in us. All these things, however, although they have their beginning here on earth, cannot be had in their fullness except in heaven. Hence, it is necessary to pray for certain necessaries which can be completely had in this life. The

[889] Ps 6:7
[890] Is 40:29
[891] Ez 2:2

Holy Spirit, then, taught us to ask for the requirements of this present life which are here obtainable in their fullness, and at the same time he shows that our temporal wants are provided us by God. It is this that is meant when we say: "Give us this day our daily bread."

In these very words the Holy Spirit teaches us to avoid five sins which are usually committed out of the desire for temporal things. The first sin is that man, because of an inordinate desire, seeks those things which go beyond his state and condition of life. He is not satisfied with what befits him. Thus, if he be a soldier and desires clothes, he will not have them suitable for a soldier, but rather for a knight; or if he be a cleric, clothes fit for a bishop. This vicious habit withdraws man from spiritual things, in that it makes his desires cleave to transitory things. The Lord taught us to avoid this vice by instructing us to ask for the temporal necessities of this present life as they are in accord with the position of each one of us. All this is understood under the name of *bread*. And so he does not teach us to pray for that which is luxurious, nor for variety, nor for what is over-refined, but for bread which is common to all and without which man's life could not be sustained: "The chief thing for man's life is water and bread."[892] And: "Having food and wherewith to be covered, with these we are content."[893]

The second sin is that some in acquiring temporal goods burden others and defraud them. This vicious practice is dangerous, because goods thus taken away can be restored only with difficulty. For, as St. Augustine says: "The sin is not forgiven until that which is taken away is restored."[894] "They eat the bread of wickedness."[895] The Lord teaches us to avoid this sin, and to pray for our own bread, not that of another. Robbers do not eat their own bread, but the bread of their neighbor.

The third sin is unnecessary solicitude. There are some who are never content with what they have, but always want more. This is wholly immoderate, because one's desire must always be measured by his need: "Give

[892] Ecclus 29:27
[893] 1 Tm 6:8
[894] Augustine, *Epistle 153*
[895] Prv 4:17

me neither beggary nor riches, but give me only the necessaries of life."[896] We are taught to avoid this sin in the words, *our daily bread*, that is, bread of one day or for one time.

The fourth sin is inordinate voracity. There are those who in one day would consume what would be enough for many days. Such pray not for bread for one day, but for ten days. And because they spend too much, it happens that they spend all their substance. "They that give themselves to drinking and that club together shall be consumed."[897] And: "A workman that is a drunkard shall not be rich."[898]

The fifth sin is ingratitude. A person grows proud in his riches, and does not realize that what he has comes from God. This is a grave fault, for all things that we have, be they spiritual or temporal, are from God: "All things are thine; and we have given thee what we received of thy hand."[899] Therefore, to take away this vice, the prayer has, "Give us" even "our daily bread," that we may know that all things come from God.

From all this we draw one great lesson. Sometimes one who has great riches makes no use of them, but suffers spiritual and temporal harm; for some because of riches have perished. "There is also another evil which I have seen under the sun, and that frequent among men. A man to whom God hath given riches and substance and honor, and his soul wanteth nothing of all that he desireth; yet God doth not give him power to eat thereof, but a stranger shall eat it up."[900] And again: "Riches kept to the hurt of the owner."[901] We ought, therefore, pray that our riches will be of use to us; and it is this we seek for when we say, "Give us our bread," that is, make our riches be of use to us. "His bread in his belly shall be turned into the gall of asps within him. The riches which he hath swallowed, he shall vomit up; and God shall draw them out of his belly."[902]

---

[896] Prv 30:8
[897] Prv 23:21
[898] Ecclus 19:1
[899] 1 Par 29:14
[900] Eccles 6:1-2
[901] Eccles 5:12
[902] Jb 20:14-15

Another great vice is concerned with the things of this world, viz., excessive solicitude for them. For there are some who daily are anxious about temporal goods which are enough for them for an entire year; and they who are thus troubled will never have rest: "Be not solicitous therefore, saying: 'What shall we eat,' or 'What shall we drink,' or 'Wherewith shall we be clothed?'"[903] The Lord, therefore, teaches us to pray that today our bread will be given us, that is, those things which will be needful for us for the present time.

One may also see in this bread another twofold meaning, viz., sacramental bread and the bread of the word of God. Thus, in the first meaning, we pray for our sacramental bread which is consecrated daily in the Church, so that we receive it in the sacrament, and thus it profits us unto salvation: "I am the living bread which came down from heaven."[904] And: "He that eateth and drinketh unworthily, eateth and drinketh judgment to himself."[905]

In the second meaning this bread is the word of God: "Not in bread alone doth man live, but in every word that proceedeth from the mouth of God."[906] We pray, therefore, that he give us bread, that is, his word. From this man derives that happiness which is a hunger for justice. For after spiritual things are considered, they are all the more desired; and this desire arouses a hunger, and from this hunger follows the fullness of life everlasting.

THE FIFTH PETITION

"And forgive us our trespasses as we forgive those who trespass against us."

There are some men of great wisdom and fortitude who, because they trust too much in their own strength, do not wisely carry out what they attempt, and they do not bring to completion that which they have in

---

[903] Mt 6:31
[904] Jn 6:51
[905] 1 Cor 11:29
[906] Mt 4:4

mind. "Designs are strengthened by counsels."[907] It must be known that the Holy Ghost who gives fortitude also gives counsel. Every good counsel concerning the salvation of man is from the Holy Ghost. Thus, counsel is necessary for man when he is in difficulty, just as is the counsel of physicians when one is ill. When man falls into spiritual illness through sin, he must look for counsel in order to be healed. This necessity for counsel on the part of the sinner is shown in these words: "Wherefore, O king, let my counsel be acceptable to thee, and redeem thou thy sins with alms."[908] The best counsel, therefore, against sin is alms and mercy. Hence, the Holy Spirit teaches sinners to seek and to pray: "Forgive us our trespasses."

We owe God that which we have taken away from his sole right; and this right of God is that we do his will in preference to our own will. Now, we take away from God's right when we prefer our will to God's will, and this is a sin. Sins, therefore, are our trespasses. And it is the counsel of the Holy Spirit that we ask God pardon for our sins, and so we say: "Forgive us our trespasses."

We can consider these words in three ways: 1) Why do we make this petition? 2) How may it be fulfilled? 3) What is required on our part?

Why Do We Make This Petition?

It must be known that from this petition we can draw two things that are necessary for us in this life. One is that we be ever in a state of salutary fear and humility. There have been some, indeed, so presumptuous as to say that man could live in this world and by his own unaided strength avoid sin. But this condition has been given to no one except Christ, who had the Spirit beyond all measure, and to the Blessed Virgin, who was full of grace and in whom there was no sin. "And concerning whom," that is, the Virgin, "when it is a question of sin I wish to make no mention," says St. Augustine.[909] But for all the other saints, it was never granted them that they should not incur at least venial sin: "If we say that we have no sin,

---

[907] Prv 20:18
[908] Dn 4:24
[909] Augustine, *On Nature and Grace*, Ch. 42

167

we deceive ourselves and the truth is not in us."[910] And, moreover, this very petition proves this; for it is evident that all saints and all men say the Our Father in which is contained: "Forgive us our trespasses." Hence, all admit and confess that they are sinners or trespassers. If, therefore, you are a sinner, you ought to fear and humble yourself.

Another reason for this petition is that we should ever live in hope. Although we be sinners, nevertheless we must not give up hope, lest our despair drive us into greater and different kinds of sins. As the apostle says: "Who despairing, have given themselves up to lasciviousness, unto the working of all uncleanness."[911] It is, therefore, of great help that we be ever hopeful; for in the measure that man is a sinner, he ought to hope that God will forgive him if he be perfectly sorry for sin and be converted. This hope is strengthened in us when we say: "Forgive us our trespasses."

The Novatiani destroyed this hope, saying that one who has sinned but once after baptism can never look for mercy. But this is not true, if Christ spoke truly when he said: "I forgave thee all the debt, because thou besoughtest me."[912] In whatsoever day, therefore, you ask, you can receive mercy if with sorrow for sin you make your prayer. Both fear and hope arise from this petition. For all sinners who are contrite and confess their guilt, receive mercy. Hence, this petition is necessary.

The Fulfillment of This Petition

Concerning the second consideration of this petition (viz., how it may be fulfilled), it must be known that there are two factors in sin: the fault by which God is offended, and the punishment which is due because of this fault. But the sin is taken away in contrition which goes with the purpose to confess and make satisfaction: "I said: I will confess against myself my injustice to the Lord. And thou hast forgiven the wickedness of my sin."[913]

[910] 1 Jn 1:8
[911] Eph 4:19
[912] Mt 18:32
[913] Ps 31:5

One has no need to fear then, because, for the remission of a fault, contrition with a purpose to confess is sufficient.[914]

But one might say: "If sin is thus taken away when a man is contrite, of what necessity is the priest?" To this it must be said that God does forgive the sin in contrition, and eternal punishment is changed to temporal, but nevertheless the debt of temporal punishment remains. If one should die without confession, not out of contempt for it but prevented from it, one would go to purgatory, where the punishment, as St. Augustine says, is very great. When you confess, the priest absolves you of this punishment in virtue of the keys to which you subject yourself in confession. When, therefore, one has confessed, something of this punishment is taken away; and similarly, when he has again confessed, and it could be that after he has confessed many times, all would be remitted.

The successors of the apostles found another mode of remission of this punishment, namely, the good use of indulgences, which have their force for one living in the state of grace, to the extent that is claimed for them and as indicated by the grantor. That the pope can bring this about, is sufficiently evident. Many holy men have accomplished much good, and they have not greatly sinned, at least not mortally; and these good deeds were done for the common use of the Church. Likewise, the merits of Christ and the Blessed Virgin are, as it were, in a treasury; and from it the supreme pontiff and they who are by him permitted can dispense these merits where it is necessary. Thus, therefore, sins are taken away not only as regards their guilt by contrition, but also as regards punishment for them in confession and through indulgences.

What Must We Do?

Concerning the third consideration of this petition, it must be known that on our part we are required to forgive our neighbor the offenses which

---

[914] Translator's note: See editor's note in English translation of *Summa Theologica Supplement*, q. 18, a. 1, which says: "St. Thomas here follows the opinion of Peter Lombard...Later in life he altered his opinion," and subsequently gives the following references: Cf. *Summa Theologiae*, III, q. 67, a. 1; q. 64, a. 1; q. 86, a. 6.

he commits against us. Thus, we say: "As we forgive those who trespass against us." Otherwise, God would not forgive us: "Man to man reserveth anger: and doth he seek remedy of God?"[915] "Forgive and you shall be forgiven."[916] Therefore, only in this petition is there a condition when it says: "As we forgive those who trespass against us." If you do not forgive, you shall not be forgiven.

But you may think, "I shall say what goes first in the petition, namely, 'Forgive us,' but that 'as we forgive those who trespass against us,' I shall not say." Would you seek to deceive Christ? You certainly do not deceive him. For Christ who made this prayer remembers it well, and cannot be deceived. If therefore, you say it with the lips, let the heart fulfill it.

But one may ask whether he who does not intend to forgive his neighbor ought to say: "As we forgive those who trespass against us." It seems not, for such is a lie. But actually, it must be said that he does not lie, because he prays not in his own person, but in that of the Church which is not deceived, and, therefore the petition itself is in the plural number. And it must also be known that forgiveness is twofold. One applies to the perfect, where the one offended seeks out the offender: "Seek after peace."[917] The other is common to all, and to it all are equally bound, that one offended grant pardon to the one who seeks it: "Forgive thy neighbor if he hath hurt thee; and then shall thy sins be forgiven to thee when thou prayest."[918] And from this follows that other beatitude: "Blessed are the merciful."[919] For mercy causes us to have pity on our neighbor.

[915] Ecclus 28:3
[916] Lk 6:37
[917] Ps 33:15
[918] Ecclus 28:2
[919] Mt 5:7

THE SIXTH PETITION

"And lead us not into temptation."

There are those who have sinned and desire forgiveness for their sins. They confess their sins and repent. Yet, they do not strive as much as they should in order that they may not fall into sin again. In this indeed they are not consistent. For, on the one hand, they deplore their sins by being sorry for them; and, on the other hand, they sin again and again and have them again to deplore. Thus it is written: "Wash yourselves, be clean. Take away the evil of your devices from my eyes. Cease to do perversely."[920]

We have seen in the petition above that Christ taught us to seek forgiveness for our sins. In this petition, he teaches us to pray that we might avoid sin—that is, that we may not be led into temptation, and thus fall into sin. "And lead us not into temptation."

Three questions are now considered: 1) What is temptation? 2) In what ways is one tempted and by whom? 3) How is one freed from temptation?

What Is Temptation?

Regarding the first, it must be known that to tempt is nothing other than to test or to prove. To tempt a man is to test or try his virtue. This is done in two ways just as a man's virtue requires two things. One requirement is to do good, the other is to avoid evil: "Turn away from evil and do good."[921] Sometimes a man's virtue is tried in doing good, and sometimes it is tested in avoiding evil.

Thus, regarding the first, a person is tried in his readiness to do good, for example, to fast and such like. Then is thy virtue great when thou art quick to do good. In this way does God sometimes try one's virtue, not, however, because such virtue is hidden from him, but in order that all might know it and it would be an example to all. God tempted Abraham in

---

[920] Is 1:16
[921] Ps 33:15

this way,[922] and Job also. For this reason God frequently sends trials to the just, who in sustaining them with all patience makes manifest their virtue, and themselves increase in virtue: "The Lord your God trieth you, that it may appear whether you love him with all your heart and with all your soul, or not."[923] Thus does God tempt man by inciting him to good deeds.

As to the second, the virtue of man is tried by solicitation to evil. If he truly resists and does not give his consent, then his virtue is great. If, however, he falls before the temptation, he is devoid of virtue. God tempts no man in this way, for it is written: "God is not a tempter of evils, and he tempteth no man."[924]

How Is One Tempted?

The temptations of the flesh. —Man is tempted by his own flesh, by the devil, and by the world. He is tempted by the flesh in two ways. First, the flesh incites one to evil. It always seeks its own pleasures, namely, carnal pleasures, in which often is sin. He who indulges in carnal pleasures neglects spiritual things: "Every man is tempted by his own concupiscence."[925]

Secondly, the flesh tempts man by enticing him away from good. For the spirit on its part would delight always in spiritual things, but the flesh asserting itself puts obstacles in the way of the spirit: "The corruptible body is a load upon the soul."[926] "For I am delighted with the law of God, according to the inward man. But I see another law in my members, fighting against the law of my mind, and captivating me in the law of sin, that is in my members."[927] This temptation which comes from the flesh is most severe, because our enemy, the flesh, is united to us; and as Boethius says: "There is no plague more dangerous than an enemy in the family circle."[928]

---

[922] Cf. Gn 22
[923] Dt 13:3
[924] Jas 1:13
[925] Jas 1:14
[926] Ws 9:15
[927] Rom 7:22-23
[928] Boethius, *Consolation of Philosophy*, Bk. 3, Ch. 5

We must, therefore, be ever on our guard against this enemy: "Watch and pray that ye enter not into temptation."[929]

The temptations of the devil. — The devil tempts us with extreme force. Even when the flesh is subdued, another tempter arises, namely, the devil against whom we have a heavy struggle. Of this the apostle says: "Our wrestling is not against flesh and blood, but against principalities and powers, against the rulers of the world of this darkness, against the spirits of wickedness in high places."[930] For this reason he is very aptly called the tempter: "Lest perhaps he that tempteth should have tempted you."[931]

The devil proceeds most cunningly in tempting us. He operates like a skillful general when about to attack a fortified city. He looks for the weak places in the object of his assault, and in that part where a man is most weak, he tempts him. He tempts man in those sins to which, after subduing his flesh, he is most inclined. Such, for instance, are anger, pride and the other spiritual sins. "Your adversary the devil, as a roaring lion, goeth about seeking whom he may devour."[932]

How the devil tempts us. — The devil does two things when he tempts us. Thus, he does not at once suggest something that appears to us as evil, but something that has a semblance of good. Thereby he would, at least in the beginning, turn a man from his chief purpose, and then afterwards it will be easier to induce him to sin, once he has been turned away ever so little. "Satan himself transformeth himself into an angel of light."[933] Then when he has once led man into sin, he so enchains him as to prevent his rising up out of his sin. The devil, therefore, does two things: he deceives a man first, and then after betraying him, enthralls him in his sin.

Temptations of the world. — The world has two ways of tempting man. The first is excessive and intemperate desire for the goods of this life: "The desire of money is the root of all evil."[934] The second way is the fears engen-

---

[929] Mt 26:41
[930] Eph 6:12
[931] 1 Thes 3:5
[932] 1 Pt 5:8
[933] 2 Cor 11:14
[934] 1 Tm 6:10

dered by persecutors and tyrants: "We are wrapped up in darkness."[935] "All that will live godly in Christ Jesus shall suffer persecution."[936] And again: "Fear not those that slay the body."[937]

How Is One Freed from Temptation?

Now we have seen what temptation is, and also in what way and by whom one is tempted. But how is one freed from temptation? In this we must notice that Christ teaches us to pray, not that we may not be tempted, but that we may not be led into temptation. For it is when one overcomes temptation that one deserves the reward. Thus it is said: "Count it all joy when you shall fall into divers temptations."[938] And again: "Son, when thou comest to the service of God,...prepare thy soul for temptation."[939] Again: "Blessed is the man that endureth temptation; for when he hath been proved, he shall receive the crown of life."[940] Our Lord, therefore, teaches us to pray that we be not led into temptation, by giving our consent to it: "Let no temptation take hold on you, but such as is human."[941] The reason is that it is human to be tempted, but to give consent is devilish.

But does God lead one to evil, that he should pray: "Lead us not into temptation"? I reply that God is said to lead a person into evil by permitting him to the extent that, because of his many sins, he withdraws his grace from man, and as a result of this withdrawal man does fall into sin. Therefore, we sing in the psalm: "When my strength shall fail, do not thou forsake me."[942] God, however, directs man by the fervor of charity that he be not led into temptation. For charity even in its smallest degree is able to resist any kind of sin: "Many waters cannot quench charity."[943] He also guides man by the light of his intellect in which he teaches him what he

---

[935] Jb 37:19
[936] 2 Tm 3:12
[937] Mt 10:28
[938] Jas 1:2
[939] Ecclus 2:1
[940] Jas 1:12
[941] 1 Cor 10:13
[942] Ps 70:9
[943] Cant 8:7

should do. For as the philosopher says: "Everyone who sins is ignorant."[944] "I will give thee understanding and I will instruct thee."[945] It was for this last that David prayed, saying: "Enlighten my eyes that I never sleep in death; lest at any time my enemy say: I have prevailed against him."[946] We have this through the gift of understanding. Therefore, when we refuse to consent to temptation, we keep our hearts pure: "Blessed are the clean of heart, for they shall see God."[947] And it follows from this petition that we are led up to the sight of God, and to it may God lead us all!

SEVENTH PETITION

"But deliver us from evil. Amen."

The Lord has already taught us to pray for forgiveness of our sins, and how to avoid temptations. In this petition, he teaches us to pray to be preserved from evil, and indeed from all evil in general, such as sin, illness, affliction, and all others, as St. Augustine explains it. But since we have already mentioned sin and temptation, we now must consider other evils, such as adversity and all afflictions of this world. From these God preserves us in a fourfold manner.

First, he preserves us from affliction itself; but this is very rare because it is the lot of the just in this world to suffer, for it is written: "All that will live godly in Christ Jesus shall suffer persecution."[948] Once in a while, however, God does prevent a man from being afflicted by some evil; this is when he knows such a one to be weak and unable to bear it. Just so a physician does not prescribe violent medicines to a weak patient. "Behold, I have given before thee a door opened, which no man can shut; because thou hast little strength."[949] In heaven this will be a general thing, for there no one shall be afflicted. "In six troubles," those, namely, of this present life

944 Aristotle, *Ethics*, Bk. 3, Ch. 1
945 Ps 31:8
946 Ps 12:4-5
947 Mt 5:8
948 2 Tm 3:12
949 Apoc 3:8

which is divided into six periods, "he shall deliver thee, and in the seventh evil shall not touch thee."[950] "They shall no more hunger nor thirst."[951]

Second, God delivers us from afflictions when he consoles us in them; for unless he console us, we could not long persevere: "We were pressed out of measure above our strength so that we were weary even of life."[952] "But God, who comforteth the humble, comforted us."[953] "According to the multitude of my sorrows in my heart, thy comforts have given joy to my soul."[954]

Third, God bestows so many good things upon those who are afflicted that their evils are forgotten: "After the storm thou makest a calm."[955] The afflictions and trials of this world, therefore, are not to be feared, both because consolations accompany them and because they are of short duration: "For that which is at present momentary and light of our tribulation, worketh for us above measure exceedingly an eternal weight of glory."[956]

Fourth, we are preserved from afflictions in this way that all temptations and trials are conducive to our own good. We do not pray, "Deliver us from tribulation," but "from evil." This is because tribulations bring a crown to the just, and for that reason the saints rejoiced in their sufferings: "We glory also in tribulations, knowing that tribulation worketh patience."[957] "In time of tribulation thou forgivest sins."[958]

The Value of Patience

God, therefore, delivers man from evil and from affliction by converting them to his good. This is a sign of supreme wisdom to divert evil to good. And patience in bearing trials is a result of this. The other virtues operate by good things, but patience operates in evil things, and, indeed, it is very

[950] Jb 5:19
[951] Apoc 7:16
[952] 2 Cor 1:8
[953] 2 Cor 7:6
[954] Ps 93:19
[955] Tb 3:22
[956] 2 Cor 4:17
[957] Rom 5:3
[958] Tb 3:13

necessary in evil things, namely, in adversity: "The learning of a man is known by his patience."[959]

The Holy Spirit through the gift of wisdom has us use this prayer, and by it we arrive at supreme happiness which is the reward of peace. For it is by patience we obtain peace, whether in time of prosperity or of adversity. For this reason, the peacemakers are called the children of God, because they are like to God in this, that nothing can hurt God and nothing can hurt them, whether it be prosperity or adversity: "Blessed are the peacemakers, for they shall be called the children of God."[960]

Amen. This is general ratification of all the petitions.

A Short Explanation of the Whole Prayer

By way of brief summary, it should be known that the Lord's Prayer contains all that we ought to desire and all that we ought to avoid. Now, of all desirable things, that must be most desired which is most loved, and that is God.

Therefore, you seek, first of all, the glory of God when you say: "Hallowed be thy name." You should desire three things from God, and they concern yourself. The first is that you may arrive at eternal life. And you pray for this when you say: "Thy kingdom come." The second is that you will do the will of God and his justice. You pray for this in the words: "Thy will be done on earth as it is in heaven." The third is that you may have the necessaries of life. And thus you pray: "Give us this day our daily bread." Concerning all these things the Lord says: "Seek ye first the kingdom of God," which complies with the second, "and all these things shall be added unto you,"[961] as in accord with the third.

We must avoid and flee from all things which are opposed to the good. For, as we have seen, good is above all things to be desired. This good is fourfold.

[959] Prv 19:11
[960] Mt 5:9
[961] Mt 6:33

First, there is the glory of God, and no evil is contrary to this: "If thou sin, what shalt thou hurt him?...And if thou do justly, what shalt thou give him?"[962] Whether it be the evil inasmuch as God punishes it, or whether it be the good in that God rewards it—all redound to his glory. The second good is eternal life, to which sin is contrary: because eternal life is lost by sin. And so, to remove this evil we pray: "Forgive us our trespasses as we forgive those who trespass against us." The third good is justice and good works, and temptation is contrary to this, because temptation hinders us from doing good. We pray, therefore, to have this evil taken away in the words: "Lead us not into temptation." The fourth good is all the necessaries of life, and opposed to this are troubles and adversities. And we seek to remove them when we pray: "But deliver us from evil. Amen."

The Hail Mary

THE ANGELIC SALUTATION

This salutation has three parts. The angel gave one part, namely: "Hail, full of grace, the Lord is with thee, blessed art thou among women."[963] The other part was given by Elizabeth, the mother of John the Baptist, namely: "Blessed is the fruit of thy womb."[964] The Church adds the third part, that is, "Mary," because the angel did not say, "Hail, Mary," but "Hail, full of grace." But, as we shall see, this name, *Mary*, according to its meaning agrees with the words of the angels.[965]

---

[962] Jb 35:6-7
[963] Lk 1:28
[964] Lk 1:42
[965] Translator's note: The Hail Mary or Angelical Salutation or *Ave Maria* in the time of St. Thomas consisted only of the present first part of the prayer. The words, *Mary* and *Jesus*, were added by the Church to the first part, and the second part—"Holy Mary, Mother of God," etc.—was also added by the Church later.

"HAIL MARY"

We must now consider concerning the first part of this prayer that in ancient times it was no small event when angels appeared to men; and that man should show them reverence was especially praiseworthy. Thus, it is written to the praise of Abraham that he received the angels with all courtesy and showed them reverence. But that an angel should show reverence to a man was never heard of until the angel reverently greeted the Blessed Virgin saying: "Hail."

The Angel's Dignity

In olden time an angel would not show reverence to a man, but a man would deeply revere an angel. This is because angels are greater than men, and indeed in three ways.

First, they are greater than men in dignity. This is because the angel is of a spiritual nature: "Who makest thy angels spirits."[966] But, on the other hand, man is of a corruptible nature, for Abraham said: "I will speak to my Lord, whereas I am dust and ashes."[967] It was not fitting, therefore, that a spiritual and incorruptible creature should show reverence to one that is corruptible as is a man.

Secondly, an angel is closer to God. The angel, indeed, is of the family of God, and as it were stands ever by him: "Thousands of thousands ministered to him, and ten thousand times a hundred thousand stood before him."[968] Man, on the other hand, is rather a stranger and afar off from God because of sin: "I have gone afar off."[969] Therefore, it is fitting that man should reverence an angel who is an intimate and one of the household of the King.

Then, thirdly, the angels far exceed men in the fullness of the splendor of divine grace. For angels participate in the highest degree in the divine

---

[966] Ps 103:4
[967] Gn 18:27
[968] Dn 7:10
[969] Ps 54:8

light: "Is there any numbering of his soldiers? And upon whom shall not his light arise?"[970] Hence, the angels always appear among men clothed in light, but men on the contrary, although they partake somewhat of the light of grace, nevertheless do so in a much slighter degree and with a certain obscurity. It was, therefore, not fitting that an angel should show reverence to a man until it should come to pass that one would be found in human nature who exceeded the angels in these three points in which we have seen that they excel over men — and this was the Blessed Virgin. To show that she excelled the angels in these, the angel desired to show her reverence, and so he said: "*Ave* (Hail)."

"FULL OF GRACE"

The Blessed Virgin was superior to any of the angels in the fullness of grace, and as an indication of this the angel showed reverence to her by saying: "Full of grace." This is as if he said: "I show thee reverence because thou dost excel me in the fullness of grace."

The Blessed Virgin is said to be full of grace in three ways. First, as regards her soul she was full of grace. The grace of God is given for two chief purposes, namely, to do good and to avoid evil. The Blessed Virgin, then, received grace in the most perfect degree, because she had avoided every sin more than any other saint after Christ. Thus it is said: "Thou art fair, my beloved, and there is not a spot in thee."[971] St. Augustine says: "If we could bring together all the saints and ask them if they were entirely without sin, all of them, with the exception of the Blessed Virgin, would say with one voice: 'If we say that we have no sin, we deceive ourselves and the truth is not in us.'[972] I except, however, this holy Virgin of whom, because of the honor of God, I wish to omit all mention of sin."[973] For we know that to her was granted grace to overcome every kind of sin by

---

[970] Jb 25:3

[971] Cant 4:7

[972] 1 Jn 1:8

[973] Augustine, *On Nature and Grace*, Ch. 42; Translator's note: Elsewhere St. Thomas says: "In the Angelic Salutation is shown forth the worthiness of the Blessed Virgin for this conception when it says, 'Full of grace'; it expresses the conception itself in the

him whom she merited to conceive and bring forth, and he certainly was wholly without sin.

Virtues of the Blessed Virgin

Christ excelled the Blessed Virgin in this, that he was conceived and born without original sin, while the Blessed Virgin was conceived in original sin, but was not born in it.[974] She exercised the works of all the virtues, whereas the saints are conspicuous for the exercise of certain special virtues. Thus, one excelled in humility, another in chastity, another in mercy, to the extent that they are the special exemplars of these virtues—as, for example, St. Nicholas is an exemplar of the virtue of mercy. The Blessed Virgin is the exemplar of all the virtues.

In her is the fullness of the virtue of humility: "Behold the handmaid of the Lord."[975] And again: "He hath regarded the humility of his handmaid."[976] So she is also exemplar of the virtue of chastity: "Because I know not man."[977] And thus it is with all the virtues, as is evident. Mary was full of grace not only in the performance of all good, but also in the avoidance of all evil.

Again, the Blessed Virgin was full of grace in the overflowing effect of this grace upon her flesh or body. For while it is a great thing in the saints

words, 'The Lord is with thee'; and it foretells the honor which will follow with the words, 'Blessed art thou among women'" (*Summa Theologiae*, III, q. 30, a. 4).

[974] Translator's note: St. Thomas wrote before the solemn definition of the immaculate conception by the Church and at a time when the subject was still a matter of controversy among theologians. In an earlier work, however, he pronounced in favor of the doctrine (I Sent., d. 44, q. 1, a. 3, ad. 3), although he seemingly concluded against it in the *Summa Theologiae* (III, q. 27, a. 2, rep. 2). "Yet much discussion has arisen as to whether St. Thomas did or did not deny that the Blessed Virgin was immaculate at the instant of her animation" (*Catholic Encyclopedia*, art. "Immaculate Conception"). On December 8, 1854, Pope Pius IX settled the question in the following definition: "Mary, ever Blessed Virgin in the first instant of her conception, by a singular privilege and grace granted by God, in view of the merits of Jesus Christ, the Savior of the human race, was preserved exempt from all stain of original sin" (*Ineffabilis Deus*).

[975] Lk 1:38
[976] Lk 1:48
[977] Lk 1:34

that the abundance of grace sanctified their souls, yet, moreover, the soul of the holy Virgin was so filled with grace that from her soul grace poured into her flesh from which was conceived the Son of God. Hugh of St. Victor says of this: "Because the love of the Holy Spirit so inflamed her soul, he worked a wonder in her flesh, in that from it was born God made man." "And therefore also the Holy which shall be born of thee shall be called the Son of God."[978]

Mary, Help of Christians

The plenitude of grace in Mary was such that its effects overflow upon all men. It is a great thing in a saint when he has grace to bring about the salvation of many, but it is exceedingly wonderful when grace is of such abundance as to be sufficient for the salvation of all men in the world, and this is true of Christ and of the Blessed Virgin. Thus, "a thousand bucklers," that is, remedies against dangers, "hang therefrom."[979] Likewise, in every work of virtue one can have her as one's helper. Of her it was spoken: "In me is all grace of the way and of the truth, in me is all hope of life and of virtue."[980] Therefore, Mary is full of grace, exceeding the angels in this fullness and very fittingly is she called *Mary* which means "in herself enlightened": "The Lord…will fill thy soul with brightness."[981] And she will illumine others throughout the world for which reason she is compared to the sun and to the moon.[982]

[978] Lk 1:35
[979] Cant 4:4
[980] Ecclus 24:25
[981] Is 58:11
[982] Translator's note: "The Blessed Virgin Mary obtained such a plenitude of grace that she was closest of all creatures to the author of grace; and thus she received in her womb him who is full of grace, and by giving him birth she is in a certain manner the source of grace for all men" (*Summa Theologiae*, III, q. 27, a. 5, rep. 1). St. Bernard says: "It is God's will that we should receive all graces through Mary" (*Serm. de aquaeductu*, n. 7). Mary is called the "Mediatrix of all Graces," and her mediation is immediate and universal, subordinate however to that of Jesus.

"THE LORD IS WITH THEE"

The Blessed Virgin excels the angels in her closeness to God. The angel Gabriel indicated this when he said: "The Lord is with thee"—as if to say: "I reverence thee because thou art nearer to God than I, because the Lord is with thee." By *the Lord* he means the Father with the Son and the Holy Spirit, who in like manner are not with any angel or any other spirit: "The Holy which shall be born of thee shall be called the Son of God."[983] God the Son was in her womb: "Rejoice and praise, O thou habitation of Sion; for great is he that is in the midst of thee, the Holy One of Israel."[984]

The Lord is not with the angel in the same manner as with the Blessed Virgin; for with her he is as a Son, and with the angel he is the Lord. The Lord, the Holy Ghost, is in her as in a temple, so that it is said: "The temple of the Lord, the sanctuary of the Holy Spirit,"[985] because she conceived by the Holy Ghost: "The Holy Ghost shall come upon thee."[986] The Blessed Virgin is closer to God than is an angel, because with her are the Lord the Father, the Lord the Son, and the Lord the Holy Ghost—in a word, the Holy Trinity. Indeed of her we sing: "Noble resting place of the Triune God."[987] "The Lord is with thee" are the most praise-laden words that the angel could have uttered; and, hence, he so profoundly reverenced the Blessed Virgin because she is the Mother of the Lord and our Lady. Accordingly, she is very well named *Mary*, which in the Syrian tongue means "Lady."

"BLESSED ART THOU AMONG WOMEN"

The Blessed Virgin exceeds the angels in purity. She is not only pure, but she obtains purity for others. She is purity itself, wholly lacking in every guilt of sin, for she never incurred either mortal or venial sin. So, too, she

---

[983] Lk 1:35

[984] Is 12:6

[985] Antiphon from the *Little Office of Blessed Virgin*.

[986] Lk 1:35

[987] "*Totius Trinitatis nobile Triclinium.*"—From a medieval hymn by Adam of St. Victor.

was free from the penalties of sin. Sinful man, on the contrary, incurs a threefold curse on account of sin.

The first fell upon woman who conceives in corruption, bears her child with difficulty, and brings it forth in pain. The Blessed Virgin was wholly free from this, since she conceived without corruption, bore her child in comfort, and brought him forth in joy: "It shall bud forth and blossom, and shall rejoice with joy and praise."[988]

The second penalty was inflicted upon man in that he shall earn his bread by the sweat of his brow. The Blessed Virgin was also immune from this because, as the apostle says, virgins are free from the cares of this world and are occupied wholly with the things of the Lord.[989]

The third curse is common both to man and woman in that both shall one day return to dust. The Blessed Virgin was spared this penalty, for her body was raised up into heaven, and so we believe that after her death she was revived and transported into heaven: "Arise, O Lord, into thy resting place, thou and the ark which thou hast sanctified."[990] Because the Blessed Virgin was immune from these punishments, she is "blessed among women." Moreover, she alone escaped the curse of sin, brought forth the source of blessing, and opened the gate of heaven. It is surely fitting that her name is *Mary*, which is akin to the "Star of the Sea" (*Maria—maris stella*), for just as sailors are directed to port by the star of the sea, so also Christians are by Mary guided to glory.

"BLESSED IS THE FRUIT OF THY WOMB"

The sinner often seeks for something which he does not find; but to the just man it is given to find what he seeks: "The substance of the sinner is kept for the just."[991] Thus, Eve sought the fruit of the tree (of good and evil), but she did not find in it that which she sought. Everything Eve desired, however, was given to the Blessed Virgin. Eve sought that which

---

[988] Is 35:2
[989] Cf. 1 Cor 7:34
[990] Ps 131:8
[991] Prv 13:22

the devil falsely promised her, namely, that she and Adam would be as gods, knowing good and evil. "You shall be," says this liar, "as gods."[992] But he lied, because "he is a liar and the father of lies."[993] Eve was not made like God after having eaten of the fruit, but rather she was unlike God in that by her sin she withdrew from God and was driven out of paradise. The Blessed Virgin, however, and all Christians found in the fruit of her womb him whereby we are all united to God and are made like to him: "When he shall appear, we shall be like to him, because we shall see him as he is."[994]

Eve looked for pleasure in the fruit of the tree because it was good to eat. But she did not find this pleasure in it, and, on the contrary, she at once discovered she was naked and was stricken with sorrow. In the fruit of the Blessed Virgin we find sweetness and salvation: "He that eateth my flesh…hath eternal life."[995]

The fruit which Eve desired was beautiful to look upon, but that fruit of the Blessed Virgin is far more beautiful, for the angels desire to look upon him: "Thou art beautiful above the sons of men."[996] He is the splendor of the glory of the Father. Eve, therefore, looked in vain for that which she sought in the fruit of the tree, just as the sinner is disappointed in his sins. We must seek in the fruit of the womb of the Virgin Mary whatsoever we desire. This is he who is the fruit blessed by God, who has filled him with every grace, which in turn is poured out upon us who adore him: "Blessed be God and the Father of our Lord Jesus Christ, who hath blessed us with spiritual blessings…in Christ."[997] He, too, is revered by the angels: "Benediction and glory and wisdom and thanksgiving, honor and power and strength, to our God."[998] And he is glorified by men: "Every tongue should confess that the Lord Jesus Christ is in the

---

[992] Gn 3:5
[993] Jn 8:44
[994] 1 Jn 3:2
[995] Jn 6:55
[996] Ps 44:3
[997] Eph 1:3
[998] Apoc 7:12

glory of God the Father."[999] The Blessed Virgin is indeed blessed, but far more blessed is the fruit of her womb: "Blessed is he who cometh in the name of the Lord."[1000]

---

[999] Phil 2:11
[1000] Ps 117:26

Medieval Manuals
of Instruction

Opening page of John Pecham's constitution Ignorancia (Ignorantia)
Sacerdotum *with commentary; MS Eng. th. c. 57 from the Bodleian*
Library, Oxford. Multiple scribes, England ca. 1450

Ignorantia Sacerdotum

Information for Priests of Simple Learning

The ignorance of priests casts the people down into the ditch of error, and the foolishness and lack of learning of clerics, whom the decrees of canon law order to teach the sons of the faithful, is all the worse when it leads to error instead of knowledge. For some blind preachers do not always see the places which stand in greatest need of the light of truth; the prophet testifies that "the little ones have asked for bread, and there was none to break unto them,"[1] and another cries that "the needy and the poor seek for waters, and there are none: their tongue hath been dry with thirst."[2]

To remedy this dangerous situation we order that four times during the year, that is, once in every quarter on one or several solemn days, each priest in charge of a parish should personally explain or have someone else explain to the people in their mother tongue, without any fancifully woven subtleties, the fourteen articles of faith, the ten commandments of the decalogue, the two precepts of the gospel (namely, the twin laws of charity), the seven works of mercy, the seven capital sins and their fruits, the seven principal virtues, and the seven grace-giving sacraments. And lest anyone, claiming ignorance, should try to excuse himself from knowledge of these things, which all ministers of the Church are required to know, we have outlined them here in a brief summary.

On the Articles of the Creed

Thus, one should know that there are seven articles of faith that pertain to the mystery of the Trinity: four concern the interrelationship of the Godhead, and three concern its effects. The first article is that there is one divine essence contained in a Trinity of three indivisible Persons. As the

---

[1] Lam 4:4
[2] Is 41:17

Creed says: "I believe in one God." The second article is to believe that the Father is the unbegotten God. The third article is to believe that the only begotten Son is God. The fourth article is to believe that the Holy Spirit is God neither born nor unbegotten, but proceeds equally from the Father and the Son. The fifth article is the belief that heaven and earth, that is, all creatures visible and invisible, are the creation of a totally indivisible Trinity. The sixth article is the sanctification of the Church through the Holy Spirit, the grace-giving sacraments, and all the other things in which the Christian Church communicates. By this is to be understood that the Church with its sacraments and laws through the Holy Spirit suffices for the salvation of every man, sinner though he be, and that outside the Church there is no salvation. The seventh article is the fulfillment of the Church through everlasting glory in the truly-resurrected soul and body; the opposite of this means the eternal damnation of the reprobate.

The remaining seven articles of faith pertain to the manhood of Christ. The first is his incarnation, or real assuming of flesh from the glorious Virgin through the Holy Spirit. The second is the birth of the truly incarnate God from the inviolate Virgin. The third is the real passion and death of Christ-God on the cross under the tyranny of Pontius Pilate. The fourth is the descent in the spirit of Christ-God into hell to harrow it, while his body lay in the sepulcher. The fifth is the true resurrection of Christ. The sixth is his true ascension into heaven. The seventh is the most certain expectation of his coming in judgment.

On Charity

Out of the ten commandments of the old testament,[3] three (called the laws of the first tablet) are ordained for God; and seven (called the laws of the second tablet) are ordained for our neighbors.

The first commandment forbids all idolatry when it says "Thou shalt not have strange gods before me."[4] Implicitly it forbids all sorcery, incantations, and superstitious uses of written letters or other types of images.

---

[3] Cf. Ex 20:3-17
[4] Ex 20:3

The second commandment, when it says "Thou shalt not take the name of the Lord thy God in vain,"[5] primarily forbids all heresy and secondarily forbids all blasphemy and irreverence for the name of God, especially in perjury.

When the third commandment says, "Remember that thou keep holy the sabbath day,"[6] it orders the promotion of the Christian religion to which clergy and laity alike are obliged. From this it should be understood that the legal obligation to fast on the sabbath along with other legally required rituals contained in the old testament completely ceased and was succeeded in the new testament by the rule for keeping Sundays (and other holy days designated by the Church's authority) free for divine worship. This new rule was not adduced from the superstition of the Jews but through the creation of the holy canons.

The fourth commandment (the first commandment of the second tablet) explicitly is to "honor thy father and thy mother,"[7] both in temporal and spiritual affairs. An implicit and secondary meaning of this commandment is that anyone should be honored by virtue of his status. One should also understand this commandment to mean that we should honor not only our natural father and mother but also our spiritual parents. Thus, our father is also any prelate of the Church, mediate or immediate, and our mother is the Church itself whose children are every Catholic person.

The fifth commandment is: "Thou shalt not kill,"[8] which explicitly forbids the illegal destruction of a person by conspiracy, word, deed, or approval; but implicitly this commandment forbids every unjust injury to someone. They commit spiritual murder who do not relieve the needy; similarly, they kill who slander, or who oppress or harass the innocent.

The sixth commandment is: "Thou shalt not commit adultery,"[9] which explicitly forbids adultery, but also implicitly fornication (which Deuteronomy 23 explicitly forbids where it says: "There shall be no

---

5 Ex 20:7
6 Ex 20:8
7 Ex 20:12
8 Ex 20:13
9 Ex 20:14

whore among the daughters of Israel, nor whoremonger among the sons of Israel"[10]). This commandment also forbids all sexual relations between men and women which the blessings of marriage do not allow, and every willful act of sexual pollution achieved in any eager or voluntary fashion.

The seventh commandment is: "Thou shalt not steal."[11] It explicitly forbids any clandestine withdrawal of another's things without the owner's consent. Implicitly, it also forbids any harmful seizure of another's things whether through fraud, usury, violence, or intimidation.

The eighth commandment is "Thou shalt not bear false witness against thy neighbor,"[12] which explicitly forbids false testimony harmful to someone. However, it implicitly forbids false testimony that speaks on behalf of someone who, based on merits, is unworthy. This commandment also condemns all lies, especially pernicious ones.

The ninth commandment is: "Thou shalt not covet thy neighbor's house";[13] that is, by damaging it. This commandment implicitly forbids greed for another's real property, especially that of any Catholic.

The tenth commandment is: "Thou shalt not desire his wife, nor his servant, nor his handmaid, nor his ox, nor his ass, nor anything that is his,"[14] which condemns greed for another's possessions, including his chattel.

The gospels add two other commands to these ten commandments — namely, love of God and of neighbor.[15] He loves God who keeps the aforesaid commandments chiefly out of love, not fear. In addition, everyone ought to love his neighbor as himself. This conjunction *as* does not mean "equally," but "similarly." So you should love your neighbor for that which you love in yourself (that is, for the good in him, not the bad), and in the manner in which you love yourself (that is, spiritually, not carnally, insofar as carnality can be called a vice), and to the degree you love yourself (that

[10] Dt 23:17
[11] Ex 20:15
[12] Ex 20:16
[13] Ex 20:17
[14] Ibid.
[15] Cf. Mt 22:37-39; etc.

is, in good times and bad, in health and sickness), and in comparison to temporal goods (insofar as you should love every single person more than any temporal wealth), and as you love yourself (insofar as you should love the soul of your neighbor or the eternal salvation of the soul more than your own earthly life—just as you should put the life of your soul above the life of your body), so that you should go to the aid of every other person in an emergency, just as you would wish to be aided in similar circumstances. All these things should be understood by the phrase, "Thou shalt love thy neighbor as thyself."[16]

There are six works of mercy revealed in the gospel of Matthew.[17] They are to feed the hungry, to give drink to the thirsty, to give shelter to strangers, to clothe the naked, to visit the sick, and to comfort those in prison. The book of Tobias adds a seventh: to bury the dead.[18]

On the Seven Deadly Sins

These are the seven deadly sins: pride, envy, wrath (or hate), sloth, avarice, gluttony, and lust. Pride is love of your own excellence, from which arises boasting, ostentation, hypocrisy, schism, and other such things. Envy is hatred for your neighbor's happiness, from which arises disparagement, querulousness, disagreement, wrongful judgments, and similar things. Wrath is a craving for vengeance against or harming another; when it endures in the heart it becomes hatred from which arises persecutions in words and deeds, fighting, murder, and things like these. Sloth is lethargy toward spiritual goods, from which a man takes delight neither in God nor in divine praises for him. From it arises listlessness, faint-heartedness, despair, and similar things. Avarice is an immoderate love of movable and immovable wealth, either by unlawfully acquiring it or unlawfully detaining it. From it arise fraud, theft, sacrilege, simony, and all ill-gotten gains.

Gluttony is the immoderate love of the pleasures of the sense of taste through eating and drinking. There are five varieties of the sin of gluttony.

---

[16] Mt 22:39
[17] Cf. Mt 25:35-36
[18] Cf. Tb 1:21

First one can sin according to interval, as when one eats too early in the morning or lingers too long when eating or is too hasty. Second, one can sin through quality when one craves sumptuous food, that is, food that is too rich. Third, one sins in quantity when one eats or drinks too much. This is the commonest type of gluttony; it is this surfeit of food and drink which aggravates the heart, impedes both the exterior and interior senses, and injures the body's health. Fourth, one can sin in the overeager voracious quality of one's eating. And finally, one can sin in the over-meticulous and exquisite preparation of food meant to arouse the savory pleasures of taste. These five circumstances for gluttony are summarized in this verse: "Too hastily, too sumptuously, too much, too ardently, too meticulously." It is not fitting to say much about lust whose infamy infects every breath we take.

On Virtue

The seven principal virtues are faith, hope, and charity (which were or-dained by God and so are called the theological virtues), and prudence, justice, temperance, and fortitude (which were ordained by man for himself and his neighbors). To act with prudence is to choose the good; to act with justice is to do the good; to act with temperance is to be unimpeded by pleasures; to act with fortitude is to do good despite whatever difficulties and troubles. These four are called the cardinal (or principal) virtues. There are many other matters concerning these four, but because we are writing here for those of only a little learning, right now we will not discuss them further.

On the Sacraments

There are seven sacraments of grace, whose ministers are the prelates of the Church, five of which all Christians ought to receive: namely, baptism, confirmation, penance, the Eucharist (at the proper time), and the last anointing. (The last anointing ought to be given only to those who seem to be in danger of death from some grave illness: however, if possible it should be given to them while they are still of sound mind. But if it happens that they are delirious or out of their minds, and before this happened they showed concern for their salvation, we nevertheless advise that this sacrament be faithfully ministered to them. For we believe and have learned by experience that the reception of this sacrament, inasmuch as it increases grace, will be of profit no matter how mad someone may be—providing he is a predestined son of God—by giving him a lucid moment or at least some spiritual benefit.) There are two other sacraments—holy orders and matrimony—the first of which is appropriate for those seeking perfection, while the second is appropriate only for the imperfect, so long as the law of the new testament endures; still, we believe it bestows grace through the power of the sacrament if it is contracted with a sincere spirit.

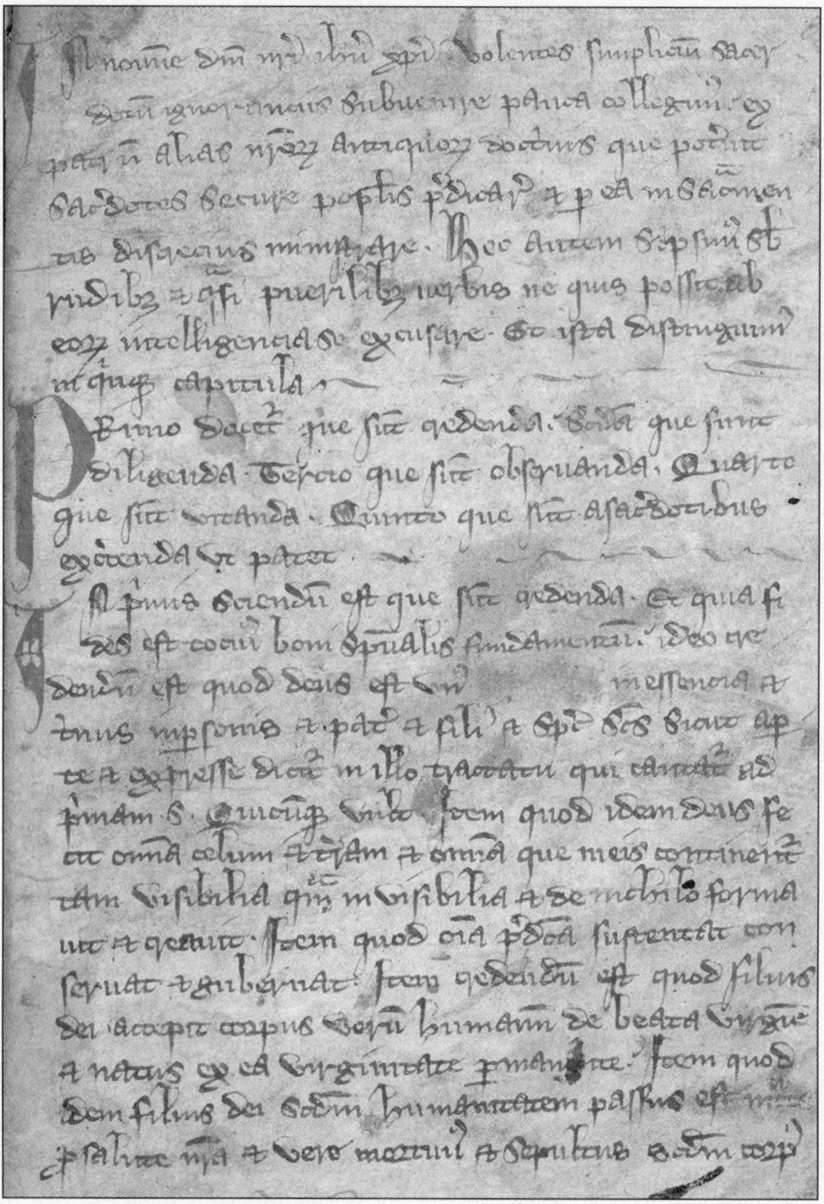

Opening page of the anonymous Quinque Verba; *MS Laud. Misc. 527 from the Bodleian Library, Oxford. Scribe unknown, England ca. 1300.*

Quinque Verba

On the Ignorance of Priests and the Remedy Thereof

In the name of our Lord Jesus Christ. In an effort to remedy the ignorance of simple priests, we have gathered a few things from the teachings of our fathers that tell priests how they can preach with confidence to the people and administer more carefully the Church's sacraments. Thus, we have written these things in a simple and almost childlike manner lest anyone try to excuse himself from knowing this material. Furthermore, we have divided these things into five chapters: in the first, an explanation of those things which must be believed; the second, the things that should be loved; the third, what works should be done; the fourth, what should be watched out for or avoided; the fifth, those things that priests should do.

On Faith

Since faith is the foundation of every spiritual good, the first thing that should be known are matters of faith. It is necessary to believe that God is one and absolute in essence, three in Persons, Father, Son, and Holy Spirit, as is clearly and manifestly stated in the hymn sung at prime, "Quicumque vult salvus esse," etc.[19] Namely that God created out of nothing and formed all things in heaven and on earth, things visible and invisible. Also, that God sustains, protects, and rules all creation. It must also be believed that the Son of God took on human form and was born of the Blessed Mary ever Virgin. Also, that the same Son of God suffered bodily on the cross for our salvation, died and his body was buried; that his soul went down to the netherworld to harrow hell and free the elect and just who had been held there. And that on the third day he truly rose from the dead, and after forty days ascended to heaven and sent the Holy Spirit upon the apostles and all who believe. He gave these same apostles and their successors

---

[19] Editor's note: The first words of the Athanasian Creed. See p. 4–5, above.

the power to bind and loose souls of all sin through the ministries of the Church he established; he also gave them power to sanctify souls through the Church's sacraments, in particular, baptism, penance, and the others. And that the same Son of God will come again at the end of the world to judge the living and the dead; and the good he shall lead into eternal life, but the wicked he shall send to the everlasting flames.

On Charity

The second thing one must know is what should be loved in true charity without which neither faith nor good works can suffice for everlasting life.

First, God should be loved above all things and, especially, more than you love yourself to the extent that you would rather lose everything including your own life than offend God through mortal sin. Second, you should love yourself, that is, out of charity you should love your soul which is true love. In this way you desire for yourself virtues and grace in order to merit eternal life. For, as the prophet says, "whoever loves (sin and) iniquity hates his soul."[20]

Third, you shall love your neighbor, which means everyone, as yourself and this is that good for which you love yourself. As the saying goes, you should love the good in every person, the noble manners and the grace through which eternal life is won, just as you love the same in yourself. As the Lord says, "Love your neighbor as yourself";[21] he does not say how much you should love yourself, but you should love your own soul more than your neighbor, and you should love your neighbor's soul more than your own property or worldly goods. Fourth, out of charity, you should love your body to the extent that it serves your soul for glorification in the life to come.

For there are seven principal virtues with which you ought to decorate your soul and which you should encourage among your neighbors: the first is faith, by which you believe in God; the second is hope, by which you confide and hope in God; the third is charity, by which, above all things,

[20] Ps 10:6
[21] Mt 22:39

you shall love God and neighbor. These are called the three theological virtues since they direct one to God. The four other virtues are called cardinal virtues and they are: first, prudence, by which good is chosen and evil avoided; second, justice, by which one gives to another his or her due; third, temperance, by which one uses all things in reasonable measure; and fourth, fortitude or magnanimity, which makes a person unafraid to suffer pain or persecution for justice's sake.

On the Ten Commandments

The third thing one ought to know are those works which need to be done, since faith without works is dead and true charity is never idle. These works include the ten commandments of the old testament.

The first commandment is: "You shall not have strange gods," in which holy Church forbids every kind of sorcery, incantations, spells, and superstitions.

The second commandment is: "Do not take the name of your God in vain," wherein lies the prohibition of false and empty oaths and any blasphemy, that is, words and sayings which are against the honor of the Divine Majesty.

The third commandment is: "You shall make holy the sabbath day," which means the devout observance of the Church's ancient feasts, worshipping God through pious acts, listening attentively to the word of God and the divine office, and doing other things that are similarly good; it also means avoiding those things which are not holy, such as all uncleanness, going to the taverns, wrestling, and dancing.

The fourth commandment is: "Honor your father and mother," which requires not only the respect due to one's natural parents, but also the honor and humble obedience due to spiritual fathers, the prelates and guardians of your soul, and the worthy veneration to the spiritual mother, that is, the Church.

The fifth commandment is: "You shall not kill," which forbids every sin of killing, in deed but also in forethought, counsel, consent or support; also, this same commandment forbids any violence done to one's neighbor, for scripture calls murderers all those who plunder the poor, oppress and subjugate the innocent. It is the same for those who hate their neighbor, who do not feed the poor or allow others to die through neglect.

The sixth commandment is: "You shall not commit adultery," by which all fornication is forbidden along with every kind of lustful and unchaste act which is intentional and willingly engaged in. This sort of act is a mortal sin.

The seventh commandment: "You shall not steal," which means not only the furtive theft of someone else's possessions, but any unjust acquisition or appropriation by means of plunder, fraudulence, usury, violence, threats, or fear.

The eighth commandment is: "You shall not give false witness against your neighbor," which includes any lie, especially slander which harms you or your neighbor.

The ninth commandment is: "You shall not unjustly covet your neighbor's property." This is a prohibition as well of the desire to possess another's immovable goods, such as land or fields.

The tenth commandment is: "You should not desire your neighbor's wife," servant or maid, ass or any moveable goods which your neighbor owns. Do not covet these things for God forbids willful sin or the sin of the heart.

On the Seven Deadly Sins

The fourth matter to be known are those things which ought to be avoided or shunned, as much in heart as well as in word and deed. These are the deadly sins and are so called because any one of them kills the soul, destroys charity and all virtue, and is deadening like poison.

The first deadly sin is pride, which is the inordinate love of one's own greatness from which all other vices are born: boastfulness, discord, quarreling, hypocrisy, vainglory.

The second deadly sin is envy, which is a yearning for another person's goods. Other sins arise from this, such as detraction, backbiting, slander, and delight in another's misfortunes.

The third deadly sin is anger, a desire or craving for the punishment or harm of another. If this endures, it gives rise to hatred in the heart. Anger's progeny are quarrels, fights, blows, harsh words, murder, and the like.

The fourth deadly sin is sloth, a lethargy about spiritual goods from which a person fails to delight in God or sing God's praises. From sloth comes laziness, evil-doing, despair, and indifference towards God's commands, and other like things.

The fifth deadly sin is greed, the inordinate love of wealth. To be greedy is to seek after something more than is necessary. Thus, greed is equivalent to desiring and holding on to more than one needs. From greed comes other sins: theft, pillage, false oaths, fraud, sacrilege, simony, and profit from base things.

The sixth deadly sin is gluttony, an excessive love of delicacies in food and drink. There are five types of gluttony: hastiness, indulgence, excess, voraciousness, and over-fondness. One is hasty when one has too little time, or is too early or eats something too quickly or too often, especially on fast days. One is indulgent when eating too many delicacies or rich foods. Excess occurs when one does more than is good for one's health or when one becomes so ill because of drink that one is unable to eat. Voracity happens when there is an excess of desire and greed. To be overfond of something is manifest in excessive preparation in the creating of delicacies.

Lust is the seventh deadly sin, and lust means the desire for illicit pleasures in many forms such as fornication, whoring, adultery, debauchery, incest, sacrilege, unnatural vices, and other horrendous sins. Still, it is not a good thing to dwell on these sins or speak of them at too great length, but, rather, to grieve over and fear them. The best antidote is to avoid at all costs the company of women and to resist any thoughts of this sort as soon as they arise.

It is important to know that the above sins are grave, dangerous, and mortal when a person gives full consent to them and knows that they are against the laws of God. But when one resists them entirely when inclinations or thoughts of them first arise, then they are venial or less serious sins.

On the Sacraments

The fifth subject that every priest ought to know for his pastoral work is the seven sacraments, which are the medicine of the soul. They are seven and were established by God for the remission of sins and the transmission of grace. A sacrament is the visible form of an invisible grace; a sacrament is also the sign of a sacred thing.

The first sacrament is baptism, which takes place only with water and these words "I baptize you N., in the name of the Father and of the Son and of the Holy Spirit. Amen." This may be done by anyone who has the intention of baptizing according to ecclesiastical form. Without these aspects, it is not the sacrament of baptism. Anything else which takes place or is said before these words is not essential for baptism but belongs to its celebration and the devotion of the people. Baptism's effect is to wash the baptized clean of every sin, original and actual. Actual sin is what a person does, namely through doing, speaking, or thinking in an evil manner, either mortally or venially. Original sin is what a person takes on or receives as a child of our first parents, Adam and Eve, on account of their disobedience to God. Original sin is the flesh's desire against the spirit's and came with the loss of original justice that had once been given to Adam and his race but which was forfeited through the disobedience of sin.

The second sacrament is confirmation, which is performed only by the bishop with holy chrism and a certain verbal formula. Its effect is to strengthen faith with the Holy Spirit.

The third sacrament is penance, which is, before all else, the tearful resolve that one will not sin intentionally again. Now penance has three aspects: contrition of the heart, confession of the lips, and making satisfaction.

Contrition is the genuine and heartfelt sorrow for one's sins; it should be profound because of the offense to God's grace and covenant, and on account of the pains of hell to which sinners are obliged because of their sins.

Confession is a full rendering of one's sins before a priest, and it ought to be complete so that everything which comes to mind may be revealed. Confession also ought to be personal and confidential, to prevent penitents from lying and to encourage them to reveal their own sins and not those of another. The penitent should confess with a heartfelt sorrow and a real determination not to sin mortally again, and to hope all the more in God's loving kindness. Without these things it is not true confession, nor is it helpful toward salvation.

Satisfaction is the performance of good works for the amendment of sins, and these good works include fasting, pilgrimages, almsgiving, and prayer. Fasting and pilgrimage counteract fleshly desires; almsgiving, the desires of the world; and prayers, an arrogant spirit. Penitents should be required to do these in a relative fashion as some are hale while others are weak, some wealthy and others indigent, some work while others have leisure.

It is important that restitution be required of all those who hold on to property that does not belong to them and which they are obliged to return, either immediately or as soon as they can. As St. Augustine says, the sin is not remitted until restitution is complete.[22] Confessors need to be careful about requiring the restitution of goods belonging to executors, heirs, or neighbors of penitents if such cases arise. But if restitution is impossible, penitents should pray all the more for those whose goods they have or else they should seek pardon from the latter without breaking the seal of confession.

It is also important to know that every mortal sin had an automatic penance of seven years, though the actual penance should be moderated depending on the number of sins and the judgment of the confessor. Those who confess many of these mortal sins ought be given penance for the rest of their lives. Still, penances ought to be harsher in the first years and lighter in the latter if they are to be carried out properly. Everyone ought to know that whenever they ponder their sins, they should be heartily sorry and beg God's pardon with a strong resolve to sin no more.

After the penance has been given, the priest should have the penitent recite the *confiteor* word for word in his or her own language and then the priest may say the *misereatur*, etc. Finally, he grants the penitent absolution

---

[22] Cf. Augustine, *Epistle 153*

in these words: "By the authority of God and the blessed apostles Peter and Paul, and with the authority and power granted to me, I absolve you of all the sins you have confessed with a contrite heart as well as those you would have confessed had you remembered them. All the good things you will do and the difficult things you will endure are your penance. May the passion of our Lord Jesus Christ and the merits of his saints strengthen you for the remission of all your sins and for life eternal. Amen."

Confessors should be careful not to interfere in cases reserved to the bishop or his penitentiary or when someone is under a sentence of general or particular excommunication, except in danger of death. Nor should they impose penance on the diseased or gravely ill, but urge them to be sorry for their sins and to accept an appropriate penance, and absolve them in the manner described above for their quick healing. If the penitent is an excommunicate and is absolved for fear of death, when the person has recovered, the priest should order the excommunicate to seek absolution from a higher authority. Indeed, the effect of the sacrament of penance is the remission of every sin.

The fourth sacrament is Eucharist, which is the body and blood of our Lord under the appearances of bread and wine; only a priest may celebrate this sacrament and with single-grain bread and unsoured wine. The bread is changed into the body of Christ through the power of these words in the Canon of the Mass: "This is my body." And the wine is changed into blood through the words that follow: "This is the chalice of my blood, of the new and eternal covenant, the mystery of faith, which is for you," etc. This sacrament is given to the laity only in the form of bread and not in the form of wine because of the danger in spilling it. When the sacrament is given to the sick, it should be emphasized to them that this is truly the body of Christ, born of the Virgin, who died on the cross, and is here under the form of bread and should be adored before they receive it. The sacrament should not be given to the sick because they might vomit, or to those who are delirious; neither should it be given to children who have no idea of its power, nor to widely-known and public sinners until their penance is equally manifest. The effect of this sacrament is that it feeds the soul and joins it to God, it strengthens virtue and, when devoutly received, takes away venial sins; but mortal sin renders one unworthy to receive it.

The fifth sacrament is holy order. There are four minor orders which an acolyte possesses and three sacred orders, namely the orders of subdiaconate, diaconate, and priesthood. And in each order worthily received through the laying on of hands by the bishop, a spiritual grace is given for ministry in accordance with the office of those ordained. The effect of this sacrament is a special power given by God.

The sixth sacrament is matrimony, and matrimony is the legitimate joining of a man and a woman by the pronouncement of these words the man says to the woman: "I take you as my spouse." When these words refer to a future event, this is a betrothal and not a marriage. There is a threefold effect to matrimony, namely: faith, offspring, and sacrament. Faith, since both are bound to give their bodies over to each another faithfully. Offspring, since they ought to intend when having sexual intercourse to bring into this world sons and daughters for the honor and worship of God. Sacrament, in that matrimony represents the joining of Christ to his Church. By means of this sacrament, a man and woman are freed from the mortal sin that arises from sexual union, so long as the bounds of marriage are not exceeded.

The seventh sacrament is extreme unction, given to the sick when they are gravely ill by the anointing of the body and the recitation of certain words. The effect of this sacrament is the alleviation of physical infirmity if it frees the soul and the remission of venial sins. If one who is sick asks for the sacrament devoutly, it should be given lest that person fall sick again.

It is important to note that baptism, confirmation, and holy orders may be received only once in life, but the other sacraments may be taken more often. Indeed, the Eucharist ought to be taken frequently; and penance should be continuous since all of us are sinners, and after baptism, penance alone can take away sins.

Here ends the treatise on the things a priest ought to know.

Page from William of Pagula's Oculus Sacerdotis; *MS Holkham Misc. 21*
from the Bodleian Library, Oxford. Scribe unknown, England ca. 1400.

Oculus Sacerdotis

The Priestly Office and How a Priest Should Instruct His Parishioners

There are many priests, yet there are few priests—many priests in name, but few in deed.[23] There are many priests in name since nothing in this life, especially in these times, is easier, more agreeable, and more acceptable to men than to perform the office of bishop or priest; but in the sight of God, nothing is more wretched, sadder, and damnable if it is done indifferently and for adulation.

On Priestly Duty

Yet there are few priests in deed since nothing in this life, especially in these times, is harder, more burdensome, or perilous than the office of bishop or priest; but nothing is holier in the sight of God if one soldiers on and does his duty in the way Christ commands. And according to a sermon of St. Ambrose, due to the disordered and undisciplined lives of many priests, the holy sacrament of the Redeemer is daily heaped with scorn by those who should be vicars of the apostles and sons of Peter but are instead companions of Judas and followers of Antichrist. In order for there to be more priests in deed, they should study holy scripture with great diligence according to the apostle Paul in his letter to Timothy where he says, always stay dedicated to "reading (the scriptures), in exhortation, and in teaching."[24] Priests should know holy scripture and at least the major canons of the Church; all their effort should be put to preaching and teaching; they should edify everyone with their knowledge both about the faith and about good behavior; and they are bound to mold their subjects with the food

---

[23] Translator's note: Citations of canon law follow almost every sentence in this text. All these references are omitted here.

[24] 1 Tm 4:13

of God's word according to how he inspires them, lest they are deservedly blamed because of their idleness. And so a pastor of the Church is told: "diligently apply the cure of souls to those over whom you happen to be in charge. Know the state of their souls and each one's deeds; if you discover any vice in them, be mindful to correct it quickly. For you will not always have the power to feed the Lord's sheep, but you will gain an eternal crown if you feed them well in your time," as it says in the gloss upon Proverb 27 ("Be diligent to know the countenance of thy flock"[25]). And according to the words of St. Ambrose in one of his letters, nothing is more dangerous for a priest in the eyes of God or so base in the eyes of men than to see the truth and not openly proclaim it.

It should especially be the duty of priests to harm no one and to be useful to everyone. For insofar as they set examples of behavior that warrant perdition, they warrant punishment. Thus, it is necessary that they carefully guard themselves as much from sin as from wickedness, since when they commit these things they are not the only ones who die from them. St. Augustine says that everyone who lives evilly in the sight of those over whom he is in charge as much as kills them.

They ought to, indeed they are bound to, obey absolutely the canons, mandates, and constitutions of bishops and superior prelates, because many things are enjoined in the canons and in various provincial constitutions that parish priests, by virtue of obedience, are obliged to announce publicly and also preach to their parishioners. Certain priests, as much out of negligence as ignorance, neither explain nor preach the things that they are bound to; they are therefore disobedient and as a consequence deserve to be punished.

Priests cannot excuse themselves due to their ignorance of the law, since no priest may ignore the canons of the Church nor do anything which opposes the rules of the fathers of the Church.

And they are especially obliged to know the penitential canons and provincial and synodal statutes. It is absolutely contemptible and dangerous for the Church's prelates and parish priests, who are given the

---

[25] Prv 27:23

governance of souls as representatives of their King, to utterly ignore these things—just as it would be disgraceful for a lawyer to be ignorant about the law he practices or for any worker to neglect looking after his duties. St. Jerome says that it should be considered a priest's duty to respond when asked a question about the law;[26] if he is a priest he should know the Lord's law. But Jerome argues that if a priest does not know the Lord's law, he is not the Lord's priest since it is the duty of his priest to know the law and to answer questions about it.

Yet today there are many priests who neither know God's law nor learn it. Carefree in their idleness, they are keen on feasting and drinking; they covet worldly things—they reek of them; they busy themselves in the streets, but rarely in church; they are slow to inquire about the sins of their parishioners, but quick to hunt the tracks of hares or other wild animals; faster at rounding up their hounds than gathering together the poor, they would sooner offer bread to a dog than to a poor man; they have more people serving them at the dinner table than at the Lord's table; they want servants and maids attending them, not clergy. These are the sort of men whose bedchamber is better furnished than their church, whose dinner table is better adorned than their altar, whose goblet costs more than their chalice, whose surcoat is finer than their chasuble, whose shirt is more delicately woven than their alb. See how the gold is dulled, the brightest color faded, and how the bricks of the temple are scattered at the head of every street, as Hugh of St. Victor says.

Priests should not behave this way; rather, what they do not know they should learn. For even a blind man can see that it is necessary to learn since, if it is better for someone to teach than to learn, it is better to learn than be ignorant, as St. Augustine writes in one of his letters;[27] and the man who is ashamed to undergo education for a short spell will remain ever after shamefully foolish. It is obvious that any workman who wishes to do well the job given him needs the proper tools for that job; otherwise, as it is plain to anyone considering it, he cannot accomplish his job or duty

---

[26] Cf. Jerome, *Letter 53 to Paulinus*, n. 3
[27] Cf. Augustine, *Letter 166 to Jerome*, Ch. 1, n. 1

properly. Exactly the same holds true for the Church's prelates and parish priests who, in assuming the job of teaching God's people, need to own and know at the very least the penitential canons and provincial and synodal constitutions. If they do not have these due to negligence and carelessness, they should be accused. If they have these and rashly do not observe them, they should be reproved and also rebuked. Priests also should perform the divine office faithfully and with good intention; as it says in Galatians, "let everyone test his own work" and diligently examine his reason for doing it; "and so he will have glory in himself only"[28] and in God who is in him.

They especially ought to be of good conscience and lead a pure life; thus, Proverb 21 says "the perverse way of a man is strange: but as for him that is pure, his work is right."[29] And priests should be pure not only inwardly but also outwardly in order to honor God and support Christ. Thus, Proverb 24: "Prepare thy work without, and diligently till thy ground"[30] and Matthew 5: "Let your light shine before men, in order that they may see your good works and give glory to your Father in heaven";[31] and so those close to you are instructed and enlightened by your good works. Thessalonians 4: "So that you may walk becomingly towards outsiders";[32] he who does good works will have eternal life. Ecclesiasticus 14: "Every excellent work shall be justified: and the worker thereof shall be honored therein"[33] and Romans 2: "Glory and honor and peace shall be awarded to everyone who does good."[34] And "the presbyters who rule well" in their lives and learning should be "held worthy of double honor"[35] by their subjects: spiritually their subjects should obey them, and outwardly they should tend them their goods. For good and faithful stewards should be rewarded not only with high honor, but also with material possessions so

[28] Gal 6:4
[29] Prv 21:8
[30] Prv 24:27
[31] Mt 5:16
[32] 1 Thes 4:11
[33] Ecclus 14:21
[34] Rom 2:10
[35] 1 Tm 5:17

that they are not distressed by their lack of finery but take delight in their devotion to spiritual things, as Augustine says in his gloss on 1 Timothy 5.

For parish priests to rule well in this regard they should be discerning, knowing how to bind and loose sins, lest, out of ignorance, the blind take it upon themselves to lead others and they both fall into the pit. Hence the verse: "If a blind man guide a blind man…"[36]

First the leader falls into the pit and then the follower. Their eyes are covered in sin so that they are blinded, and their backs are always bent.[37] For when the leaders who bear all their sins are blind, those following them are easily led astray. Therefore, prelates and priests should strive to slough off ignorance from them as if it were some disease. For, according to Augustine, "he who is ignorant will be disregarded,"[38] by which he means those who have an aptitude for learning but do not apply themselves to it.

Therefore, so that no prelate or parish priest, by claiming ignorance, will excuse himself in any way from knowing about these things, everything that the canons and provincial councils particularly order them to explain to their parishioners and preach in church is contained briefly and easily in this modest summary.

On Baptism

First, a parish priest should frequently explain to his parishioners on Sundays the English words for the baptismal ritual so that they can baptize someone who is in danger of dying. They should know this formula and be able to use it. The ritual for baptism consists not only in the action of baptizing but also in the order of the words spoken, through which this sacrament is divinely instituted. Here is what should be said while baptizing someone: "Ich cristen the in the name of the Fader and the Sone and the Holi Gost," or similar words in the vernacular using the local dialect. And they should immerse the child in water one to three times or sprinkle the water on it. And people who baptize a child with these words should take

---

[36] Mt 15:14
[37] Cf. Ps 68:24
[38] Augustine, *Letter 169*, Ch. 1; Cf. 1 Cor 14:38

care that the child is not baptized a second time as some foolish women do, since someone doing this in effect crucifies Christ twice. Still, the exorcism and catechism should be said over a child baptized by a layman, and the child should be anointed by the priest out of respect for the rituals of the Church, because exorcism and anointing have been and still are effective in preventing the devil from harming the baptized child. Nor should anyone wonder why the devil is adjured to depart the body of the baptized child and do it no harm even though he is no longer in it, because this is in the sense of the words "depart from him," that is, "you may have no power to do harm."

If someone immerses a child in water three times and says, "In the name of the Father, and of the Son, and of the Holy Spirit," but fails to say, "I baptize you," the child is not baptized. Understand that the ritual formula for baptism prescribed by the Church must be strictly observed. And no one may be baptized in any other liquid than water.

Second, a priest should explain to his parishioners that not only a priest but any other cleric or even the child's own father or mother — with no impediment to their marriage — may baptize in an emergency; the effect of baptism is still imparted to the child. And if a baby is baptized by a layman, the priest should supply those parts of the rite omitted.

Third, the priest should warn his parishioners that children born eight days or less before Easter or Pentecost should be reserved to be baptized on the Holy Saturday before Easter or on Pentecost if baptism can be delayed without endangering them. But children born at other times of the year may be baptized sooner or later according to their parents' wishes.

Duties of Parents and Godparents

Also, the priest should warn his parishioners that the men and women who stand as sponsors for children at baptism are responsible for them before God. Thus, their sponsors should always admonish them to guard their chastity, love justice, and maintain charity; above all they are obliged to teach them the Creed and the Lord's Prayer.

Those who stand as sponsors by receiving the child from the baptismal font should not also sponsor them at their confirmation unless necessity demands it.

Also, priests should warn their parishioners not to put their little ones in the same bed with them so that they will not accidentally roll over on them or suffocate them and thereby be found guilty of homicide. Nor should they carelessly restrain them in their cradles or leave them unattended day or night because of the danger that the baby's mouth might be covered by the bedding, even for a short time which could easily prove fatal. It is the custom in some places for women who have overlain their children through negligence to go to the bishop on Ash Wednesday to be confessed. If their sin is widely known then they are enjoined public penance; if their sin was kept secret, they are given private penance.

A priest also should warn his parishioners and effectively persuade them to take care to have their children confirmed by a bishop within five years of birth if they have the opportunity to see the bishop. If they neglect to do this, they should be forbidden entrance to the church until they have their children confirmed. But according to the canon law, those to be confirmed should have reached the age of majority and should fast before coming to confirmation. They should be warned to confess their sins first so that, thus purified, they may be worthy to receive the gift of the Holy Spirit.

He should also explain to them that a spiritual consanguinity is created between a child's godparents and real parents, and between the godparents and the child, both at baptism and at confirmation; because of this relationship, they are prohibited from marrying one another.

Therefore, so that a parish priest ignorant of canon law can understand among which people a spiritual affinity exists because of baptism and confirmation, he should realize that such a spiritual relationship is created between ten people through baptism, namely: between the baptized child and the person who sponsored it at baptism; between the baptized child and the children of its sponsor; between the sponsor and the wife he had carnal relations with before he was made sponsor; between the sponsor and the mother (and father) of the baptized child; between the baptized child and the one who baptized it; between the baptized child and the children of its baptizer; between the baptized child and the baptizer's wife (with whom the baptizer had previously had carnal relations); between the baptizer and the baptized child's father; and between the baptizer and the baptized child's mother. Thus, there are ten kinds of spiritual affinity established through baptism. This affinity is an impediment to contracts of marriage made between these people and it annuls contracts already made.

Likewise, know that the same kinds of affinity are established by confirmation (the anointing of the forehead). Namely, between the confirmed child and the one holding or sponsoring it before the bishop confirming it; between the confirmed child and the children of its sponsor; between the confirmed and its sponsor's wife; between the sponsor and the confirmed child's father; between the sponsor and the confirmed child's mother; between the person confirming and the confirmed child; between the confirmed child and the children of the one confirming it; between the confirmed child and the wife of the one confirming it; between the one confirming it and the confirmed child's father; and between the one confirming it and the confirmed child's mother. Thus, these are the cases forbidden because of spiritual affinity: ten cases through baptism, ten through confirmation. Any one of these cases prevents a marriage between these people from being contracted and annuls one if it has been contracted.

But baptism or confirmation does not prevent marriage from being contracted between people other than the ones just mentioned, nor does it annul ones already contracted, customs to the contrary notwithstanding.

On Marriage and Purity

Also, he should explain that if legitimate consent is exchanged through words of the present tense between a man and a woman for the purpose of contracting marriage, even though no trothplight or oath has been exchanged nor has there been carnal consummation, nevertheless it is a truly legitimate marriage. And if one of the parties afterwards contracts a second marriage, even if that marriage is carnally consummated, the couple should be separated and the first marriage should be corroborated.

And he should explain that all carnal relations between a man and a woman outside of legal marriage are a mortal sin. Also, he should warn them that boys and girls over the age of seven should not sleep together in the same bed because of the danger of fornication or, if the girl is the boy's sister, incest.

He should explain that marriage should be solemnized with a priest, legitimate witnesses, and banns announced before the members of the parish on three prior solemn days. And if a parish priest or any clergyman, regular or secular, dares to be present at a clandestine marriage or fails to prevent one when he has the power to, he should be suspended from office for three years. Also, he should announce frequently that a man having carnal relations with his wife or another woman should do nothing to prevent his wife from conceiving a child; if he does this, he sins more seriously than if he had committed adultery.[39]

He should also tell his parishioners that since human nature is always prone toward evil, every person is flawed by sin. For the path of man inclines towards pleasure and in his nature he mirrors the vices. Some men and even some women ejaculate semen or sperm in various ways either while sleeping or while awake. Thus, anyone to whom this happens, either while sleeping or awake, is bound to confess it to his confessor, saying whether he did this willfully or with pleasure, since it can happen in many and various ways. Then their confessor should tell those confessing how serious and detestable this sin is. Since sperm or semen can be ejaculated in various ways, he should tell him that in [intenionally] doing this, he sins more seriously than he would by having sexual relations with his mother or sister. But a priest should not tell everyone the ways that people can sin against nature, since — as bishops' penitentiaries know well enough — these days there are many people who believe that in many cases a sin against nature is not really a sin, which is a deplorable state of affairs. Thus, a priest can confidently tell his parishioners that they should be aware that anyone who ejaculates semen knowingly and willingly in

---

[39] Editor's note: In antiquity, both contraception and abortion were commonly viewed as species of murder.

any manner other than the normal way with his wife sins gravely, and he should tell his confessor how he did this.

He should warn them that no game warden or bailiff should hold scot-ales[40] or collect or make someone else collect the garb tithe; if he does this he is *ipso facto* excommunicated because he has violated the Charter of the Forest[41] and anyone violating the Charter of the Forest is *ipso facto* excommunicated. [This is made explicit both in the Charter and in the general excommunication issued by Archbishop Boniface of Canterbury and his suffragan bishops in the great hall at Westminster (in 1258.)]

On Penance and the Holy Eucharist

He ought to announce this statute in church frequently: each of the faithful, when they reach the age of discretion (i.e. fourteen) and so are able to commit sins, ought to confess all their sins to their own priest at least once a year and fulfill the penance given to them. And at Easter they should receive the body of Christ, unless at the counsel of their priest they have been advised to abstain from receiving at this time for some reasonable cause. If they do not do this, they are to be forbidden entrance into the church while they are living and denied Christian burial at their death.

If for some justifiable reason a parishioner wishes to confess his sins to a priest who is not his parish priest, he should first seek and obtain license from his parish priest when that priest is otherwise unable to bind or loose him from his sins.

A priest should explain that pregnant women, because of the danger of death that threatens when they are giving birth, should go to confession so that they will be prepared in such an emergency to receive the Eucharist.

---

[40] Translator's note: A scot-ale (i.e., "ale payment") was a festival sponsored by a manorial lord, bailiff, or game warden. Villagers were forced to attend and to pay a fee for drinking the ale served there.

[41] Translator's note: The royal forests were vast tracts of woodland and pasture spread across England meant for the sport of the king, who rigidly safeguarded his rights to the wild animals (venison) and timber (vert) within them. The Charter of the Forest (1217, with subsequent re-issues) developed those clauses in the Magna Carta that restrained the more tyrannical royal abuses of this forest land.

For it is unseemly for a priest to stay with them too long while they are in labor.

And a priest should frequently teach his people that when he elevates the saving host during the celebration of Mass, they should reverently genuflect if they can comfortably do so, and they should be able to say these words: "Hail, salvation of the world, Word of the Father, true host, living flesh, fully God, truly man," or "Glory to you, Lord, who was born of the Virgin," etc. or the Lord's Prayer. They should say these same things when they see the saving host, the body of Christ, as the priest is carrying it to the sick. Both coming and going, the priest, decently dressed, should openly and honorably carry the host with all reverence and honor in a clean linen cloth held before him, always being preceded by a lamp representing the splendor of eternal light; by doing this the faith and devotion of everyone may be increased. Prelates should gravely punish violators of this mandate.

The parish priest should teach his parishioners that when the body of Christ is given to them at Easter or some other time, they receive both Christ's body and blood under the appearance of bread, and that it is Christ, fully and truly man, who is contained in the sacrament. He also should teach them that what they drink from the chalice is not a part of the sacrament but only ordinary wine or wine mixed with water that is given to them to drink to help them swallow the host more easily, for only the celebrant is allowed to drink the blood under the appearance of consecrated wine.[42]

He should instruct them that when the sacrament is in their mouth, they should not crush it too much with their teeth; instead, they should gently chew it, swallowing it completely so that no particles get stuck between their teeth and remain there. Parishioners should be urged to look freely and frequently upon the body of Christ. The priest should announce to his parishioners that whoever yearns to see the body of Christ will merit the following according to St. Augustine in his book *The City of God*: he

---

[42] Editor's note: Out of heightened veneration and care for the Eucharistic species, the practice of offering the sacred chalice to the laity had faded in the West already by the twelfth century. However, sips of ordinary wine and/or water were taken in many places, as a kind of additional ablution for those who received the sacred host.

who sees it will get whatever food he needs; on that day too, his idle words will be forgiven, unwitting oaths canceled; on that day he will not lose his sight; on that day he will not meet with sudden death; on that day, he will not grow older while he hears the Mass; angels will guard the footsteps coming and going of whoever sees the body of Christ or who even is on his way devoutly to church.

On Tithing and Fasting

He should warn them that they should not knowingly protect or shelter in their houses or villages anyone they know to be, or who obviously is, a thief.

He should admonish his parishioners to pay tithes faithfully on all goods legally acquired. Unless they do this completely and lovingly, many bad consequences will follow, according to Augustine, who says that is a transgression against divine command since tithes were instituted by God, not man. Secondly, in past times men paying tithes of all their goods had abundance; but now because they do not faithfully and willingly pay their tithes, they are compelled to tithe. The third reason is so that God does not send forth locusts nor stir up plagues that destroy the crops. The fourth is that what Christ does not get, taxes will. But they who faithfully pay their tithes are rewarded fourfold. The first reward is an abundance of crops; the second is bodily health; the third is indulgence for sins; the fourth is an everlasting reward.

He should also teach his parishioners how they should faithfully give to God and to his holy Church tithes from all their goods, since many people have been found to tithe badly due to ignorance. Thus, so that henceforward they will not sink down into a pit of such danger out of ignorance, the priest should inform his parishioners and tell them that, because quarrels, disputes, scandals, and great animosity once arose between rectors of churches and their parishioners due to the many different customs for claiming tithes, Boniface, former Archbishop of Canterbury of good memory — with the consent and assent of all his suffragan bishops and the whole clergy at the Council of Lambeth — decreed and ordered that through the whole province of Canterbury there should be a uniform rule for seeking tithes.[43]

The priest should publish and announce those days which are feast days and those which are days of fasting.

Likewise, a priest ought to admonish his people that magical practices and incantations cannot remedy any sort of human sickness or cure sick, lame, or dying animals. Instead, such things are the snares and traps of the ancient enemy by which that treacherous enemy works to deceive the human race; and he who violates this, if he is a cleric, should be degraded; if a lay person, he should be anathematized.

On Usury

And he should warn his parishioners that none of them should loan money, wine, oil, grain, or anything else by usury. If a cleric does this he should be suspended from his office and his benefice. If a lay person does this, he shall be excommunicated until he makes suitable restitution. Usury is when someone receives more in repayment of a loan than he lent.

Also, he should warn them that if anyone receives land or dwellings as a pledge for the loan of some amount of money and he then recovers the whole amount or its equivalent value from the proceeds of that land or the dwellings, after he has deducted his expenses he should return the land to the person who borrowed from him, because a creditor is obliged to credit all the profit that he received from the possessions pledged to him into the debt for the principal; if he refuses to give it back, it is considered usury and he should be compelled to make restitution through ecclesiastical censure.

And he should warn his parishioners both that they should be hospitable and that they should not sell their goods to travelers at a higher price than they could receive at market.

Also, he should warn them that no one should wait to sell his goods at a higher price, since if he does this on purpose it is deemed usury; and when he goes to confession he should be strongly persuaded that he is

---

[43] Translator's note: Here William of Pagula inserts almost verbatim Archbishop Boniface's mid-thirteenth-century *Statute on Tithes*.

bound to make restitution for profit he has received due to having delayed the date of the sale.

Note that usury is contrary to the teaching of the old testament. And so, when the prophet asks, "Lord, who shall dwell in thy tabernacle," he answers, "he who does not lend out his money with usury."[44] It is likewise contrary to the gospels where it says, "lend, not hoping for any return."[45] It is also contrary to the prohibitions of all the saints. And it is contrary to the constitutions of the Church. Thus, he who commits usury is a damnable sinner. It also violates civil law.

And note that, according to St. Ambrose, usurers are called robbers.[46] According to St. Augustine they are called crucifiers of the poor. Also they are called minions of filthy lucre driven by avarice. They are called thieves, because they steal their souls from God. They are called the devil's children, not by birth but by joining in his work through sin alone. They are called accursed; John Chrysostom says that usurers should be cursed more than any other sinners. This is why usury is forbidden both in the old and the new testament, since if usury were allowed, all sorts of evils would follow from it. In particular, since the rich would care more for usurious profits than agriculture, there would be such a dearth of food that all the poor would starve to death. For, although they could get land for farming, they could not get the animals and tools necessary to farm it. Since these poor people would have nothing and the rich would lack nothing — partly because of their greed and partly safeguarded by the profits of their usury — then food would cost so much that the poor could not afford it. This is usury's greatest and most serious danger.

Also, another reason is that it is hardly possible for someone indebted to a usurer to survive for long without falling into poverty, which is an especially dangerous condition unless the desire for poverty is given to someone as a special gift from God.

Many other evils arise from usury, for in lending and loving money, idolatry can scarcely be avoided. For "where thy treasure is, there also will

[44] Ps 14:1; Cf. Lv 25:37
[45] Lk 6:35
[46] Cf. Ambrose, *De Bono Mortis*, n. 56

thy heart be."[47] For these reasons, therefore, usury is forbidden in both testaments.

On Priestly Aspirants

Also, the priest should publicly announce to his parishioners three times yearly in church that those men who wish to enjoy the privilege of the clergy should wear a decent tonsure and have the crown of their head suitably shaved, especially in the presence of their ordinaries and in their churches and in congregations of the clergy. Nor should they be ashamed to bear the mark of that man who, obedient even unto death, deigned to wear a crown of thorns for them so that they could share in his resurrection. Whoever would presume to disobey this warning, ashamed to bear the sign of the Savior impressed upon his brow, will beseech the Savior's help in vain, since he deserves to lose that privilege which, after he received it, he betrayed by abusing its dignity.

And the priest should publicly explain the meaning of the Creed to his parishioners on one of the days of Lent.

On Reverencing the Church

Also, he should announce to his parishioners that they should enter the church humbly and devoutly and should stand there quietly and respectfully, since this is how you behave even in the presence of a temporal lord. And they should hold in great reverence that name above every name, given to no one else on earth, from which mankind receives salvation, namely, the name of Jesus Christ who saved his people from their sins, and about which it is said that at the name of Jesus Christ all creatures in heaven, earth, and hell bow down.[48] Therefore, each and every person when he hears that glorious name of Jesus, especially during the celebration of Mass, should genuflect deep in his heart by striking his breast and

[47] Mt 6:21
[48] Cf. Phil 2:9-10

bowing his head. He should listen to the divine office with great presence of mind and he should offer up devout prayers.

They should also be admonished that they should not cause a quarrel, disturbance, assault, nor hold a conference in the church or graveyard, nor secular courts or gatherings; nor should they have disputes, fights, conversations, or anything else that could disturb divine services or offend God, so that an opportunity to sin does not arise in the very place where people ought to beg forgiveness for their sins.

And he should warn his parishioners that they should not conduct business in the church or graveyard nor, in particular, should they allow fairs or markets to be held there; and lay people should not be allowed to hold their courts or any sorts of judicial actions there; and there should be no dishonorable dancing in the church or graveyard, nor any singing of improper songs as is the custom during the vigils of certain saints' feast days; no games should be played there, nor should rocks be thrown, nor should they do any other things which could lead to the violation of the church or the graveyard.

On Marital Chastity

He should announce to them that, without the other's consent, a husband or wife may not take a vow of chastity or a vow to make a pilgrimage or to fast (except for the vow to go to Jerusalem), since a man and a woman are not judged according to the same standards. But a husband should be careful that he does not consent to his wife's vow; in fact, he should immediately oppose it if he wishes. For once he has given his consent to her vow, she is obliged to fulfill it, since he has not opposed it. But a husband does not sin by revoking his wife's vow, because it is within his rights; power over her body rests with him, not her. For if you abstain from sexual relations with your wife without her consent, you are granting her license to fornicate, and her sin will be blamed on your abstinence.

Finally, a parish priest should announce frequently on Sundays and other solemn feast days during the celebration of Mass, the articles of general excommunication issued at the Council of Oxford and the Council of Lambeth.

And note that there are many crimes for which someone incurs excommunication *ipso facto*: these cases are noted in the *Speculum Prelatorum*,[49] Part Two, Title 21.

[49] Translator's note: William of Pagula's own *Mirror for Priests*, a massive pastoral compendium combining both the *Oculus Sacerdotis* and his handbook for canon law, the *Summa Summarum*.

ABOUT THIS SERIES

Tradivox was first conceived as an international research endeavor to recover lost and otherwise little-known Catholic catechetical texts. As the research progressed over several years, the vision began to grow, along with the number of project contributors and a general desire to share these works with a broader audience.

Legally incorporated in 2019, Tradivox has begun the work of carefully remastering and republishing dozens of these catechisms which were once in common and official use in the Church around the world. That effort is embodied in this *Tradivox Catholic Catechism Index*, a multi-volume series restoring artifacts of traditional faith and praxis for a contemporary readership. More about this series and the work of Tradivox can be learned at www.Tradivox.com.

SOPHIA INSTITUTE

Sophia Institute is a nonprofit institution that seeks to nurture the spiritual, moral, and cultural life of souls and to spread the Gospel of Christ in conformity with the authentic teachings of the Roman Catholic Church.

Sophia Institute Press fulfills this mission by offering translations, reprints, and new publications that afford readers a rich source of the enduring wisdom of mankind.

Sophia Institute also operates the popular online resource Catholic Exchange.com. *Catholic Exchange* provides world news from a Catholic perspective as well as daily devotionals and articles that will help readers to grow in holiness and live a life consistent with the teachings of the Church.

In 2013, Sophia Institute launched Sophia Institute for Teachers to renew and rebuild Catholic culture through service to Catholic education. With the goal of nurturing the spiritual, moral, and cultural life of souls, and an abiding respect for the role and work of teachers, we strive to provide materials and programs that are at once enlightening to the mind and ennobling to the heart; faithful and complete, as well as useful and practical.

Sophia Institute gratefully recognizes the Solidarity Association for preserving and encouraging the growth of our apostolate over the course of many years. Without their generous and timely support, this book would not be in your hands.

www.SophiaInstitute.com
www.CatholicExchange.com
www.SophiaInstituteforTeachers.org

Sophia Institute Press® is a registered trademark of Sophia Institute.
Sophia Institute is a tax-exempt institution as defined by the
Internal Revenue Code, Section 501(c)(3). Tax ID 22-2548708.